US INTELLIGENCE
and
THE POLISH CRISIS
1980 – 1981

Douglas J. MacEachin

Center *for the* Study *of* Intelligence
Washington, DC 20505
2000

Acknowledgments

This project would not have been possible without the major effort of Tom Troy, a friend and former colleague who undertook the challenging task of reviewing an enormous body of intelligence documents for declassification. His subsequent interpretation of some of the events and the US intelligence reporting during the formation of Solidarity and the Soviet threats of military intervention provided much of the stimulus for addressing the crisis in its full dimensions. And his comments and suggestions during the drafting process were also of great value.

Thanks also must be given to Mark Kramer of the Davis Center for Russian and International Studies, whose exhaustive research and translation of documents from the archives of Poland and the former USSR and East Germany provided new insights into the events that unfolded. I am in addition indebted to Tom Blanton and Malcom Byrne of the National Security Archive—and to their colleague Sue Bechtel who did the heavy lifting—and to the many scholars of the Cold War International History Project, without whose work and support this project would not have been possible. I must also express my gratitude to Professors Ernest May and Philip Zelikow at Harvard's John F. Kennedy School for their encouragement throughout this effort.

Most of all, special thanks to Wendy Hilton-Jones at the Center for the Study of Intelligence, whose work and patience are responsible for turning this work in progress into a deliverable product. Thanks also to John Hedley for his editing and indexing skills.

Author's Note

I would like to record a view on an issue that has been a subject of considerable debate among many who are aware of the role of former Polish military officer, Col. Ryszard Kuklinski. Recently, some American scholars and Polish officials have asked me if I did not believe that Colonel Kuklinski's reporting for the United States did not represent in effect a "betrayal." This same view has been expressed in articles by former Polish dissidents, who were the same people whom Colonel Kuklinski was trying to help.

For those who are wedded to a view, perhaps out of a personal need for the relief that holding such a view provides, there is little to say. For those who are genuinely willing to examine the question, I would ask that they consider the following.

First of all, the entity against which Colonel Kuklinski was "conspiring" was not his homeland of Poland. It was the dictatorial alliance whose governing power was exerted to bring about the participation of the armed forces of his homeland in a military intervention to suppress a political liberalization movement in the neighboring country of Czechoslovakia. It was this same dictatorial power and military alliance that 12 years later was threatening the same kind of military intervention in his homeland, in an attempt to coerce Polish state and party leaders to employ their own military forces to crush the Polish civil opposition movement. And it was the alleged "inevitability" of this military intervention by the dictatorial alliance that was cited later by Poland's supreme leader, General Jaruzelski, as the reason for employing Poland's own military forces—as a "lesser evil"—to crush the civil opposition of Polish workers and farmers.

As this study seeks to demonstrate, the information possessed by the US at the time—most importantly the information provided by Colonel Kuklinski—offered a chance to derail the military suppression of the civil opposition movement. If the military suppression had been deterred because efforts taken by Colonel Kuklinski at the risk of his own life, would he be judged a hero or a villain? It should be noted that this question does not rest on judgments as to whether the Polish leadership could have been deterred from military oppression. The question is—was it worth trying? And how does a person who tried, at the risk of his life, become condemned?

Contents

Acknowledgments iii
Author's Note v
Copyright and Attribution Statement ix
Foreword xi
Chapter 1: The Burgeoning Confrontation 1
Chapter 2: The Confrontation Escalates 17
Chapter 3: US Launches Public Policy and Diplomatic Offensive 31
Chapter 4: Filling Out The Picture 45
Chapter 5: Intelligence and Policy 61
Chapter 6: Escalating Challenges to the Polish Regime 69
Chapter 7: Jaruzelski Takes the Government Reins 83
Chapter 8: A Setup for Military Crackdown 95
Chapter 9: A Close Call? 113
Chapter 10: Liberalization Infects the Party 125
Chapter 11: Solidarity Charges Ahead, and the Regime Digs In ... 141
Chapter 12: Bringing Down the Curtain 159
Chapter 13: Caught Off Guard 179
Chapter 14: Would It Have Made a Difference? 195
Sources 205
Index 209

Copyright and Attribution Statement

This study was written by Douglas J. MacEachin for professors Philip Zelikow and Ernest May (the project's principals), under the auspices of the Harvard Intelligence and Policy Project, with support from the Central Intelligence Agency, under contracts 1999-Y012400-000, 2000-Y0552000-00, and 2000-Y081200-000. The John F. Kennedy School of Government, Harvard University, takes sole responsibility for the content of this case. (1099)

Copyright 1999 by the President and Fellows of Harvard College. To request permission to reproduce materials, contact the Case Program Office, John F. Kennedy School of Government 79 John F. Kennedy Street, Cambridge, MA 02138. No part of this publication may be reproduced, revised, translated, stored in a retrieval system, used in a spreadsheet, or transmitted in any form or by any means—electronic, mechanical, photocopying, recording, or otherwise—without the written permission of the Case Program Office at the John F. Kennedy School of Government.

Foreword

Doug MacEachin has used his considerable skill as an intelligence analyst and historian to detail the intriguing story of the 1980-81 Polish crisis. The description of actual events on the ground, the assessment of these events by intelligence analysts and policymakers, and the US policy process, provided an interesting commentary on both the strengths and weaknesses of the process.

The book describes the problem faced by intelligence analysts when they try to forecast decisions made by foreign actors before the actors themselves have decided what those decisions will be. It also highlights the danger of a current intelligence process that provides a blizzard of information without context and absent a systematic overview of events.

Perhaps the key lesson is the consequence of analysts and policy makers alike staying with a "going in" judgment and over time pushing new evidence to make it consistent with that judgment.

Mr. MacEachin also offers an alternative intelligence product that might have influenced a different policy outcome.

This book is an important addition to the literature of intelligence.

— Richard Kerr,
former Deputy Director
of Central Intelligence

CHAPTER 1

The Burgeoning Confrontation

On 1 July 1980, Poland's Communist government, without advance notice, announced that it had raised prices of food and other consumer goods. Meat prices were increased by as much as 60 to 90 percent. The next day, strikes for compensatory wage increases erupted throughout Poland. To Western observers these events appeared to put the Polish workers and ruling powers on the same kind of collision course they had gone through twice in the last decade.[1]

In December 1970, a government-directed increase of more than 35 percent in staple food prices had been immediately followed by widespread worker protests. The regime's response at that time had been a crackdown by police and soldiers that resulted in the shooting of workers in front of the Lenin Shipyard in Gdansk. Less than a week later, Edward Gierek replaced Wladyslaw Gomulka, the First Secretary of the Polish United Workers Party (PZPR),[2] who had ordered the crackdown. These events have been subsequently viewed as perhaps the most important precursor to the development of the independent Polish trade union federation known as Solidarity.[3]

In June 1976, strikes had quickly spread across the country after unexpected food price hikes. Public demonstrations by workers included the burning of the Polish party headquarters in Radom, south of Warsaw. The breadth of opposition ultimately compelled the regime to back down from price hikes,

---

[1] Extensive descriptions of the political, social and economic dynamics shaping the internal situation in Poland in 1980-81 include Nicholas G. Andrews, *Poland 1980-81: Solidarity vs. the Party*, (Washington, DC: National Defense University Press, 1985); Neal Ascherson, *The Polish August*, (New York: Penguin, 1982); Timothy Garton Ash, *The Polish Revolution: Solidarity*, (New York: Vintage Books, 1982). All three authors were in Poland and had direct observation of the events – Andrews as deputy chief of the US Mission, and Garton Ash and Ascherson covering events for the British press. For the reader with the time and dedication, extensive details can be obtained by reviewing the major US press publications for the summer and fall of 1980.
[2] PZPR is the Polish acronym for "Polska Zjednoczona Partia Robotnicza" or "Polish United Workers Party."
[3] Lech Walesa, *A Way of Hope* (New York: Henry Holt and Co., 1987), p. 10. Also Garton Ash, *The Polish Revolution*, pp. 10-13.

but police and security forces imposed harsh retaliatory measures on the striking workers, particularly in Radom and at the Ursus tractor factory near Warsaw.

The violence experienced in these earlier episodes had a significant impact on participants in the struggle. Labor groups began to seek greater coordination and centralization to strengthen their hand in confronting the party. A group of dissident intellectuals formed the Committee for the Defense of Workers (KOR)[4] for the specific purpose of supporting the labor groups. It established an advisory channel on political strategy and tactics between the workers and intelligentsia that would prove to be influential in the development and shaping of Solidarity, and would ultimately include people who were members of Solidarity. Other groups that sprang up included the Movement in Defense of Human and Citizen Rights (ROPCiO), whose purpose was the monitoring of compliance with the Helsinki Final Act, and the Young Poland Movement (RMP).[5]

For senior Polish political and military officials the experiences of 1970 and 1976 presented a vivid demonstration of the volatility and potential costs of using force to bring popular uprisings under control. The perception of Polish attitudes toward the use of force would also become an important variable in the calculations of Western governments and the Soviet leadership.

The July 1980 announcement of price increases occurred at a time when tensions between opposition groups and the government had already been mounting. Two months earlier some members of the RMP and the ROPCiO had been arrested. Their organizations responded with a campaign of leaflets demanding, among other things, recognition of the rights of Polish citizens, and a major economic reconfiguration aimed at ending price increases and inflation. Other groups such as the KOR threw their support to these demands. (One participant in these campaigns was an electrician named Lech Walesa, who had been fired from the Lenin Shipyard at Gdansk in 1976 for making a confrontational speech at a meeting there of the government-sanctioned union.[6] He would shortly begin a trek to an enduring place in the history of Poland.)

As the strikes were breaking out in July, the political evolution in the labor movement quickly became evident when the KOR declared it would use its resources to keep the public informed on the progress of the strikes, becom-

---

[4] KOR stands for Komitet Obrony Robotnicza or Committee for the Defense of Workers.
[5] ROPCiO is the Ruch Obrony Praw Czlowieka I Obywatela or Movement in Defense of Human and Citizen Rights; RMP or Ruch Mlodej Polski, means Young Poland Movement. See Garton Ash, *The Polish Revolution*, pp. 17-25; and Walesa, *A Way of Hope*, p. 10.
[6] Walesa, *A Way of Hope*, pp. 104-105.

ing, in effect, an alternate news service. The publicity would prove to be of considerable help to the strikers in countering regime efforts to splinter their unity by cutting separate deals with workers at different enterprises. It also helped keep the Western press informed of ongoing events.

In contrast to the swift imposition of force in 1970, this time the Polish authorities sought some degree of appeasement. They initially had some success: strikers at individual enterprises agreed to return to work after being offered wage hikes of 10 to 15 percent. But in what would be a continuing pattern, as soon as a strike at one factory was settled, another began somewhere else. This contagion appears to have been at least partly the result of the KOR communication effort, with increasing numbers of workers resorting to strikes after learning that strikers elsewhere had obtained some concessions.

By mid-July the strikes had expanded to Lublin, the site in western Poland of a major junction of rail links between the Soviet Union and East Germany. The initial strike there was at a truck factory, where workers submitted some 35 demands to the government. Many of their demands involved issues beyond prices and wages, such as press freedom and curbs on privileges of security organizations. As soon as the Lublin truck workers strike was settled by offers of wage increases, the local railway workers launched a strike that shut down the rail lines. Reflecting the prominence of this development, a deputy prime minister, Mieczyslaw Jagielski, was dispatched to negotiate a solution with the strikers.[7]

On 20 July the US Intelligence Community prepared an Alert Memorandum warning that the labor disputes in Poland could become even more intense and widespread. It said that tensions were increasing throughout the country and that agreements that had appeared to settle some disputes were coming unglued. It characterized the situation as potentially degenerating into a violent confrontation between the unions and the regime. The Memorandum said that while Soviet leaders would be reluctant under any circumstances to take military action, Moscow would intervene as a last resort if the Polish leadership proved incapable of restoring order in a situation that appeared to be deteriorating into violent confrontation. The Alert Memo also pointed out that so far no unusual activity had been observed in Soviet military units based in or near Poland.[8]

---

[7] See Andrews, *Poland 1980-81*, pp. 25-26, and Garton Ash, *The Polish Revolution*, pp. 33-34.

[8] Alert Memorandum: Poland, declassified *National Intelligence Daily* (hereafter cited as decl. *NID*), 21 July 1980. Alert Memoranda appeared in the *NID* one day after they were received by the President. Declassified *NID* articles on the Polish crisis were released by CIA in August 1999 and are on deposit at the National Security Archive (Gelman Library, Suite 701, 2130 H St. NW, Washington, DC). *NID* articles were almost always drafted by CIA analysts, but were required to be coordinated with analysts from other intelligence agencies.

At about the same time that this intelligence assessment was being disseminated, a compromise settlement was being reached in the negotiations between Deputy Prime Minister Jagielski and the rail strikers at Lublin. The strikers agreed on 20 July to return to work. The Lublin strikes had lasted nine days, during four of which the entire town had been paralyzed.

Less than a month later, on 14 August, a strike began at the Lenin Shipyards in Gdansk—the site of the December 1970 tragedy. Until that day, workers there had not joined the widespread strikes in reaction to the July announcement of price hikes. The fuse that set them off was the firing of Anna Walentynowicz, a popular employee of long standing at the shipyard, on blatantly bogus charges in connection with her efforts promoting a memorial to the protesters killed in the strikes of 1970. The next two weeks would produce a fundamental evolution in the nature of the labor movement and popular opposition in Poland.

Solidarity Evolves as a Political Force

Many of the factors shaping developments at Gdansk in August 1980 were not clear at the time. Nonetheless, it did seem evident, even then, that what was unfolding had the potential to become an historical watershed.

On the first day of the strike, Lech Walesa vaulted into a leading role in the unfolding events. The preceding December he had made an impromptu appearance at a ceremony held at the Lenin Shipyard to commemorate the 1970 tragedy, delivering a speech that drew rousing applause from the crowd (and resulted in his dismissal from his latest job). On 14 August his timely intervention and delivery of another rousing speech was instrumental in causing what was initially a protest demonstration to quickly become an occupation of the factory.[9]

Within a few days the confrontation took on a new dimension with the creation of an Inter-Factory Strike Committee (MKS).[10] This was composed of two representatives from each of the diverse striking enterprises in Gdansk and the nearby cities of Gdynia and Sopot. Its meeting site was a large hall at the Lenin Shipyard. On the weekend of 16-17 August, the MKS issued a communiqué describing its purpose as the coordination of the actions and demands of workers at all striking enterprises. The communiqué said that a

---

[9] Garton Ash, *The Polish Revolution*, p. 39. Garton Ash arrived on the scene on 18 August 1980, covering events for *The London Times*. His accounts of events throughout 1980-81 in Poland also appear in *Der Speigel*, and *The Spectator*. His chapter entitled "Inside the Lenin Shipyard" draws on his direct knowledge derived from his presence there during the strikes.

[10] In Polish, Miedzyakladadowy Komitet Strajkowy.

common list of demands would be drawn up, and that all workers represented by the MKS would remain on strike until all demands on the list were settled.[11]

By Monday morning, 18 August, the MKS had agreed upon and released a list of 21 demands. At the top of the list were:

- Free trade unions that would be independent of the party and employers, in accordance with the convention of the International Labor Organization.

- A guaranteed right to strike, and guarantees of security for strikers and those who supported them.

- Regulation of censorship through guarantees for free speech and protection of printing and distribution of independent publications.[12]

- Restoration of jobs and rights for those who had been dismissed from their jobs or expelled from universities in the 1970 and 1976 crackdowns, the release of political prisoners, and legal prohibition of reprisals for political beliefs.

- Access to the mass media for publication of worker views and demands.

- Provision of full and accurate information on the economy, and opportunities for all social groups to participate in discussions of economic reforms.

These were not simply demands tied to specific work-related concerns of the specific strikers represented by the MKS. They addressed political, social and economic issues central to the entire citizenry of Poland—what one European scholar has described as a "civil crusade."[13] Issues such as wages, strike

---

[11] These developments and the formulation of the demands that resulted are described from different vantage points in Walesa, *A Way of Hope*, pp. 128, 131-132; Andrews, *Poland 1980-81*, pp. 28-29; and Garton Ash, *The Polish Revolution*, pp. 41-43.

[12] The unions would later be charged by the Soviet Politburo with seeking to "abolish" censorship. Some Western writers also described this as one of the workers demands, and reportedly some MKS representatives did press for including such a provision. MKS leaders, however, recognized the explosive potential of such a demand, and the wording of their final list sought only legal restrictions.

[13] Garton Ash, *The Polish Revolution*, p. 74. For a similar outlook written at the time, see John Darnton, "Strikers in Poland Defy Gierek Appeal," *The New York Times*, 20 August 1980, p. A1; and Darnton, "Warsaw Averts Main Dissidents," *The New York Times*, 21 August 1980, p. A1. Mr. Darnton was also in Poland then, covering events for *The New York Times*. He has not written a book on the subject, but his articles at the time were particularly insightful—they look all the better with the test of time—and read in sequence they equal the books of his colleagues.

compensation, work and holiday regulation, (including the demand that Saturdays be work free) and other worker benefits appeared further down on the list of demands. Even some of these demands were framed to affect a much broader segment of Polish society than just the workers at the striking facilities. They included, for example, provisions dealing with food pricing and distribution, and demands for reining in the preferential treatment and privileges of PZPR officials and security forces. The provisions addressed the complaints of all Poles who were not the beneficiaries of party *nomenklatura* privileges. Many of the demands articulated long-standing objectives of the KOR.

US intelligence descriptions of these developments said that while the Polish regime was willing to offer concessions on purely economic issues like wages, prices and working conditions if this would defuse the crisis, the leadership would not give ground on the demands that were seen as crossing into the political sphere. Free trade unions in particular were "politically unacceptable," according to intelligence analysts.[14]

Some 300 enterprises in the Gdansk region signed up with the MKS within the first week of its existence. Workers on strike at factories in Gdansk alone numbered about 120,000. Strikes also had spread to every major Polish industrial center. In some of the larger ones, such as Szczecin near the East German border, Elblag southeast of Gdansk, and later at Wroclaw in southwestern Poland, the workers copied the Gdansk idea by forming their own MKSs. On 23 August, the Gdansk MKS distributed the first issue of its strike bulletin under the title "Solidarnosc," or Solidarity.[15]

The regime initially refused as "a matter of political principle" to negotiate with the unified MKS, continuing instead to pursue a "divide and conquer" strategy aimed at getting separate agreements with workers at different plants—trying, in effect, to buy them off with nominal wage increases. This scheme soon came to be seen as exacerbating the standoff. It had in fact been these government tactics that contributed to the creation of the MKS. Also on 23 August—the same day that the first "Solidarnosc" bulletin was issued—Deputy Prime Minister Jagielski, who again had been put in charge of government negotiations with the strikers, began dealing directly with the Gdansk MKS. This de facto official recognition of the authority of the MKS to represent the collective unions was a new dimension of achievement for the labor movement.[16]

---

[14] "Poland: Labor Unrest," decl. *NID*, 16 August 1980; "Poland: Situation Report," decl. *NID*, 18 August 1980; and "Poland: Prospects for Confrontation," decl. *NID*, 22 August 1980.

[15] Decl. *NID* Situation Reports on Poland, 21and 23 August 1980; Joseph Held, *Dictionary of East European History Since 1945*, (Westport, Connecticut: Greenwood Press, 1994), pp. 304, 338; Garton Ash, *The Polish Revolution*, pp. 49-50; Andrews, *Poland 1980-81*, p. 34.

[16] Decl. *NID* Situation Reports of 21, 22, and 23 August 1980; Andrews, *Poland:1980-81*, p. 32.

A day later came a major overhaul in the membership of the ruling party Politburo and Secretariat, and in the composition of the government ministers. Prime Minister Edward Babiuch was offered up as a scapegoat for the failure of economic policies, and Josef Pinkowski was nominated as his successor. Several individuals viewed as impeding constructive dealings with the workers were dropped from the party Central Committee, even though most of them were also First Secretary Gierek's allies. The individuals who were promoted included at least two of Gierek's strongest critics. One of them—Stefan Olszowski—had challenged Gierek some years earlier and had since then been exiled as ambassador to East Germany. Olszowski was described by US intelligence analysts as a candidate to replace the politically weakened Gierek, and as a "forceful supporter of far-reaching economic reforms." Intelligence analysts described the personnel changes as having shifted the balance within the regime toward "the moderate and pragmatic end of the political spectrum," but said that this offered no guarantees for resolving the crisis.[17]

On 31 August Deputy Prime Minister Jagielski and Walesa signed what became known as the "Gdansk agreement." By any standard it was a landmark event.[18] On its face it essentially committed the government to all 21 of the demands put forward by the MKS. Many of these provisions, such as the right to establish independent unions, the right to strike without reprisals, and the right of "freedom of expression," were without precedent in member states of the Soviet Bloc. (As events would demonstrate, implementing these provisions would involve further struggle.) The government had already reached a settlement with strikers in Szczecin a day earlier, and three days after the signing at Gdansk an agreement was reached ending strikes at Jastrzebie in the Silesian coal fields.

The widespread perception of the agreement's historical dimensions was reflected in a *New York Times* article the following day that said "the idea of independent unions and the right to strike [in a Soviet Bloc country] is so revolutionary that it is impossible to say where it will lead."[19] Intelligence assessments said the Gdansk agreement would "usher in a period of political turmoil that could last for several years." Analysts pointed out that allowing free and

---

[17] "Poland: Situation Report," decl. *NID*, 25 August 1980. See also Garton Ash, *The Polish Revolution*, p. 55; Michael Dobbs, *Down With Big Brother: The Fall of the Soviet Empire* (New York: Alfred A. Knopf, 1997), p. 49. Mr. Dobbs also was in Poland at the time, covering events for *The Washington Post*. For Babiuch this was the end of the "what goes around" cycle. He had been appointed prime minister under exactly the same circumstances in February 1980 to replace Piotr Jaroszewiecz when it had been the latter's turn to be offered up as the scapegoat.

[18] "Excerpts from Polish Agreement," *The New York Times*, 31 August 1980, p. 1. The full text of the Gdansk Agreement is in Ascherson, *The Polish August*, pp. 288-299.

[19] "Polish Strikers Agree to End Walkout After Government Yields on Final Key Demand," *The New York Times*, 1 September 1980, p. A1.

independent trade unions would "differentiate Poland even more from its Warsaw Pact allies, giving it an independent workers' lobby to go along with an independent church and independent farmers," and resulting in Poland's movement "toward a more liberal and open society." One intelligence assessment said that "so far, the workers are clearly the winners.... They have wrung from the regime a settlement that offers them a chance to institutionalize their right to represent the industrial work force of Poland over the longer term."[20]

Less than a week after the signing of the Gdansk agreement, Poland had both a new prime minister and a new party first secretary. On the afternoon of 5 September, the Polish Sejm (parliament) went through the formality of voting to confirm Josef Pinkowski as Prime Minister. This was followed that afternoon by a public announcement that PZPR First Secretary Gierek was ill and in the hospital. A meeting of the party Central Committee took place that evening, and the next day the public was informed that Stanislaw Kania had been named as the new First Secretary. Other personnel changes in the Politburo, Central Committee and party Secretariat were also announced. The unmistakable signal was that this was the PZPR's reaction to a failed leadership that had permitted the situation to reach the point where the party's authority clearly was in jeopardy. In hindsight, Gierek's ouster probably had begun to be set up by the Central Committee shakeup two weeks earlier.

The National Intelligence Daily reported that there was a strong possibility Moscow had a hand not only in Gierek's ouster, but also in the selection of Kania as his successor. Earlier intelligence reports had posited Olszowski as the strongest candidate to replace Gierek, but he was described as having probably been passed over because of his "mounting enthusiasm for free trade unions." Kania had a long tenure as a party apparatchik, including 10 years in the party Secretariat position overseeing military and security affairs, and intelligence reports pointed out that he had] close contacts with the KGB and with Soviet leaders in general. Intelligence analysts suggested that he had been chosen as party leader in the belief that he would take a strong line toward restoring public order. Western journalists offered similar assessments. The intelligence reporting also said, however, that despite Kania's "hard-line reputation" he was likely to show considerable flexibility, and that the party

---

[20] *The New York Times,* 1 September 1980, *op. cit.*; "Poland: Settlement Implications," decl. *NID,* 2 September 1980; and "Poland: Post Strike Prospects," decl. *NID,* 5 September 1980.

leadership continued to be "largely moderate and pragmatic."[21] As later events would show, neither Kania nor Olszowski would quite live up to the images that intelligence analysts initially built of them. In Kania's case, the same seems to have been true of Moscow's hopes for him.

The next few weeks offered ample demonstration of the level of challenge to party supremacy that had been opened by the Gdansk agreement. On 17 September, 35 newly formed independent Polish trade unions declared their intent to register as a single Independent Self-Governing Trade Union (NSZZ),[22] under the name Solidarity (Solidarnosc). Delegates at the founding meeting announced that some 3 million workers from 3,500 factories had joined or had applied to join Solidarity. To head what was in effect intended to be a national union confederation, a National Coordinating Commission (KKP) was set up with Walesa as its chairman. "Inter-Factory Founding Committees" (MKZ) were set up on the regional level, and "Factory Commissions" (KZ) were set up at the individual enterprises.[23] By 24 September, the National KKP had approved language for Solidarity's founding statutes and submitted them to the Warsaw Provincial Court for formal registration of its status as an independent trade union. This would set the stage for the next round of confrontation.[24]

---

[21] "Poland: New Party Chief," decl. *NID*, 6 September 1980; and "Poland: Implications of Change in Party Leadership," 8 September 1980. It should be noted that contrary to the intelligence view, most observers on the scene regarded Olszowski as a hard liner. For example, Ascherson, in *The Polish August*, p.180-185, suggests that Moscow was in the process of engineering the accession of Olszowski or some other similar "hardliner" to head the party, but that Gierek's sudden heart attack caused the change to take place before the Soviets could get the support lined up for their preferred candidate. Thus, according to this view, Moscow had to settle for a more "moderate" Kania. Records now available of Soviet leadership discussions of the Polish leaders tend to cast doubt on this theory, but do confirm their view of Olszowski as equally tough. In discussions at the time, the Soviet leaders described Kania as one of the "best available," and while appreciative of Olszowski's hard line, they expressed reservations about his potential to provoke rather than to manage the confrontations. See for example, the record of the CPSU CC Politburo meeting of 29 October 1980 in Mark Kramer, "Soviet Deliberations During the Polish Crisis, 1980-81," Cold War International History Project (CWIHP) Special Working Paper No. 1, (Washington, DC: Woodrow Wilson Center, April 1999).

[22] NSZZ stands for Niezalezny Samorzadny Zwiaczek Zwodowy.

[23] KKP stands for Krajowa Komisja Porozumiewawcza; MKZ equals Miedzyzakladowa Komisja Zalozycielski; KZ stands for Komisja Zakladowa.

[24] For more detail on this event see Andrews, *Poland 1980-81*, p. 286; and Garton Ash, *The Polish Revolution*, pp. 74-75. The initial intelligence perspective is in the decl. Situation Report from the *NID*, 19 September 1980.

The Washington Perspective: Threat of Soviet Intervention

In the last week of August, a few days before the Gdansk agreement was announced, President Jimmy Carter sent a letter to British Prime Minister Margaret Thatcher, West German Chancellor Helmut Schmidt, and French President Giscard d'Estaing proposing that the four Western leaders share views and coordinate actions with regard to ongoing events in Poland. He said that "what is going on in Poland could precipitate far reaching consequences for East-West relations and even for the future of the Soviet Bloc itself."

The President also stressed that "the matter is for the Poles themselves to resolve, without any foreign interference," and that "We must of course be concerned about possible Soviet reactions." The letter concluded with the recommendation that economic aid from the West be "designed to encourage the Poles to undertake a more fundamental and systemic reform of their economic system." The dispatch of this letter prompted the US State Department to begin consultations with Allied governments on contingency plans for the possibility of Soviet military intervention.[25]

Shortly after this letter was sent, but still before the agreement at Gdansk, CIA disseminated a Special Analysis that said Moscow "could not...tolerate genuinely independent trade unions or legal restrictions on censorship" in a Soviet Bloc state. This intelligence assessment correctly forecast that the Soviets would exert pressure on Gierek to adopt a tougher stance, and that if this failed to produce results they would seek his removal. The assessment also said Moscow probably would pose the specter of Soviet military intervention as a means of driving home to the Poles the need to impose their own solution, including if necessary the use of force. The ramifications of military intervention would lead the Soviets to exhaust all possibilities first, according

---

[25] Declassified State Department Cable 232803, NODIS, 1 September 1980, to US Embassies in London, Bonn and Paris, included in Malcom Byrne, Pavel Machcewicz and Christian Osterman, eds., *Poland 1980-82: Internal Crisis, International Dimensions, A Compendium of Declassified Documents and Chronology of Events*, (Washington, DC: National Security Archive, 1997). Hereafter referred to as *Poland 1980-82: Compendium*. This cable provided to the US Embassies the text of the President's private letter, informing them that it had been sent on 27 August, and alerting them that "indications that the letter has been sent are already appearing in the press." The letter's contents were in fact described in a *New York Times* article two days later. ("Carter Urges Allies to Assist Poles," *The New York Times*, 3 September 1980, p. A1.) The comment about it having prompted contingency planning regarding Soviet intervention is in Zbigniew Brzezinski, *Power and Principle: Memoirs of a National Security Advisor, 1977–1981* (New York: Farrar, Straus, and Giroux, 1983), p. 464. Brzezinski describes the letter as being done on 25 August, but the difference in dates may simply be a matter of when it was prepared versus when it was transmitted or delivered to the addressees.

to the intelligence assessment, but if they reached a conclusion that the Communist system in Poland was at risk of collapsing, they would nonetheless be willing to accept the enormous costs.[26]

The possibility that the events in Poland could result in Soviet military intervention had been a concern for U.S officials virtually from the time the strikes first broke out in July, as was reflected in the 20 July 1980 Intelligence Community Alert Memorandum. Intelligence assessments gave little prospect that the Polish regime could successfully carry out its own forceful crackdown, even if it was willing to try, which most analysts doubted. Although police units and Internal Security officers had been moved from Warsaw to the Gdansk area within a week of the outbreak of the Gdansk strike, intelligence analysts said any attempt to use the security forces – especially the military – carried the risk that the units might not perform reliably. Even before the Gdansk agreement, intelligence analysts concluded that the reliability of the police and other security forces had been further eroded. An attempt to use force, concluded the intelligence assessments, could result in violence quickly spreading beyond the regime's control. It was that prospect which, at least in the formative stages of the union movement, was seen as most prominently creating the risk of Soviet military intervention.[27]

After the signing of the Gdansk agreement—which included the provisions on independent trade unions and legal restrictions of censorship that intelligence analysts said Moscow could not accept—CIA again raised the issue of potential Soviet military intervention. A Special Analysis of 5 September concluded that the longer term prospects essentially came down to:

- Continued aggressive strikes by the workers against an increasingly enfeebled regime, leading inevitably to Soviet intervention, or

- The union and regime would work out some accommodation for a balance of power, motivated to a substantial degree by the explicit recognition of the danger of Soviet military intervention as the alternative.[28]

Even before this intelligence assessment was disseminated, President Carter's National Security Advisor, Zbigniew Brzezinski independently concluded that the Gdansk agreement represented a serious undermining of the

---

[26] "Poland: Implications of the Labor Crisis," decl. *NID*, 28 August 1980.
[27] Declassified Alert Memorandum, 20 July 1980, *op. cit.*; "Poland: Prospects for Confrontation," decl. *NID*, 22 August 1980; "Implications of the Labor Crisis," decl. *NID*, 28 August 1980.
[28] "Poland: Post Strike Prospects," decl. *NID*, 5 September 1980.

basis for party authority in Poland. He asked Director of Central Intelligence Stansfield Turner for an updated Intelligence Community assessment of the prospects for Soviet military intervention.[29]

For the Intelligence Community, this task went beyond examining the factors that might cause the Soviets to intervene, and calculating the odds that they would do so. That was a function that could be done—and was being done daily—by policy makers and outside experts on the basis of diplomatic reporting and public sources of information from observers on the scene. (Brzezinski himself would have been at the top of the list of those doing such analysis.) The specific extra dimensions expected from the Intelligence Community included detailed calculations of the specific steps that would be involved in preparations for such measures, and the detection and assessment of actions revealing Soviet preparations to actually carry them out.

During the first half of September, the Intelligence Community began to detect and report Soviet military activity in the western parts of the USSR that seemed unusual compared to past patterns. Analysts cautioned that the evidence was relatively sparse and that it was possible that the activities observed were part of the normal training cycle. Perhaps the most significant activity disclosed in this time frame was that of civilian vehicles exercising with heretofore low-strength ground force divisions, a sign that the Soviets were at least practicing mobilization. The CIA reported that there was no evidence that mobilization was as yet actually taking place, and that the activities observed to date did not indicate imminent military operations against Poland. The activities did, however, suggest that the Soviets were taking some preparatory measures with the expectation that the use of military force might be necessary, according to intelligence analysts. Measures that seemed related to increasing readiness continued in certain units throughout the month of September.[30]

An updated Alert Memorandum that Turner sent to the President and other senior officials on 19 September cited some of this activity, two days after Solidarity announced its intent to register as an independent trade union. The DCI attached his own cover note to this Memorandum, saying that "Soviet military

---

[29] Robert Gates, *From the Shadows: An Insider's Story of Five Presidents and How They Won the Cold War* (New York: Simon and Schuster, 1996), p. 163.

[30] "Military Activity," decl. *NID*, 13 September 1980; "Poland," decl. *NID*, 17 September 1980; "Special Analysis: Crisis at Another Peak," decl. *NID*, 18 September 1980; and "Poland," decl. *NID*, 25 September 1980. Other than the few snippets exemplified in these four documents, most of the descriptions of Soviet military activities relating to the Polish crisis prior to 1 December 1980 have been excluded from the declassified intelligence documents.

activity detected in the last few days leads me to believe that the Soviet leadership is preparing to intervene militarily if the Polish situation is not brought under control in a manner satisfactory to Moscow." The text of the Alert Memorandum said that Soviet military preparations so far were well short of the requirements for a large-scale military intervention, although they had increased their preparedness. The Memorandum said Moscow would be likely to give Kania more time to establish control, but "if the Soviets conclude the [Polish] regime is losing control of the country or that Poland's loyalty to the Warsaw Pact is in question, they will intervene militarily." According to Gates, this alarming message was accompanied with a cautionary note pointing out that cloud cover over much of the western USSR was impeding efforts to acquire detailed information on Soviet military developments.[31]

This intelligence assessment was specifically cited in (and included as an attachment to) a White House memorandum setting up a meeting of the senior US national security officials four days later. Brzezinski chaired this meeting, which included the Secretary of Defense, the Deputy Secretary of State, the Acting Chairman of the Joint Chiefs of Staff, and the DCI. The stated purpose of the meeting was to "review the current intelligence on Soviet troop movements and the state of our contingency planning" for Soviet military intervention.[32]

According to the official White House Summary of the meeting, the DCI stressed that Polish political leaders had not begun to bring the situation under control and that unrest was, in fact, spreading. He said that the Soviet military was taking steps similar to those that had been seen prior to Soviet intervention in Czechoslovakia in 1968, although Moscow was not believed to have yet reached a decision on an invasion of Poland.

Turner said the Intelligence Community estimated that a Soviet military intervention force would include at least 30 divisions—more than twice the number of Polish divisions. He said US intelligence resources would be able to detect the readying of such a large force in time to provide two or three weeks' warning. The meeting participants expressed a consensus that the Poles would fight any Soviet military intervention, although they were uncertain as to how organized the resistance would be.[33]

---

[31] "Polish Trends and Soviet Perceptions and Reactions," decl. Alert Memo, *NID*, 20 September 1980; Gates, *From the Shadows*, p. 163, describes Turner's note and the admonition on cloud cover.

[32] Memorandum from Steve Larrabee to Zbigiew Brzezinski, 22 September 1980, "SCC on Poland, Tuesday, September 23, 10:45," declassified, in *Poland 1980-82: Compendium*. The declassified version of the memo does not include the CIA attachments, but it lists the DCI's memo as an attachment to the original.

[33] Summary of Conclusions, Special Coordinating Committee meeting, Tuesday, September 23, 1980, *Poland 1980-82: Compendium*.

Turner's description of the probable size of the potential invasion force was based on CIA's calculation that:

- The Soviets would be uncertain about reactions of Polish armed forces, which had 13 ground divisions plus one airborne division; the airborne division and eight of the ground divisions were kept at a fairly high manning level. The Poles also had sizable internal defense militia.

- The Soviet General staff was very conservative and would seek a force of sufficiently overwhelming size to constitute a deterrent to organized opposition and provide the power to quickly suppress any resistance that did occur, as the Soviets had done in their 1968 intervention in Czechoslovakia.

The expected warning time for the preparation of such a force was based on the belief that the Soviet units employed would come mainly if not exclusively from the western USSR. The forces there were not normally kept at full wartime manning levels, and also relied on the civilian economy to provide the motor transport vehicles needed for major deployments. Soviet divisions stationed in East Germany and Czechoslovakia routinely had their full manpower and equipment complements, but most intelligence analysts believed that Moscow would be reluctant to deplete its forces facing NATO. The Soviets probably would not expect NATO to react, but would not be willing to take this for granted, in the analysts' view. [34]

CIA analysts also posited some Soviet military measures short of invasion that might be employed to heighten pressure on the Polish regime. These included high-visibility exercises in the western USSR, including the call up of some reservists, movements of air transport and airborne forces, and deployment of some additional divisions into Poland under the guise of exercises. All of these moves had been seen prior to the Soviet intervention in Czechoslovakia in 1968.[35]

According to Robert Gates, who was the DCI's Executive Assistant at the time, Turner also said at the 23 September White House meeting that Moscow viewed the developments in Poland as a threat to the entire communist system. He said the Soviets feared a ripple effect elsewhere in Europe and in the USSR. Turner postulated that the labor movement's demonstration of an ability to extract fundamental concessions from the communist government had led the Soviets to see the current situation as potentially more contagious than the earlier crises in their East European bloc (apparently referring to Hungary

---

[34] Author's description.
[35] "Special Analysis: Crisis at Another Peak," *op. cit.*

in 1956 and Czechoslovakia in 1968.) Gates says that Turner concluded by stating his belief that because the Soviets saw the developments in Poland as threatening the fabric of the Warsaw Pact, they could not let it spread. But Turner also added that there were signs of disagreement among the Soviet leaders on what to do about it.[36]

Brzezinski stressed that strong Western reaction and the likelihood of strong Polish resistance might well deter the Soviets. It was then agreed that a letter was to be prepared for President Carter to send to some of his NATO counterparts, urging that they weigh in to make clear to Moscow the repercussions of a Soviet military intervention. Exactly one month later, this group of senior officials met again to review a series of proposed steps designed to penalize the Soviet Union severely in the event military intervention was actually carried out. Brzezinski's personal account of that meeting stresses that it was important "... not [to] discuss how likely such an intervention is but focus on what we would do (1) to deter it if it was imminent and (2) how we should react if it took place." The proposals agreed upon at the meeting were then sent to the Allies for consultation and coordination.[37]

---

[36] Gates, *From the Shadows*, p. 164.
[37] Summary of September 23 1980 Special Coordinating Committee (SCC) meeting, op. cit., Brzezinski, *Power and Principle*, p. 465. See also Brzezinski's day-to-day notes for the period from 4 October through 12 December 1980, published in the Winter 1988 edition of *Orbis*, "A White House Diary," pp. 32-48. The description of the 23 October SCC meeting is on p. 33.

Chapter 2

The Confrontation Escalates

In the last week of September, Soviet media attacks began portraying the Polish situation in the context of an East-West confrontation. Western "forces" were accused of "inciting anti-socialist actions in the [Polish Peoples Republic]," attempting to "drive a wedge in the relations with the fraternal states of the socialist commonwealth," and propagating "slanderous fabrications put out by the West's sabotage services." A long-scheduled joint Soviet–East German military exercise was given an unusual amount of television coverage. It concluded with a broadcast by the Soviet officer in overall command of the Warsaw Pact military forces, Marshal Kulikov, who declared that the exercise demonstrated that the Warsaw Pact countries were "ready to defend the revolutionary achievements of socialism and fulfill their international duty."[1]

The rhetorical temperature was sufficiently high to prompt Brzezinski personally to discuss the sensitivity of the situation with the head of the US national labor federation AFL–CIO, which was then organizing support for the Polish trade unions. This had already come to the attention of the public media at the time of the Gdansk agreement.[2] US policy officials were concerned that the AFL-CIO's efforts could give Moscow an excuse to portray the growing power of the Polish labor forces as a product of Western scheming.[3]

A benchmark event occurred on 3 October, when Solidarity carried out a one-hour "warning strike" to protest the regime's delay in implementing the Gdansk agreement. The effect of the strike itself was mainly symbolic, but Intelligence Community analysts pointed out that it demonstrated vividly the evolution that had occurred in the national support and organizational effectiveness of the Polish labor movement. A single, national "command center" had organized and carried out a strike implemented simultaneously throughout

---

[1] Thomas Cynkin, *Soviet and American Signaling in the Polish Crisis* (New York: St. Martin's Press, 1988), pp. 48, 51.
[2] "US Unions Ship Money into Poland," *The New York Times*, 1 September 1980, p. A4.
[3] Gates, *From the Shadows*, p. 164. According to Gates, the AFL–CIO question was raised at a 29 September SCC meeting.

the country. This demonstration added significant weight to Solidarity's threat a few weeks later to call a general strike in response to the regime's manipulation of Solidarity's registration as an independent trade union.[4]

On 24 October, receiving what they were told was Solidarity's official registration, union leaders learned that the Warsaw Provincial Court had unilaterally inserted a clause into the charter text that stipulated union recognition of the party's leading role in matters of state. Language to this effect had been part of the agreement signed at Gdansk, but that agreement had not extended to incorporation of the same language as a "party supremacy" clause in the official founding charter of the independent trade unions. The issue of including it in the charter had been a matter of contention in the weeks preceding the court ruling. The union's leaders had been led to believe in mid-October, however, that the government accepted their compromise offer to include in an appendix to the charter a statement on the "leading role" of the party. Solidarity leaders saw the Provincial Court's move as the first step in a regime walkback strategy, and responded by threatening a general strike beginning 12 November if talks before then had not resolved the issue. The union and the regime appeared to be on another countdown to a clash that could include a violent breakdown in public order if one or both sides did not give ground.[5]

On 30 October the US Government learned that First Secretary Kania and Prime Minister Josef Pinkowski had made an unexpected trip to Moscow to meet with the Soviet political leadership. This was described in the Polish media as an "emergency trip," but its origins and purpose were obscured in the public communiqués from both Warsaw and Moscow. The officially released statement following the meeting (31 October 1980 in the official Soviet party newspaper, *Pravda*) was crafted to avoid any overt indication that Moscow was putting pressure on the Poles. Intelligence Community analysts nonetheless concluded that the meeting had been "hurriedly arranged" by the Soviets

---

[4] "Poland," decl. *NID* article of 4 October 1980. Regarding the significance of the event, see also assessments by Andrews, *Poland 1980-81*, p. 48; Garton Ash, *The Polish Revolution*, pp. 80-81; Ascherson, *The Polish August*, p. 189-190; and Jane Leftwich Curry, *Poland's Permanent Revolution: People vs. Elites, 1956-1990* (Washington, DC: American University Press, 1995), p. 269.
[5] The ongoing battle over this issue was tracked in the now decl. *NID* articles entitled "Poland" of 17, 18, 20, 21, 22, 25, 27, and 29 October 1980. See also Andrews, *Poland 1980-81*, p. 61; Garton Ash, *The Polish Revolution*, p. 81; and Ascherson, *The Polish August*, pp. 193-197.

to press Polish leaders to exert their own muscle to bring an end to the erosion of party power, with Soviet military intervention threatened if they failed to do so.[6]

Scenarios for Use of Force

While these events were unfolding, CIA was reporting that the Soviet military was continuing to improve the readiness of selected divisions in the western USSR and testing much of the basic structure necessary to invade Poland. The reporting described evidence from mid-October that some forces subordinate to each of the three armies in the western part of the Ukraine were exercising. This activity lasted about a week, and was followed by similar exercises involving at least some units in the Baltic republics and Belorussia. CIA also described training that had given Soviet command and staff personnel an opportunity to review and update contingency plans centered on Poland.

The CIA reporting pointed out that the level of troop training was still well short of what analysts believed would be Soviet requirements for a large-scale military intervention into Poland. The reports also called attention to the fact that the normal troop rotation taking place would offset the increased preparedness for some time. In the last week of October, the CIA's overall assessment was that the Soviets had not yet prepared an invasion force approaching the size CIA estimated would be employed to intervene in Poland. Nonetheless, CIA also reported that while "Soviet intervention was not inevitable…the chances for it are high enough that we should be prepared for it."[7]

By this time, however, CIA was aware that the Polish regime had started constructing its own plans for suppressing popular opposition through the use of force. A small group of Polish General Staff officers had been assigned the task of drafting plans to impose martial law. One of those assigned to this

---

[6] "Poland," declassified *NID* articles, of 30 and 31 October 1980. The press ("Top Polish Leaders Fly to Soviet Union," *The New York Times*, 30 October 1980, p. A6) attributed the meeting to Kania's initiative to discuss issues of concern to him. Minutes of the Soviet Politburo discussions preceding and following this meeting, however, specifically state that the meeting on 30 October was held at the Politburo's "invitation," for an agenda worked out in detail beforehand. See the comments by Gorbachev and Tikhonev in the records of the CPSU CC Politburo sessions of 29 and 31 October 1980, Documents 2 and 3 in Kramer, "Soviet Deliberations During the Polish Crisis," CWIHP Special Working Paper No. 1, April 1999.

[7] "Special Analysis: Poland: Crisis at Another Peak," decl. *NID*, 31 October 1980, and author's descriptions.

group was Colonel Ryszard Kuklinski, who had been a clandestine source reporting to CIA for many years.[8]

According to Kuklinski, a "Party-State Leadership Staff," headed by new Prime Minister-designate Josef Pinkowski, had been established on 24 August to oversee the design of measures for employing force to reassert the Party's power.[9] The timing of this strongly suggests that initiation of plans for imposing force was one of the actions accompanying the leadership appointments on that same date. Others on this staff included Defense Minister Jaruzelski, Internal Affairs Minister Milewski, and Deputy Prime Minister Jagielski, who had been the point man for negotiations with Solidarity. The drafting of the martial law plans was initially assigned to a group of five general staff officers, one of whom was Kuklinski. It was headed by the chief of the Polish General Staff, General Siwicki. Kuklinski has stated that the actual drafting began on 22 October. By early November, according to Kuklinski, a preliminary plan—detailed enough to have included language for decrees to be broadcast upon implementation—had been completed.[10]

The question of the willingness and ability of the Polish leadership to use its own forces to reassert party authority was the linchpin of CIA's assessment of likely Soviet courses of action. CIA postulated that if the Poles were willing (and able) to use coercive force, the Soviets could opt for sending in a few divisions to provide backup—as a reserve force and as an intimidating presence. The prevailing view in CIA, however, was that the Polish leadership would not or could not make this commitment.

The dominant view among CIA's analysts was that while the Polish internal security forces probably would be willing to carry out orders for a forceful crackdown, the regular Polish military would be loath to do so. Analysts frequently referred to a phrase that one scholar on Polish affairs has described

---

[8] Kuklinski escaped from Poland on the evening of 7 November 1981, just a month before the imposition of the martial law plan that he had been working on, when it became evident that a Polish counterintelligence investigation was about to close in on him. His critical contribution to US efforts to head off violence in the resolution of the Polish crises has been publicly known since 1987, when he granted an interview to the Paris-based Polish émigré magazine *Kultura*, portions of which were printed a year later as "The Crushing of Solidarity," *Orbis*, Vol. 32, No. 1, Winter 1988, pp. 7-31. This presentation also appears as "The Suppression of Solidarity," in Robert Kostrzewa, ed., *Between East and West: Writings from Kultura* (New York: Hill and Wang, 1990). References herein are from this printing. Gates, *From the Shadows*, ch. 13, makes many references to the importance of Kuklinski's reporting in 1981.

[9] Kuklinski, Suppression of Solidarity, Kostrzewa, *Between East and West*, p. 80. According to Mark Kramer the formal title of this group was "Party-State [Government] Crisis Staff." Re this and other archival documents confirming Kuklinski's report, see Kramer, "Soviet Deliberations on the Polish Crisis," Translator's Notes 3 and 17.

[10] Kuklinski, *op. cit.*, p. 81.

as an "unwritten commandment of the national tradition"—"Poles won't shoot Poles." Jaruzelski was alleged to have used it to describe the military services' reaction to the events in 1976.[11]

CIA intelligence analysts continued to believe, therefore, that if the Polish political leaders ordered a military crackdown, part or all of the military might refuse orders to carry it out. The analysts suggested, in fact, that an attempt by the Poles to impose force would actually increase the prospect that the Soviets would be compelled to intervene. The analysts believed, therefore, that even though the Soviets wanted the Poles to be the ones to use force, and even though the possibility of a Polish attempt was not ruled out, the uncertainties of virtually any situation for use of force would drive Moscow to ready a sizable invasion force of 30 or more divisions, if only as a safety net.

CIA assessments acknowledged the possibility of alternative scenarios in which the initial Soviet intervention force might be less than the 30 divisions, although these were regarded as much less likely. One alternative was an approach more similar to that done in Czechoslovakia in 1968. This would entail sending airborne units to seize Warsaw and perhaps a few other major centers, while a small number of divisions took key positions in eastern Poland. This might even be done under the guise of an exercise or an ostensible "request for assistance" by the Poles. Introduction of the larger forces would follow more gradually. CIA analysts viewed this as high risk, however, given that Poland was so much larger territorially than Czechoslovakia, with more than twice the population and armed forces. It was thus considered mainly a plan the Soviets might adopt if faced with rapid deterioration in public order and regime control, where time would not permit readying the full force Moscow would prefer. A variant of this "quick reaction" course postulated the insertion of 10 or so divisions drawn from Soviet forces based in Eastern Europe, which were routinely kept at high readiness levels, with additional forces brought in from the western USSR as soon as they could be readied. This option, however, had the drawback of reducing the Soviet forces facing NATO.[12]

US policy officials, as indicated in the minutes of the 23 September Special Coordinating Committee meeting, generally shared the intelligence analysts' belief that Polish authorities would not use force to crush the labor movement,

---

[11] Declassified *NID* Special Analysis, 31 October 1980, *op. cit.* Regarding the "unwritten commandment," see Garton Ash, *The Polish Revolution*, p. 248. Mark Kramer, Director of the Harvard Project on Cold War Studies, has questioned the validity of the statement attributed to Jaruzelski. See "Top Secret Soviet Deliberations During the Polish Crisis, 1980-81," CWIHP Special Working Paper No. 1, April 1999, footnote 22.

[12] "Poland: Crisis at Another Peak," decl. *NID,* Special Analysis, 31 October 1980, supplemented with author's description of the analytic background.

and that armed resistance to a Soviet intervention would be likely. One notable departure is recorded by Gates in his description of views expressed by Brzezinski in a conversation with DCI Turner on 30 October. According to Gates, Brzezinski said he believed that rather than an outright invasion, the Soviets probably would attempt a "coup" in collaboration with Polish hardliners, Soviet supporters inside Poland, and Polish police. Turner responded that this would be very risky for the Soviets because of the potential for Polish army opposition. Brzezinski said the Polish army would react in a unified way only if ordered to do so from the top, and that the Soviets would subvert the top.[13]

This contrasts with Brzezinski's own description of a discussion he had with Turner the previous day, in which he says he pressed the DCI for the Intelligence Community's latest assessment of the chances of Soviet intervention in Poland, because he was "becoming increasingly concerned that this is likely." The alternative scenario he gave to Turner on 30 October may have been stimulated by his having recently learned that the Poles had begun preparing plans for martial law. Nonetheless, his own accounts indicate that he continued to hold some skepticism on the willingness of Polish authorities to collaborate in the use of force against Polish workers.[14]

Whatever the differences in specific scenarios, these discussions reflected the common concern over the threat of Soviet-imposed force to crush the growing popular movements in Poland. The analytic question was whether the Soviets would impose force directly and unilaterally, or the Poles themselves would under Soviet pressure, or if there would be some collaborative effort between Moscow and Warsaw. The prevailing view was that the Poles would not be willing or able to carry out a forceful suppression solely on their own. Thus, Soviet military force would be required, and the prevailing view was that any Soviet military intervention would include the mobilization of a large force.

A Collision Course

Soon after Kania and Pinkowski returned from their hasty meeting in Moscow, Solidarity added new demands to its already existing one that there be no change in the statute for its registration as a free trade union. The union leadership insisted that independent farmers be allowed to register as another independent union—"Rural Solidarity"—and added some demands from their summer list, such as access to the media and an end to repression of union and opposition activists. Solidarity also reaffirmed its intent to launch a national

---

[13] Gates, *From the Shadows*, p. 165.
[14] Brzezinski, "White House Diary," *Orbis*, p. 34 (on subversion from the top), and pp. 39-40 (on skepticism of collaboration).

strike on 12 November if these issues were not resolved. The confrontation seemed to be building to the point where events could spin out of control and result in the use of force.

On 10 November, however, the Polish Supreme Court ratified Solidarity's compromise proposal to exclude the "supremacy" article from the text of its legal charter and instead include a "leading role" reference in an appendix. This court decision was actually the result of closed-door negotiations between Solidarity and the government that did not reach settlement until 3:00 a.m. on the morning of the court's announcement. Western media reported that while such negotiations had been widely known, Solidarity and government officials refused to talk about it to avoid undermining the myth of an independent court.[15]

The national strike threatened for 12 November—its potential weight demonstrated in the one-hour national strike on 3 October—was canceled. The court ruling was widely seen as another major victory for the union. Western media described Solidarity as "a powerful labor movement that forced the government to back down," and as having become "a sanctioned part of Polish life."[16]

Moscow's unhappiness with this outcome was evident. A day before the ruling was announced, the Soviet Ambassador in Warsaw made a last-minute effort to influence the court's decision. At the same time, in a clumsy public-pressure move that may have been initiated in connection with the Ambassador's last-ditch effort, Warsaw and Moscow announced that Soviet and Polish troops had held joint exercises inside Poland in the past few days. Film clips purportedly of these exercises were shown prominently on Polish television. The films, however, showed tanks and soldiers operating in what was obviously a summer climate (leaves on the trees, troops in summer clothing) when conditions in Poland were cold and snowy. Western media described the exercises as "fake."[17]

---

[15] "Warsaw and Union Fail to End Dispute on Statute Wording," *The New York Times,* 10 November 1980, p. A1; "Court Backs Union in Poland's Dispute Over Role of Party," *The New York Times,* 11 November 1980, p. A1; Ascherson, *The Polish August,* p. 198-199, provides some detail on these negotiations. Among on-site observers, Ascherson had exceptional access to some of the internal machinations of events during this period, and his book is regarded by most scholars as one of the central sources on the subject.

[16] "Court Backs Union," *The New York Times,* 11 November 1980, p. A1; "Polish Crisis Only Delayed?" *The New York Times,* 12 November, p. A1. See also Garton Ash, *The Polish Revolution,* pp. 84-85.

[17] Decl. "Situation Reports" in *NID*s of 8 and 10 November 1980; "Polish Crisis Only Delayed?," *The New York Times,* 12 November 1980, p. A1, and "Poland's Union Leaders Appeal for an End to Strikes," *The New York Times,* 17 November 1980, p. A1.

Soviet reaction after the announcement of the court ruling was illustrated in a diatribe delivered over Moscow television by Leonid Zamyatin, the head of the International Information (i.e. propaganda) Department of the Soviet Communist Party Central Committee. He painted developments in Poland in standard Cold War terms, describing them as the product of "anti-socialist elements in the West pouring millions of dollars into Poland to support opposition groups." He claimed this was an effort to "structurally and legally formalize opposition to the existing social system"—in effect, subversion by the western Cold War opponent.[18]

Any expectations that the court ruling would produce a respite were quickly squelched. New confrontations between regional party and government authorities and the regional union representatives broke out almost immediately. Medical workers, nurses, and even some doctors staged a sit-in strike in Gdansk; representative of some 70 factories in Lublin demanded wage increases; textile workers in Lodz (southwest of Warsaw) clamored for negotiating higher wages, and Polish journalists continued to challenge the regime's censorship regulations.[19]

On 24 November, just two weeks after the Polish Supreme Court compromise, railway workers demanding renegotiation of pay raises staged a two-hour strike on the commuter lines. They threatened a longer walkout for the next day if a meeting was not convened. It had been the threat to railway connections that had most alarmed Moscow back at the time of the July strikes in Lublin, and this time the Soviet media were even more strident. A *Pravda* article reiterated long-standing Soviet sensitivity to potential threats to the transport system, and for the first time attacked Solidarity by name. TASS said that a general railroad strike could affect Poland's national security and disrupt transit links between East Germany and the USSR.[20]

The actions of Walesa and Kania during this turmoil seemed to demonstrate that both recognized the situation could easily erupt and lead to repercussions neither wanted. Solidarity leaders sought to moderate what they saw as provocative actions directly threatening the party's authority, and cautioned workers against uncoordinated strikes. Kania demonstrated some willingness to engage in a dialog to implement the Gdansk agreement. He also replaced over

---

[18] "High Soviet Aide Warns Poland on Liberalization," *The New York Times*, 16 November 1980, p. 14.
[19] Andrews, *Poland 1980-81*, p. 62; "Polish Governor Offers Resignation in Response to Worker Demands," *The New York Times,* 18 November 1980, p. A12; "Polish Provincial Aides Resign in Disputes With Union," *The New York Times*, 20 November, p. A8.
[20] "Poland," decl. *NID,* 24 November 1980. The TASS article was also described in "Poland's Rail Workers in a two Hour Work Stoppage," *The New York Times*, 25 November, p. A1.

a third of the provincial party secretaries with people he portrayed as willing to implement the provisions. (His efforts in this regard were undermined, however, when he appointed as Warsaw party leader the individual who had been the party's regional leader in Gdansk at the time of the 1970 crisis.)[21]

In this volatile atmosphere, aggressive action by either side was bound to be incendiary, and that was indeed the impact of what became known as the "Narozniak affair." On the night of 20 November, just as the prospect of railroad strikes was rising, the Polish police conducted a night search of Solidarity's Warsaw offices and confiscated what was described as a classified document containing information on how the regime intended to deal with dissidents. The next day they arrested young mathematician Jan Narozniak, who worked as a volunteer printer for Solidarity, and a clerk from the public prosecutor's office, Piotr Sapielo, who was accused of passing the document to Narozniak.

Reactions to the arrests initially were local, but over the next few days they gained momentum and quickly raised the confrontation between the regime and the union to a new level. On the evening of the day Narozniak and Sapielo were arrested, the Warsaw region's Inter-Factory Founding Commission (MKZ) threatened a strike alert if the two were not released. Three days later, the same day as the railroad strike, the workers at the Ursus tractor factory near Warsaw went on strike to protest the arrests. The head of the Warsaw Solidarity Commission held a press conference at which he expanded the list of demands to include the release of other jailed Solidarity activists and other dissidents; the disclosure of the origins of the seized document; establishment of a joint commission to investigate the powers of the police, and a limitation on the budget of the prosecutor's office.[22]

The Warsaw Solidarity chapter set the regional strike to begin at noon on 27 November, and the Solidarity National Commission announced its support for the strike threat of the Warsaw chapter. The extended list of demands constituted a direct challenge to the security apparatus, and most outside observers did not believe that even a party leadership inclined to compromise could accept those demands and still survive politically. This was also the view of some of Solidarity's national leadership, who tried to moderate the actions of

---

[21] Declassified articles "Poland" from *NID*s of 19 and 22 November 1980. "Polish Union Leaders Appeal...," *The New York Times*, 17 November 1980, p. A12; "Purge in Poland Called Broadest Since '56 Crisis," *The New York Times*, 22 November, p. A1.

[22] "Poland," decl. *NID*, 21 November 1980, and "Challenge to Polish Leadership Increases," Alert Memorandum, decl. *NID*, 26 November 1980. Some coverage is also in "Polish Unions Warn of Stoppages," *The New York Times*, 24 November 1980, p. A4; and "Poland's Rail Workers in a two Hour Stoppage," *The New York Times*, 25 November 1980, p. A1. For the most part, however, the Western media did not pick up on the full impact of the Narozniak affair until after the implications of the regime concessions became apparent. Detailed accounts of this event and reactions to it are in Ascherson, *The Polish August*, pp. 204-208; and Garton Ash, *The Polish Revolution*, pp. 90-91.

the Warsaw unions. Their ability to find a way out, however, was constrained by the pressures from much of their own constituency, reinforced by strikes and confrontations taking place in other regions of the country. The union and the regime once again seemed to be in a countdown to collision.

The Intelligence Picture in Washington

An Intelligence Community Alert Memorandum on 25 November 1980 described the situation as "...the gravest challenge to its authority [the Polish regime] since the strikes on the Baltic coast ended in August." The Memorandum said the demands of the Warsaw Solidarity chapter went beyond what intelligence analysts believed the regime could accept. Thus, the union's de facto ultimatum of a regional general strike, if the regime did not enter into talks on those demands, seemed to have set a win-lose proposition that moved the situation closer to "coercive measures by the regime or a possible Soviet military invasion." The regime's flexibility seemed even more constrained by Moscow's public denunciation of the threatened railroad strike. This Alert Memorandum reiterated that there was as yet no evidence of large-scale mobilization or logistics activity indicating a Soviet decision to intervene militarily. It also said, however, that exercises and preparatory measures in the preceding month or so had positioned the Soviets to ready an invasion force rapidly.[23]

The next day, Brzezinski—after consulting with the President—proposed to the Secretaries of State and Defense that a background briefing be given to the press, to spotlight for the Soviets the adverse consequences of a military intervention in Poland. Brzezinski proposed listing consequences, including the rupture of political détente and East-West economic cooperation in Europe, increased NATO defense budgets, and overt US-Chinese cooperation. He also suggested pointing out to the Soviets the friction that could result in their relations with the non-aligned states.[24]

The State Department issued a press statement that day— apparently on its own initiative—although it did not take the approach Brzezinski was proposing. It described Solidarity as making itself a rival of the party, and said that "resolution is an internal matter for the Polish people and the Polish Government ..." and that "we intend to refrain from any words or actions that could possibly hinder the earliest possible solution of that problem and we expect others to do the same." The State Department spokesman said that the US had no indication that any Soviet troop action was imminent, but pointed out that the Soviets had taken recent steps to improve their readiness.[25]

---

[23] Decl. Alert Memorandum, *NID*, 26 November 1980, *op. cit.*
[24] Brzezinski, "White House Diary," *Orbis*, p. 34.
[25] "US Worried, Hopes for Calm in Poland," *The New York Times*, 27 November 1981, p. A11. The statement was given by State Department spokesman John Trattner.

Before any specific actions appear to have been taken on Brzezinski's recommendations, another eleventh-hour deal in Warsaw seemed again to have at least temporarily defused the situation. Early on 27 November (the evening of the 26th in Washington), the Kania regime released Narozniak and Sapielo, and agreed to begin talks by noon that day on the other demands. A settlement was also reached with the railroad workers. The potentially disastrous consequences of the threatened regional shutdown were averted at least for the time, but this was viewed by intelligence analysts as merely a respite. The "capitulation" to Solidarity was expected to lead to new divisions in the party. Observers outside the Intelligence Community shared this view.[26]

The regime had gone further than many Western observers had expected. Solidarity still showed no flexibility on its remaining demands for curtailing the internal security organs. And however constructive the regime concessions on the Narozniak affair might have been in pulling back from a confrontation, Western analysts expected that Moscow would see it as yet another indication of the Polish leadership's inability or unwillingness to stem the erosion of party supremacy.

In the weeks preceding the Narozniak affair, CIA had described military activity in the western USSR as indicating that Soviet concern about Poland remained high. The reports said the Soviets were continuing to increase the preparedness level of some units near Poland. About the time Narozniak was arrested, intelligence reporting specifically identified two normally low-strength divisions, one in Belorussia and one in the Carpathian area of Ukraine, where it appeared that the Soviets had brought in some reservists.[27]

CIA pointed out, however, that weather conditions were continuing to impede efforts to determine the status of most of the Soviet divisions garrisoned in the western USSR. CIA said it had evidence of the status of only 12 of the 39 divisions based in the western USSR, and that activity had been observed in six of them. As small as this sampling was, using the same ratio, about 20 divisions probably would have been engaged in some level of activity. Even then, however, determining how much of the observed activity was not scheduled training would have been difficult.

---

[26] "Poland," decl. *NID*, 28 November 1980. See also "Poland Frees Two Jailed Workers in the Face of New Strike Threats," *The New York Times*, 27 November 1980, p. A1, and subsequent recording of similar views by observers on the scene such as Garton Ash, *The Polish Revolution*, p. 93.

[27] The activity in the division in the Carpathian area is described in the declassified *NID* of 15 November 1980, "Poland," and also is referred to in the declassified Situation Report in the *NID* of 12 December 1980. The fact that one division was also seen at this time mobilizing in Belorussia is reported in the declassified retrospective analysis "Approaching the Brink."

For CIA's military analysts, the most important barometer of preparations for large-scale intervention in Poland was the status of the military support facilities. This was the strongest indicator before the intervention in Czechoslovakia in 1968. The search for indications of Soviet intentions on military intervention continued to be dominated by the expectation of a force large enough to overwhelm any potential military opposition and deter or suppress spontaneous opposition from the civilian populace. Such a force would require activation of a large logistic and rear-echelon support structure. In normal peacetime posture, these support elements were at an even lower state of readiness than the least ready combat divisions, thus requiring a proportionally greater mobilization of reservists and civilian vehicles.[28]

In the last week of November 1980, the Intelligence Community reported that CIA had direct evidence of, at most, only sparse activity at the Soviet military support facilities in the western USSR. This relatively low level of activity in the support elements, coupled with the admittedly small sample of combat units, led to the conclusion that preparations for an imminent invasion were not underway at that time.

The Intelligence Community also informed policy officials, however, that the Soviets' continuing military preparations had enabled them to be able under urgent circumstances to carry out final preparations for a large-scale military intervention in less than a week. The activities described included raising the preparedness of some units considered likely candidates for any invasion of Poland, and establishment of an important part of a command structure for an invasion. The mobilization activities previously observed in a division in Belorussia and in a division in the Carpathian area of Ukraine were reported to be continuing, and similar activity had begun at a normally low strength division in the Baltic region.[29]

CIA concluded that Moscow's continued inability to influence developments was pushing it toward a decision to use coercive measures—to be applied by either the Polish regime or the Soviets themselves. The intelligence reports pointed out that while the adverse political and military effects of an invasion might give the Soviets pause, they would not forestall an invasion if Moscow saw the Polish authorities losing control or conceding more to the unions.

---

[28] Author's description.
[29] "USSR-Poland: Moscow's Deepening Concern," decl. Special Analysis, *NID*, 28 November 1980, and decl. Situation Reports in *NID*s of 29 November 1980 and (about the Baltic Division) 1 December and 2 December 1980. Also some of author's description. The identification at this time of a third division being mobilized is described in the declassified retrospective analysis "Approaching the Brink."

On 29 November the commanding general of the Group of Soviet Forces in East Germany announced that through 9 December almost all of East Germany along the Polish border would be closed to travel by members of the Western Military Liaison Missions in East Germany. East German air defense personnel reportedly had their leaves restricted pending a "big action" that might be called in the coming week. Referring to these developments in his daily notebook the next day, Brzezinski characterized the situation as "gathering clouds over Poland are getting darker." He records that he had openly stressed to the press the "calamitous consequences of a Soviet military intervention," even though there was still disagreement within US policy agencies whether anything should be said publicly.[30]

---

[30] Declassified Situation Report, *NID*, 1 December 1980. Brzezinski, "White House Diary," *Orbis*, p. 34.

CHAPTER 3

US Launches Public Policy and Diplomatic Offensive

At the beginning of December, the fast-breaking pattern of events accelerated. On 1 December, the PZPR began a Central Committee plenum meeting, the same day the annual Warsaw Pact Defense Ministers meeting convened in Bucharest.

Also on that day an intelligence Situation Report reported observing "an unusually high level of Warsaw Pact military activity" taking shape in and around Poland involving Soviet, East German, Polish, and possibly Czechoslovak forces. The activity was unprecedented for this time of year, according to the Situation Report, and could involve further preparations leading to military intervention in Poland or at a minimum serve as an intimidating signal to the Polish population. The same report, however, said that while the observed measures improved Soviet readiness, the available evidence did not yet suggest the extensive mobilization and logistics buildup that would be needed to support a large-scale invasion. According to Gates, poor weather was still adversely affecting the Intelligence Community's collection of information on activities in Soviet military units.[1]

Brzezinski called attention to this latest intelligence during his briefing of the President that morning. He said he believed US officials needed to ask themselves if their government had been clear enough in its public statements on Poland and had done enough in pressing the issue with its allies. The President responded by drafting a letter that was sent that same day to British Prime Minister Thatcher, German Chancellor Schmidt, and French President Giscard D'Estaing. In this letter the President described his concerns over activities that had been observed in Soviet and East European military forces, citing such indicators as "unprecedented travel restrictions in East Germany along the border with Poland." He characterized these events as indicating that

---

[1] "Poland," decl. Situation Report and European Brief *NID*, 1 December 1980. Gates, *From the Shadows*, p. 166.

"the Polish situation has entered its most critical stage," and that "preparations by the Soviets for possible intervention have progressed further than at any previous time."[2]

The President's letter said that the US Government "will take every opportunity to express to the Soviet leaders our deepest concern about any possible military intervention by them into Poland." He asked the Allied leaders to "consult very closely with us on your actions to prevent Soviet intervention." Simultaneous with the sending of this letter the US embassies in those capitals were told they would be receiving intelligence which was to be shared with their host governments, and that they were to urge those governments to express their views—publicly or privately—about the consequences of Soviet intervention.

On 2 December, the Intelligence Community disseminated another Alert Memorandum, this time accompanied by a cover note from DCI Turner to the President. The DCI declared that "I believe the Soviets are readying their forces for military intervention in Poland. We do not know, however, whether they have made a decision to intervene, or are still attempting to find a political solution."[3]

The Alert Memorandum repeated the earlier descriptions of military activities in and around Poland that were "highly unusual or unprecedented for this time of year," and of preparations for an imminent unscheduled joint exercise involving Soviet, East German, Polish and possibly Czechoslovak forces. In a significant addition to the earlier reporting, it said that a substantial buildup of forces "could now be underway" in the western areas of the USSR. At the same time, however, it pointed out that "we do not know the status of most of the ground forces that would be used to invade Poland." In fact, the only new activity in the western USSR described in that day's situation report involved the division based in the Baltic region, where some mobilization activity had been observed in late November.

The Alert Memorandum said the judgment that a substantial buildup "could" be underway was an inference from the pattern of mobilization observed in a few divisions, which suggested that "additional mobilization or training is likely to be taking place undetected." The memo concluded with

---

[2] Brzezinski, "White House Diary," *Orbis*, p. 35, describes the genesis of the letter. The text of the President's letter and the instructions to the Embassies are in a declassified State Department cable, State 31696, in *Poland 1980-82: Compendium*.

[3] "Poland," decl. Alert Memorandum, *NID*, 3 December 1980. Turner's cover note is described in Gates, *From the Shadows*, p. 166.

the hedged judgment that the activities seen to date did not "necessarily indicate that a Soviet invasion was imminent...[but] these preparations suggest that a Soviet intervention is increasingly likely."

After receiving these reports, Brzezinski sent the President a memo saying Soviet intervention had become quite probable. He included a draft of a public statement that he recommended the President issue jointly with President-elect Reagan. In his memo Brzezinski acknowledged that there was not unanimous support among the national security cabinet for taking such a public step. He told the President he nonetheless believed that it was time for such a statement, and that there was a need to establish a clear historical record that the US did everything it could to deter the Soviets.[4]

In fact, despite the disagreement among senior policy officials on the merits of official public statements, "unofficial" descriptions of intelligence on Soviet military preparations for intervention had begun appearing in the press. On 2 December, for example, a *Washington Post* front-page article described a call up of reservists in Soviet divisions in the western Ukraine near the Polish border. A *Post* article the next day reported that it was the "widely held view" among unnamed "senior US officials" that "Moscow will move militarily if necessary." The same article described the 30-division invasion scenario that had been presented in several CIA assessments since September, saying the information was from unnamed "specialists." *The New York Times* said that US intelligence showed increased activity by the Polish security forces.[5] What Brzezinski was seeking from the President, however, went beyond such "backgrounders," and would in effect constitute a de facto demarche delivered through the public media.

That evening in Warsaw the Central Committee plenum concluded with the announcement of major changes in the composition of its Politburo. Most prominent among these was the elevation of two known hardliners—Mstislaw Moczar and Tadeusz Grabski. CIA reported that both individuals seemed to have been strong advocates of greater discipline in the party, and their elevation was interpreted as an effort to stem a process of disintegration at the lower ranks of the party. Brzezinski called these changes to the President's attention in their morning meeting the next day.[6]

---

[4] Brzezinski, "White House Diary," *Orbis*, p. 35.
[5] "Soviet Reservists Activated Since August," *The Washington Post*, 2 December 1980, p. A1; "US Warns Soviets Against Invasion of Poland," *The Washington Post*, 3 December 1980, p. A1; "US Cautioning on Intervention in Polish Crisis," *The New York Times*, 3 December 1980, p. A1.
[6] Decl. Situation Report, *NID*, 3 December 1980; "Polish Communists Oust 4 Key Leaders; General Get Top Post," *The New York Times*, 3 December 1980, p. A1; Brzezinski; "White House Diary," *Orbis*, p. 36.

On 3 December, a Situation Report said US intelligence had received information that Soviet forces in East Germany had been ordered into position to move within the next two to five days (5 to 8 December) if Moscow decided to invade Poland. According to this information, the movement of forces into Poland would be under the cover of combined exercises involving Soviet, East German, Czechoslovak, and Hungarian forces.[7]

The President approved the text of the public statement that Brzezinski had proposed to him the previous day, deleting reference to consultations with the President-elect. At a noon meeting, Brzezinski, Secretary of State Edmund Muskie, and Secretary of Defense Harold Brown agreed that the President should precede this public statement with a private letter to Soviet leader Leonid Brezhnev. By early afternoon, a letter had been drafted and approved by the President and dispatched to Moscow, informing Brezhnev that President Carter intended to release that day a "public statement of concern regarding the developments in Poland." The letter said that "[b]efore doing so, I wish to convey to you the firm intention of the United States not to exploit the events in Poland nor threaten legitimate Soviet security interests in the region... At the same time I have to state that our relationship would be most adversely affected" if force were used in Poland. The US Embassy in Moscow confirmed the letter's delivery to Brezhnev shortly before 4:30 p.m. EST, and the White House immediately released the following statement:

> The United States is watching with growing concern the unprecedented buildup of Soviet forces along the Polish border and the closing of certain frontier regions along the border. The United States has also taken note of Soviet references to alleged "anti-socialist" forces within Poland. We know from postwar history that such allegations have sometimes preceded military intervention.
>
> The United States continues to believe that the Polish people and authorities should be free to work out their internal difficulties without outside interference. The United States, as well as some Western Governments, and also the Soviet Union, have pledged economic assistance to Poland in order to alleviate internal Polish difficulties. The United States has no interest in exploiting in any fashion the Polish difficulties for its political ends.
>
> Foreign military intervention in Poland would have most negative consequences for East-West relations in general and US-Soviet relations in particular. The charter of the United Nations establishes the

---

[7] Declassified Situation Report, *NID*, 3 December 1980, *op. cit.*

right of all states, both large and small, to exist free of foreign interference, regardless of ideology, alliances, or geographic location. I want all countries to know that the attitude and future policies of the United States toward the Soviet Union would be directly and very adversely affected by any Soviet use of force in Poland.[8]

As was the case with the 1 December presidential letter to Allied leaders, the 3 December public statement was followed by the dispatch to US embassies of a summary of the latest intelligence with instructions to share it with Allied governments. The embassies were also instructed to inform allied governments that the United States "would anticipate a strong and adverse reaction throughout the world to any Soviet intervention."[9]

That same afternoon, Brzezinski provided a background briefing to the media. In describing the intelligence evidence, he emphasized that the United States viewed the Soviet intervention as neither imminent nor inevitable. In his daily notes he recorded that he did this because he felt it was important not to create the impression an invasion is "about to happen," because "[a] sense of inevitability in a way makes such a strike more likely and in a curious psychological way almost legitimates it."[10]

While this was taking place in Washington, the Polish party was issuing what was perhaps its harshest public statement to date in terms of an outright threat of a crackdown. Stating that "the future of Poland was at stake," it lashed out at Poles "who do not hide their counterrevolutionary plans," and vowed to upset the schemes for "anarchy and chaos." In the party lexicon, a charge of being "counterrevolutionary" was equivalent to being labeled an enemy of the state. The Polish media also announced that the Military Council of the Ministry of National Defense had met and expressed "profound concern" over the "serious threat" to social and national order. The intelligence Situation Report the next day described this diatribe as suggesting that some decisions on the conditions for the use of force had been made at the recently concluded Polish Party Central Committee Plenum.[11]

On 5 December, a Friday, Brzezinski received a morning phone call from the DCI informing him, according to Brzezinski's notes, that CIA had just

---

[8] The text of the letter is reproduced in Brzezinski, "White House Diary," *Orbis*, pp. 36-37, along with the account of its preparation and release. The presidential statement is in *The New York Times*, 4 December 1980, p. A10, "Text of US Statement on Poland."

[9] The guidance to US embassies can be found in a declassified State Department cable, State 323419, in *Poland 1980-82: Compendium*.

[10] Brzezinski, "White House Diary," *Orbis*, p. 37. Descriptions of the press briefings are in "Carter Expresses Concern of US on Soviet Stance," *The New York Times*, 4 December 1980, p. A1.

[11] Cynkin, *Soviet and American Signaling*, p. 63; "Leaders in Poland Make Urgent Plea for End of Unrest," *The New York Times*, 4 December 1980, p. A1; decl. Situation Report, *NID*, 4 December 1980.

received "from a very reliable source" a report that "18 divisions will enter Poland Monday morning" (8 December). As Brzezinski recorded it, the report indicated that "[t]he Polish General Staff is apparently debating whether to offer any national resistance." He immediately passed this information to the President, then informed Secretary of Defense Brown and Deputy Secretary of State Christopher and scheduled a meeting with them for the following afternoon.[12]

The information on the planned intervention was from Kuklinski. He reported that at a meeting with the General Staff of the USSR, the Deputy Chief of the Polish General Staff, General Hupalowski "...in accordance with orders from General Jaruzelski's Defense Ministry, endorsed a plan to admit into Poland (under the pretext of maneuvers)..." military forces of the Soviet Union, East Germany and Czechoslovakia.[13] According to Kuklinski, the forces would consist of 15 Soviet Army divisions, two divisions from the Czechoslovak Army, and one division from the East German Army. The operational plan envisaged that the intervening forces would first regroup at all major Polish Army bases, ostensibly to conduct maneuvers with live ammunition, (presumably to insure the support or neutralization of the Polish units there). The next step would the sealing off of all major Polish cities. Four Polish divisions were to be brought into the operation "at a later point." Kuklinski said "[a] state of readiness to cross the Polish border was set for 8 December."

Kuklinski's message did not at the time specify the date or place of this meeting, but analysts presumed (correctly, as Kuklinski would later confirm) that it had taken place in Moscow on 1 December, the same time that the Defense Ministers were meeting in Bucharest. Kuklinski added that while everyone who had seen the plans—"a very restricted group"—was "crestfallen...no one is even contemplating putting up active resistance" (contrary to the impression Brzezinski had recorded from the DCI's phone call.) Kuklinski said there were even some individuals, including a Colonel Puchala who had accompanied the Polish Deputy Chief of Staff to the meeting in Moscow, who were saying that the presence of such enormous military forces on the territory of Poland might calm the situation.

This report meshed with the information reported by the Intelligence Community two days earlier indicating preparations for moving Warsaw Pact forces into Poland under the cover of combined joint exercises. The 8 December date given in Kuklinski's message also matched the earlier report that the forces were to be ready to move sometime from 5 to 8 December, and fit with

---

[12] Brzezinski, "White House Diary," *Orbis*, p. 38. Also *Power and Principle*, p. 466.

[13] The description here is taken from Mark Kramer's translation of Kuklinski's original reporting cable, "Colonel Kuklinski and the Polish Crisis," *CWIHP Bulletin 11*, Winter 1998, p. 50.

the announcement that the closing of the East German border with Poland was to remain in effect through 9 December. The Intelligence Community also reported that same morning that convoys of cargo vehicles had been observed moving through the Baltic region toward Kaliningrad, near the Polish border, and said this might represent the start of a mobilization of motor transport units to support an invasion force. The previous day, however, the intelligence Situation Report said that evidence had been obtained on the status of 11 of 25 divisions in the western USSR which would be likely to provide the bulk of any Soviet invasion force, and mobilization had been implemented at only two of them.[14]

Some hours after Turner's call to Brzezinski, a public communiqué from Moscow confirmed that an unannounced meeting of the Warsaw Pact political leaders (the "Warsaw Pact Political Consultative Committee") had taken place there that day. At the time, little was known of what transpired at the meeting. Rumors of such a session had been around for a few days, and the Moscow Embassy had reported activities on 4 December suggesting some kind of "VIP" session was about to occur.[15]

On first learning of the meeting, CIA analysts tended to view it as another indicator of a potential crackdown on Solidarity, quite likely involving the introduction of Soviet military forces. A similar Moscow summit had preceded the 1968 intervention in Czechoslovakia. Coming on the heels of the Polish party plenum and the Warsaw Pact defense ministers meeting in Bucharest, and with defense ministers in attendance with the political leaders, even outside observers who were not privy to the reporting from Kuklinski assumed that the meeting in Moscow was focused not just on the situation in Poland but with the security aspects of that situation.

The communiqué issued that evening at the end of the Moscow summit, however, was interpreted by CIA—and most Western observers—as indicating that the Soviets had decided to give the Poles more time to solve their own problems, albeit under pressure of outside "assistance" if they failed to do so. The statement expressed agreement by "meeting participants...that [the Poles] will be able to overcome the current difficulties and ensure the development of the country along a socialist path." At the same time it said that the Polish government "can firmly count on the fraternal solidarity and support of the Warsaw Treaty Organization states"—i.e., on outside intervention.[16]

---

[14] Declassified Situation Reports in *NID*s of 4 and 5 December 1980.

[15] See declassified State Department cable, Moscow 19252, 12/5/80, *Poland 1980-82: Compendium.*

[16] The communiqué appeared in *Pravda*, 6 December 1980. The portion of its text referring to Poland was printed in *The New York Times*, 6 December 1980, p. A4. The decl. Situation Report, *NID*, 6 December 1980, and "Soviet Bloc Nations Meet Unexpectedly in Moscow on Crisis in Poland," *The New York Times*, 6 December 1980, p. A1, offer the same interpretations.

On 6 December, the Situation Report on Poland said there was "additional evidence of increased Soviet preparedness for an invasion...." Soviet military units in the area around the East German town of Templin, near the northwestern Polish border, were described as being at an increased state of readiness. Increased training activity and vehicle bivouacs had been seen at or near the garrisons of three Soviet divisions there. Also reported was the loading of equipment on pallets at the garrison of a Soviet airborne unit in the Baltic region of the USSR. A mobile military hospital had been set up on the grounds of a large civilian hospital at Kaliningrad.[17]

The meeting of the top US national security officials, which Brzezinski had set up after hearing of the Kuklinski message, took place that afternoon.[18] It included Secretary of Defense Brown, DCI Turner, Deputy Secretary of State Christopher, and Joint Chiefs of Staff representative General Pustay. The discussion began with a briefing by Turner, who stated that a Soviet military buildup east and west of Poland was continuing, and that CIA had *concluded* that the Soviets "*will* go into Poland on Monday or Tuesday" (emphasis added). Turner gave three central conclusions: (1) under the cover of an exercise, 15 Soviet divisions—mainly from the western USSR—would move into Poland in the next 48–72 hours; (2) the Polish security forces would crack down on Solidarity; (3) the intervention would result in bloodshed.

Turner's briefing was followed by a discussion of the need to inform the Allies of US economic and political sanctions that would be imposed on the USSR if the intervention occurred. Brzezinski said that the inadequacy of US communications in this regard before the Soviet intervention into Afghanistan a year earlier had led to complaints from Allied governments that they had not been brought in on US planning.

Brzezinski raised the question of whether the US should publicize the intelligence on the planned interventions "once we are confident it is accurate." He also suggested that sending a message to the UN Secretary General, or calling a Security Council meeting, would at least alert Polish dissidents and trade unionists to take refuge. He said he believed the US had a moral obligation to forewarn them "if we are fairly certain in our own minds that this is about to happen." Brzezinski emphasized that it was very important to avoid the kind of situation that occurred before Afghanistan, and to be as specific as possible with regard to the US response to a Soviet intervention in Poland.

After some discussion, however, he, Brown and Christopher agreed to suspend action because to some extent they were "still hesitant about the accuracy of the CIA analysis." He described the source of his own doubts as arising from questions about the willingness of the Polish leadership to col-

---

[17] CIA Situation Report, decl. *NID*, 6 December 1980.
[18] The description of this meeting is from Brzezinski, "White House Diary," *Orbis*, pp. 39-40.

lude with the Soviets to the extent reflected in the reported plan. He also questioned the Polish regime's ability to keep knowledge of such collusion from being leaked to the Polish population by individuals in the leadership who opposed it.

A number of intelligence analysts held similar reservations. The intelligence estimate of the size of the Soviet force that would be assembled for a military intervention in Poland was directly pegged to the premise that Moscow could not and would not count on Polish cooperation. This premise was in direct contradiction to the reports of Polish collaboration in constructing an "exercise" cover for moving troops into Poland, and Kuklinski's statement that Polish military forces would actually participate in the "exercise." The size of the force Kuklinski said would be inserted into Poland under the guise of an exercise was little more than half of the Intelligence Community's estimate of the most likely force the Soviet would choose. Skepticism regarding reports of Polish collusion, and the absence of convincing evidence of invasion preparations large enough to quickly overwhelm the potential resistance capability of the Polish armed forces, led many analysts privately to conclude that an intervention was not imminent. Kuklinski's earlier reporting that the Polish leadership was developing martial law plans had little impact on these calculations.[19]

Nonetheless, Kuklinski's proven reporting credentials, combined with what appeared to be corroborating reports from other sources, and preparations detected in an admittedly limited number of Soviet units in the western USSR, left little room to challenge the widely held conviction of near term intervention. Cloud cover over much of the western USSR also forced the analysts to confront the possibility that they had only seen a fraction of the force being readied.

Brzezinski called President Carter at Camp David the evening of 6 December to report on his afternoon meeting with the other senior national security officials. He described to the President the latest intelligence relating to Soviet plans for intervention, but said the meeting participants recommended against briefing members of Congress or President-elect Reagan. This recommendation also meant there would be no official public statement. Brzezinski's account of the phone conversation strongly implies that the

---

[19] This description of the analysts' outlook is based on the author's direct involvement in the deliberations at the time and recent discussions with others who also were involved. The author confesses to guilt in this regard. So long as one accepted the "Poles won't shoot Poles" dictum, it was almost impossible not to look for the assembly of a force large enough to discourage and/or overwhelm the potential resistance. A force that had about a one-to-one ratio with the Polish army did not fit this description. At the end, our predictions that intervention was not about to occur were right for the wrong reasons.

President had problems with the recommendation. Brzezinski told him it was based on concern for causing needless panic and damaging the administration's credibility. The President said that he still wanted a meeting the next morning to discuss the matter.[20]

This meeting convened on 7 December at 9:00 a.m. in the White House Cabinet Room. In addition to the President and Brzezinski it included Secretary of State Muskie and Deputy Secretary of State Christopher, Defense Secretary Brown, and DCI Turner. Brzezinski opened by summarizing for the President the intelligence information and the three main points given in the DCI's brief the day before. According to Brzezinski's account of the meeting, a prolonged discussion followed on whether to take the story to the public.[21]

The President was strongly in favor of doing so, according to Brzezinski. As the discussion progressed, Brzezinski also argued in favor of it. He describes Secretaries Muskie and Brown as continuing to express some reservations, but mainly inclined to support a public statement. A decision was reached to begin with a briefing of congressional leaders and follow with a public statement and diplomatic initiatives, including a message to the UN Secretary General.

According to Brzezinski, while the discussions were taking place, the DCI was called out to answer a phone call. He returned at 9:34 to say that CIA had just received additional information that preparations for Soviet military intervention had been completed on 5 December and on that day a "joint decision" had been made to carry out the intervention. Turner said that the report indicated units were to enter Poland simultaneously from the USSR, East Germany, and Czechoslovakia as early as the next morning, or perhaps that same evening. Allowing for the six-hour time zone difference with Poland, this would mean within the next eighteen hours, possibly the next six hours.

This report was roughly consistent with the scenario described in Kuklinski's report received the day before, except that this most recent report seemed more certain that the decision for military intervention had definitely been made. The fact that a Warsaw Pact summit had taken place on the day that the report claimed this decision had been made presumably added to its credibility, even though the communiqué at the end of the summit had seemed conciliatory.

Brzezinski's account does not explicitly indicate whether or to what extent the DCI's interjection affected the discussions at the meeting. Nonetheless, what Brzezinski has described as the consensus decision at this meeting with the President was exactly the opposite of the consensus view reached by mostly the same people at the meeting late the previous afternoon. Certainly,

---

[20] Brzezinski, "White House Diary," *Orbis*, p. 40.
[21] *Ibid.*, pp. 41-42.

the President's views would have had a powerful impact on the discussion. The interjection of the new information, however, half an hour into what Brzezinski described as a "prolonged discussion," would seem likely to have added to the case for actions that his advisors had been unwilling to take the previous day.

After a break of a couple of hours, the President and his National Security Council met again to review and approve the draft texts of the public statement and of the message to be sent to various heads of state and the UN Secretary General. Senior members of the Senate and House of Representatives joined the meeting and were given a detailed description of the evidence and of the actions to be taken.[22]

Brzezinski led off by reading to the participants an *Associated Press* dispatch that had just been received through the wire system. It began with the words "The Soviet news agency TASS, in an unusual report Sunday, confirmed a joint Soviet-Polish military..." The wire transmission cut off at that point. While staff members worked to get the remainder of the text from the wire transmission, the partial text was, according to Brzezinski, considered by "everyone...to be a very important item of intelligence suggesting confirmation of CIA's analysis." Indeed, it appeared to be the opening line in an announcement of the combined exercise that intelligence reporting had said would be the cover for the introduction of Soviet forces into Poland, and its timing was consistent with the reporting that this was to occur the following day, 8 December.

At the conclusion of this meeting a presidential message was sent simultaneously to allied governments including the UK, Germany, France, Italy, Canada, Australia, and Japan, as well as to the Secretaries General of NATO and the UN. It provided a summary of the intelligence that lay behind the President's statement, saying that US now had intelligence indicating that:

> The Soviet Union had made the decision to intervene with military force and that entry into Poland by a substantial Soviet force, possibly under the guise of a joint maneuver, may be imminent. This may be accompanied by widespread arrests by Polish security forces. We cannot be confident that this is the case, but the probability is sufficiently high that in my view Western nations should take whatever steps they can to affect Soviet decision-making and thus try to prevent the entry of Soviet forces into Poland.

---

[22] The afternoon meeting is described both by Brzezinski, "White House Diary," *Orbis*, pp. 42-43, and by Gates (who attended the meeting with the DCI) in *From the Shadows*, pp. 167-168. The official minutes also have been declassified. See Special Coordination Committee Meeting and National Security Council Meeting, 7 December 1980, *Poland 1980-82: Compendium.*

> Accordingly, I am issuing the following statement at 2:00 p.m. today Washington time. I trust that you will be able to issue similar statements soon. Such statements will demonstrate to the Soviets the resolve of the Western Alliance and will serve to warn the Polish people of the serious nature of the current situation.[23]

Promptly at 2:00 p.m., the White House released the following statement:

> Preparations for possible Soviet intervention in Poland appear to have been completed. It is our hope that no such intervention will take place. The United States Government reiterates its statement of December 3, regarding the very adverse consequences for US-Soviet relations of a Soviet military intervention in Poland.[24]

The release of the statement was accompanied by a briefing to the press on additional details of the intelligence behind the President's statement. Front-page stories carried by *The Washington Post* and *The New York Times* the following day, attributed to "informed US sources," described extensive movement of Soviet and Warsaw Pact military units; Soviet divisions out of garrison in the western military districts of the USSR; the call up of Soviet reservists; and the bringing to full readiness of command and communications facilities linking military headquarters in the USSR to other headquarters in East Germany, Czechoslovakia, and Poland itself.[25]

By the time the press briefing was being given, CIA analysts had received the written text of the report that the DCI had described after receiving the phone call during the meeting with the President that morning. The analysts discovered that while the report did describe plans for a military intervention, it did not include a statement that "a joint decision to invade has been made." The DCI was informed of the error. There is no record of what was subsequently done to inform the policy officials.

A short while later, CIA analysts learned that the AP dispatch that seemed to confirm the plans for an exercise the next day was also erroneous. It was the result of a wire service computer error producing a re-transmission of the 9 November announcement of a pretended exercise (see page 19 above). The error in the transmission had been almost immediately detected by the wire service and cut off. The cut off in mid-sentence inadvertently led to the confusion as to what was being communicated. Brzezinski's notes show he also learned of this error, but do not state when he learned it.[26]

---

[23] The text of the letter is given in the National Security Archive document cited in the preceding footnote.
[24] The statement is attached to *The New York Times*, 8 December 1980, p. A1, "Russians Ready for Possible Move on Poland, US Says."
[25] *Ibid.*; "Concern Grows On Soviet Plans in Poland," *The Washington Post*, 8 December 1980, p. A1.
[26] Brzezinski, "White House Diary," *Orbis*, p. 43.

Over the course of the next week, intelligence reports continued to characterize activities in Warsaw Pact military units around Poland as heightening their readiness to mobilize and deploy in minimal time if called upon to do so. The reports described Soviet divisions based in East Germany and Czechoslovakia being moved out of their garrisons. In the western USSR the number of mobilized divisions appeared to have increased to four, and perhaps five, and some civilian vehicles appeared to have been called up to flesh out logistic support elements. Various maneuvers were also observed, which could have been exercises but could have been positioning. A steady stream of briefings was provided to the press. The fervor appears to have generated some exaggerations, as exemplified by a 10 December story that five Soviet divisions were camped in tents on the Soviet-Polish border.[27]

On 12 December, a NATO communiqué directed at the USSR announced that any violation of the "basic rights of any state to territorial integrity and independence" would result in the end of détente. The communiqué said any threat of intervention will force the Allies to react in a manner which the gravity of this development would require." That same day *The Wall Street Journal* carried a leaked account of senior US officials discussing the possibility of economic measures against the USSR. This information had been provided by Brzezinski as a deliberate measure to let the Soviets know such steps were being contemplated.[28]

By this time the Intelligence Community determined that some of the Soviet divisions what had been engaged in mobilization and exercises in the latter half of November were returning to their garrisons. Information also had been received reinforcing earlier intelligence interpretations that the Warsaw Pact leaders had agreed at their Moscow summit to grant Polish leaders time to use their own means to put down the challenge to party authority. The reports also indicated that this was accompanied by an implied threat of Soviet military intervention if the Poles did not act decisively.[29]

---

[27] Declassified Situation Reports from *NID*s of 8-13 December 1980. The stream of press briefings is reflected in "Russians Ready For Move, US Says;" *The New York Times*, 8 December 1980; "Moscow and Allies Activate Reservists; Invasion Fear Rises;" *The New York Times*, 9 December 1980; and "Russian Forces Around Poland Termed Ready," *The New York Times*, 10 December, 1980.
[28] Brzezinski, "White House Diary," *Orbis*, p. 47.
[29] CIA Situation Report, decl. *NID*, 13 December 1980.

CHAPTER 4

Filling Out The Picture

In mid-December, the weather conditions impeding assessment of the status of most of the Soviet forces in the western USSR dissipated. Imagery obtained at that time showed that only three regular ground force divisions in the western USSR were fully mobilized—one each in the Baltic region, Belorussia, and the Carpathian area of Ukraine.[1] These were the same three that had been observed mobilizing in the latter half of November. The fourth division in the western USSR which had been seen preparing for movement in early December, an airborne division in the Baltic region, had stood down. (Airborne divisions were normally maintained at or near full manning and thus would not have required a notable influx of reservists.) The heightened alert conditions that had been observed in many of the military installations in the area in late November and early December had ended, and most components were in normal peacetime posture.

CIA concluded that most of the Soviet divisions and support units in the western USSR had not undergone the mobilization required to bring them to full readiness for movement into Poland. The military preparations that had been observed over the preceding months were judged to have been contingency measures, undertaken in case it became necessary to carry out a full mobilization in response to a political decision to introduce forces into Poland.

---

[1] Except where otherwise noted, the intelligence described in this section is drawn from a declassified *Intelligence Memorandum* produced by CIA's National Foreign Assessments Center, "Approaching the Brink: Moscow and the Polish Crisis, November-December 1980" (late December 1980 or early January 1981), which is now available at the National Security Archive. Another, less detailed presentation is in "Poland's Prospects Over the Next Six Months," declassified *National Intelligence Estimate*, No. 12.6-81 (January 1981), National Security Archive, Washington, DC, which was included as Document 38 in the materials for the 1997 Jachranka conference.

Standard Soviet military procedures called for units subject to being ordered to full combat readiness to take time-cutting preparatory steps to complete the process, if the orders are issued. These steps included establishing command and communications centers, reconnaissance of dispersal areas, and in some cases, partial mobilization. Such intermediate measures were particularly important for divisions normally kept at low peacetime manning levels. Most of the activities observed in the western USSR in October and November fell into this category of "intermediate" steps, and most of the divisions reported as taking such steps were in the category maintained at lowest peacetime manning.

In CIA's view, these preparatory steps brought overall military readiness to the point at which as many as 20 Warsaw Pact divisions could have deployed to Poland within a week of receiving a full mobilization order. The evidence also showed, however, that except for the three divisions previously identified, the order for full combat readiness—which would have entailed extensive activation of reservists—had not been given.

Skeptics might posit that the reservists and vehicles necessary to bring forces to full readiness had been called up, but returned to the civilian sector by the time the weather cleared (i.e., after only a week or so of active duty). CIA acknowledged that this was physically possible but judged it highly improbable, and it still seems so. As CIA's analysis at the time pointed out, once a brink was reached at which Soviet leaders were willing to bear the cost of such a large mobilization, there would have been strong resistance to immediately reversing it. At a minimum, having already borne the main cost of the call up itself, it seemed implausible that the personnel would not have been retained at least through the normal reservist training period. Supporting this conclusion was the fact that the three divisions seen mobilizing in late November were the three that still had their reservists in the third week of December, when the rest of the forces in the western USSR were clearly not in a mobilized status.

CIA continued to maintain that an intervention carried out at Moscow's initiative, without Polish cooperation, would require some 30 divisions, and that preparations for such an intervention would exceed those observed in December. These preparations would have included a far more extensive mobilization of reservists and civilian vehicles, and other large-scale logistic activity.[2]

Nonetheless, while concluding that the Soviets had not prepared the necessary forces for such an intervention, CIA also judged that Moscow had indeed been preparing to deploy some forces into Poland. In addition to the planning

---

[2] This judgment is articulated in a recently declassified CIA document originally disseminated 28 March 1981, "Poland: Warning of Intervention."

and preparations already described, CIA pointed out that the Soviets had been detected reconnoitering movement routes and assembly areas in Poland. Also, a signal brigade and part of the General Staff auxiliary command center attached to the Soviet Group of Forces permanently based in Poland had been deployed to the field.

Acknowledging uncertainty as to how many troops Moscow actually intended to send in and what they would do once there, CIA said that the USSR "presumably" intended to conduct an "exercise in Poland...to jolt the [Polish] principals in the crisis into realizing that [Moscow] meant business. The Soviets may also have been planning to use the Warsaw Pact troops, once in Poland, to back up a crackdown by Polish security forces." The CIA assessment said Moscow's intent apparently was to introduce the forces "in a highly visible manner and as 'legitimately' as possible, by obtaining an official invitation from the Kania regime and the cooperation of the Polish military authorities."[3]

Earlier CIA assessments had postulated that the Soviets might engage in exercises on Polish territory as a means of coercing the Poles. Estimating that this may actually have been the Soviets' intention in December reflected the reports from Kuklinski and other sources describing a greater than expected level of Polish collaboration, and imagery revealing how little mobilization had actually been carried out.

CIA posited that the decision to defer even this military action probably was not taken by the Soviet leadership until the day before the 5 December Warsaw Pact summit in Moscow. The intelligence assessment said the Soviets appeared to have interpreted recent public and private statements by the Polish leaders (for example, on 3 December, following their plenum) as signaling that they recognized Moscow's tolerance limit had been nearly reached and that they needed to take more assertive measures to counter Solidarity. CIA said that the Soviets saw the Moscow summit itself as a mechanism for coercion, providing a forum to make clear to the Poles that if they failed to act effectively, Warsaw Pact military "assistance" would be forthcoming.[4]

Soviet and East European Records on Military Contingency Planning

Three documents from this period describing the forces to take part in the "maneuvers" in Poland are now available—two from East German records and one from Czechoslovak files. All three list the same East European forces that Kuklinski reported—one East German division, two Czech, and four Polish. The documents vary, however, in their descriptions of Soviet forces. One

---

[3] "Approaching the Brink," pp. 4-5.
[4] *Ibid.*, pp. 7-8.

of the East German documents gives the same total reported by Kuklinski—fifteen.[5] The other two documents describe the same Soviet forces that US intelligence saw being readied at the beginning of December—four divisions from the western USSR, including one airborne division.[6] The Czech document states that a fifth Soviet division—from Soviet forces permanently based in Czechoslovakia—was also slated to participate in the first phase of the maneuvers in Poland. Preparations to commit this division would have been less visible to Western intelligence because Soviet divisions based in East Europe were maintained at full manning, thus no reservist mobilization would have been required.

The different figures may reflect a distinction between the full Soviet force called for in the contingency plans for implementing the crackdown, and the portion of the plan to be exercised in December. The two East European documents that refer to the four Soviet divisions from the western USSR explicitly state that the activity in which they are to engage is an exercise. Kuklinski, however, said in his public interview that he based his description of the intervention forces on information he had received from other military officers and "...the registered blueprints of the final invasion plans taken from Soviet maps."[7] It seems likely that, given his role in martial law planning, the charts that he saw—and which are described in the one East German document—showed not just the exercise but the full contingency plan for introduction of external forces when the actual military crackdown was implemented.

This interpretation would be consistent with the plans described in a document now available from Soviet archives showing Moscow's contingency measures for mobilizing divisions in the western military districts of the USSR. On 25 August, about a week before the Gdansk agreement, the Soviet Party Central Committee established a commission charged with tracking developments in Poland and recommending courses of action. This commission was chaired by senior party ideologue Mikhail Suslov, and included Defense Minister Ustinov, KGB Chief Andropov, Foreign Minister Gromyko, Deputy Party Secretary Chernenko, "Information" Director Zamyatin, and

---

[5] Michael Kubina, Manfred Wilke, and Reinhard Gutche, *Die SED-Feuhrung und die Unterdrueckung der polnischen Oppositionsbewegung 1980/81*, [*The German Socialist Unity Party Leadership and the Suppression of the Polish Opposition Movement, 1980/81*] (Cologne: Bundesinstitute fuer Ostwissenschaftliche und Internationale Studien, 1994), pp. 30-31.

[6] Michael Kubina and Manfred Wilke, *Hart und kompromisslos durchgreifen: die SED contra Polen, 1980-81*," [*Tough and Uncompromising Crackdown: The German Socialist Unity Party Against Poland 1980-81*], (Berlin: Academie Verlag) pp. 134-137; and "Report of the Chief of the General Staff of the Czechoslovak Army, Colonel General Miroslav Blahnik, to Minister of National Defense, Army General Martin Dzur, 3 December 1980," *CWIHP Bulletin 11*, Winter 1998, p. 67.

[7] Kuklinski, "Suppression of Solidarity," Kostrzewa, *Between East and West*, p. 82.

various others.⁸ Three days after it was formed, this commission forwarded to the Central Committee a Ministry of Defense plan for preparing nine to 11 divisions in the western military districts of the USSR for possible commitment in Poland.⁹

Adding these divisions to the one division that the Czech document said was to be committed from the Soviet forces based there, plus the two Soviet divisions permanently based in Poland, would provide twelve to fifteen divisions for the Polish operation. As described above, intelligence in early December disclosed that there were also three Soviet divisions based in East Germany that appeared to be engaged in contingency preparations for movement, which would bring the total of Soviet divisions earmarked for commitment to Poland to fifteen to eighteen.

According to the "Suslov commission" plan, four of the divisions from the western USSR would be immediately brought to full combat readiness by requisitioning "from the national economy up to 25,000 reservists and 6,000 vehicles..." The reason given for the urgency was the "tense" situation in Poland. The Ministry of Defense said that to carry out their tasks "during the entry of these divisions into the territory of Poland," the divisions would have to receive their combat manpower five to seven days before undertaking the operation. Contingency measures would be taken to prepare another five to seven divisions for rapid activation "if the situation in Poland deteriorates further." This required preliminary steps for the call up of as many as 75,000 additional reservists and another 9,000 vehicles from the civilian economy. All of this is consistent with the indication in the East European documents of contingency measures for a two-phased implementation, with about four divisions initially being committed from the western USSR and the others readied for rapid deployment if the situation demanded.

There has to date been no independent confirmation that the August mobilization of reservists and civilian vehicles for four divisions was actually implemented, but the possibility cannot be ruled out. No description of such a mobilization appears in any of the US intelligence documents declassified to date, although in the first part of September 1980, CIA did report that some Soviet units appeared to be practicing mobilization, some of which involved civilian vehicles exercising with military units.¹⁰ The complete fleshing out of

---

⁸ "Extract from Protocol No. 210 of the Session of the CPSU CC Politburo on 25 August 1980," *CWIHP Bulletin 5*, Spring 1995, p. 116.

⁹ The text of this Soviet Ministry of Defense mobilization request is given in Mark Kramer's "In Case Military Assistance is Provided to Poland," *CWIHP Bulletin 11*, Winter 1998, pp. 102-109. The request noted that the initial 6,000 vehicles included replacements for 3,000 that were normally kept with the divisions but which at the time had been detached to assist in the annual harvest.

¹⁰ The declassified *NID* of 27 August 1980 does have a relatively large section under the heading of "Military Activity," but the text of the section is redacted.

only a few divisions that had already been seen at least partially mobilized could have gone undetected for some time, particularly if the divisions did not fully deploy out of garrison. The weather problems would have compounded the difficulty in confirming full mobilization.

If the full mobilization had been carried out at the end of August, the reservists would have been released if the forces were not employed within about six weeks. Even this period would have exceeded the normal reservist tour of duty. An emergency situation would permit them to be kept on duty longer than the normal training period, but eventually they would have to have been used or released. The evidence clearly shows that the divisions slated for mobilization in response to the Soviet Ministry of Defense request in August were not the same ones that were seen to be fully mobilized in mid-December.[11]

It is now known that in mid-August, the Polish leadership had established an Interior Ministry task force to begin preparations for implementing a forceful suppression of the strikes and protests. The actions being readied by this task force, codenamed *"Lato '80,"* ("Summer '80") included the storming of the Gdansk shipyard with the assistance of helicopters. By the end of August, the Polish Interior Ministry task force believed it was ready, subject to a go-ahead from the party, to impose its crackdown, and the issue was being discussed at meetings of senior party officials.[12] The Polish party backed down from the action at the last minute, reportedly because both Kania and Jaruzelski argued that the Poles were not yet ready for such a step.[13]

---

[11] The MOD requested mobilization of three tank divisions and one motorized rifle division, and the short time span for the mobilization and the number of reservists allotted indicates most of the four were from the higher peacetime readiness category. According to CIA ("Approaching the Brink," p. 2), the three observed to have been mobilized in December were all motorized rifle divisions from the lowest peacetime readiness category.

[12] See Translator's No. 2 to Mark Kramer's translation of the CPSU Politburo Protocol No. 213 of 3 September 1980, "Soviet Deliberations on the Polish Crisis, 1980-81," Document No. 1. The descriptions therein of the planning of and debates over Lato '80 are drawn from PZPR Central Committee Politburo Protocols No. 17 (15 August 1980) and No. 28 (29 August 1980), pages 24 34 and 84-90 respectively, of Zbigniew Wlodek, ed., *Tajne Dokumenty Biura Politycznego: PZPR a "Solidarnosc" 1980-1981* [*Secret Documents of the Politburo: Polish United Workers Party versus Solidarity*] (London: Aneks, 1992); and a Polish Ministry of Internal Affairs document of 29 August 1980 (Posiednie Sztabu MSW, 29.viii.1980) in Polish archives (Archiwum Urzedu Ochrony Panstwa). These events are also described in Garton Ash, *The Polish Revolution*, p. 62; Dobbs, *Down With Big Brother*, pp. 42-44, 51; and Ascherson, *The Polish August*, p. 162. Dobbs notes that the files of the "Summer '80" Task Force have now been published in I Zycie Warszawy, 12 May 1994, "Ekstra," pp. 1-3.

[13] *Ibid.*, especially PZPR Politburo Protocol No. 28. Also see Dobbs's additional material in his notes, p. 461.

Moscow was fully aware of these plans and the fact that they were being discussed at the highest echelon of the Polish party. On the surface, it appears that the Soviets were at the time readying a few divisions in case it became necessary to rapidly deploy a backup or reinforcing effort, with contingencies for mobilizing an even larger force if the situation began to spin out of control. Within a day or so of the mobilization request they would have been aware that the Polish crackdown had at a minimum been put off. They may, therefore, have eased off on the urgency of their own mobilization, while still going ahead with a "practice," which may have been what US Intelligence detected as under way in September.

Regardless of whether the mobilization was actually completed, what is most significant about the August mobilization plan is the size of the force it was intended to prepare. Together with the descriptions in the East European documents and US intelligence on the actual force preparations that were undertaken later, it raises serious doubts that Moscow was at any time truly contemplating the kind of overwhelming invasion force that the Intelligence Community had estimated as most likely. The intelligence analysts' model for the intervention was based on the premise that the Soviets could not and would not count on the Polish leadership to actively support the use of force, let alone impose it themselves. The Soviets, however, appear to have been developing their plans on the premise of just such Polish action. Their military preparations were being shaped in terms of whether and how much back up they would have to provide to the Polish effort, not on the forces they would need to carry out the operation unilaterally.

Polish Military Involvement In December "Exercise" Planning

Kuklinski's 4 December message disclosing plans for moving Warsaw Pact forces into Poland included what appears to have been a direct reference to Polish leadership involvement in the planning for those movements. As noted above, the message said that the deputy chief of the Polish General Staff had, *"in accordance with orders from General Jaruzelski's Defense Ministry, endorsed a plan"* to admit forces into Poland under the guise of an exercise (emphasis added).

Kuklinski has now provided more details on this. In responding to a question in his first public interview in 1987, he said that Jaruzelski had been engaged in discussions with the Soviets on the general outlines of the plan prior to the 1 December Moscow meeting where the detailed "blueprints" for the "exercise" were passed out. He said Jaruzelski had opposed the Soviet plan for maneuvers on the grounds that both the timing and the inclusion of foreign troops (especially East German) would have an inflammatory effect on the volatile conditions in Poland. Jaruzelski insisted that if the Soviets could not be dissuaded from conducting the maneuvers, Polish forces needed to participate. As a result of this argument, according to Kuklinski, the exercise scenario passed out at the Moscow meeting called for four Polish divisions to be brought into the operation. Kuklinski emphasized that the "blueprints" (apparently referring to charts or schematic maps) brought back from Moscow on 1 December confirmed "what had been known earlier from conversations between the Russians and Jaruzelski."[14]

This contrasts with a general perception that at the beginning of December the Soviets unilaterally presented Jaruzelski with an "ultimatum" that "shocked" him into locking himself in his office.[15] While Kuklinski does describe Jaruzelski's depressed state and his seclusion in his office, he says this occurred on 30 November and 1 December, while Jaruzelski was awaiting delivery of the detailed plans from Moscow.

Records of Soviet leadership meetings show that the main problem the Soviets perceived with the Polish leadership was not its political stance on the need to suppress the civil challenge, but rather its will to take the necessary action. This is reflected in the minutes of a 29 October Soviet Politburo meeting held for the specific purpose of reviewing the arguments and tactics that would be used in the next day's scheduled "emergency" visit to Moscow by Polish Party Chief Kania and Prime Minister Pinkowski. Brezhnev, Ustinov, Gromyko and Suslov all made remarks about Kania, Pinkowski and Polish Defense Minister Jaruzelski being "reliable...committed...the best among the core" of the Polish party officials. Each of the favorable comments, however, was accompanied by remarks about the Polish leaders being "without resolve," not "sufficiently strong," and "at loose ends."[16]

The records of this discussion clearly confirm the judgment of intelligence analysts at the time that the meeting with Polish leaders scheduled for the next day had been called for the specific purpose of galvanizing them to act. Brezhnev, Ustinov and Gromyko all referred to the need for the Poles to impose martial law. Ustinov said that "if they do not introduce martial law the matter will become very complicated." The back up role of Soviet military forces was also alluded to by Ustinov, who said that there is a "good deal of vacillation" in the Polish army, but "we have prepared the Northern Group of Forces [the two Soviet divisions permanently based in Poland]...." Concern about the Soviets being seen as the instigators of a Polish use of force was implied by

---

[14] Kuklinski, "Suppression of Solidarity," Kostrzewa, *Betweeen East and West*, p. 82.
[15] For example, see Dobbs, *Down With Big Brother*, p. 57.
[16] "Session of the CPSU CC Politburo," 29 October 1980, *op. cit.*

Gromyko's comments that martial law "doesn't have to be done immediately, and particularly not right after their [Kania and Pinkowski] return from Moscow...but we should steer them to that...."

Following the 30 October meeting with the Polish leaders, Brezhnev reported to the Politburo that Kania had said the Poles did have a plan for martial law ("state of emergency"), that they "knew who should be arrested," and that they knew "how to use the [Polish] army." (This was about a week after the date when Kuklinski said the Polish task force actually began drafting the martial law plans.) While characterizing his discussion as positive, Brezhnev again commented that Kania still seemed hesitant regarding the imposition of martial law. He described the Polish leaders as particularly anxious to "forestall hints that they were acting at the behest of Moscow."[17] All of this took place more than a month before the Moscow summit in December, and the issues clearly intensified during the interim.

The Warsaw Pact Summit in Moscow

Several accounts of what transpired at this meeting, including minutes and descriptions by official participants, have become available since the end of the Cold War. The most detailed record so far available is the stenographic record of the East German delegation—virtually verbatim minutes. A somewhat less detailed record was prepared by the Hungarian delegation.[18] All of the accounts generally confirm the intelligence interpretation (and Western media descriptions) at the time.

The Poles were subjected to intense pressure to use their own forces to restore party authority. Kania gave an extensive discourse asserting that the Poles agreed with the recommendations for a forceful crackdown and were in the process of preparing to take the necessary steps. The threat of intervention by the other Warsaw Pact military forces seems more muted than was presumed at the time, however, coming across mainly in the atmosphere and "double entendres" (at least as presented by the record scribes). No mention appears of any plans for joint military maneuvers on Polish territory.

---

[17] "Session of the CPSU CC Politburo," 31 October 1980, in Kramer, "Soviet Deliberations on the Polish Crisis, 1980-81," Document No. 3.
[18] Kubinka and Wilke, *Hart und kompromisslos durchgreifen*, pp. 140-195. A translation of large excerpts from this stenographic record by Christian Ostermann of the Woodrow Wilson Center is at the National Security Archive. A somewhat more abbreviated version is the report of Hungarian Party leader Janos Kadar to his own Central Committee, obtained by the CWIHP from the Hungarian National Archives Department of Documents on the Hungarian Workers Party and on the Hungarian Socialist Workers Party. Both documents were included in *Poland 1980-82: Compendium*. Both are in close agreement, the only difference being in Kadar's version of what he personally said at the meeting and the order in which he spoke.

Kania described the Polish leadership group chaired by the Prime Minister that had been established to manage the "emergency measures," and he insisted that it was preparing specific steps. He also outlined plans for the arrest of the "most active functionaries of the counterrevolutionaries," and the creation of "special groups of particularly trustworthy party members which, if necessary, can be armed." Kania said some 19,000 already had been selected and the number was expected to reach 30,000 by the end of the month.

Each of the other Warsaw Pact leaders emphasized that it was up to the Polish leadership to resolve the problems in Poland. There were specific urgings (e.g., by Todor Zhivkov of Bulgaria, and Eric Honecker of East Germany) that the Polish armed forces and security forces be used to crush the civil resistance. The party leaders of Hungary (Janos Kadar) and Czechoslovakia (Gustav Husak) cited the previous crises in their own states as a means of impressing on the Poles the potential consequences of failing to take timely decisive action on their own. Brezhnev and Honecker stressed what they saw as the Polish leaders' failure to follow through on the promises they had given—at their meeting in Moscow at the end of October—to draw a line on the concessions to Solidarity and to take more decisive action. The implication was that there was a limit to how many times such promises could be taken seriously, and that patience had its limits.

This plenary meeting was followed by a private session between Brezhnev and Kania. Personal descriptions given by participants in this meeting and in a parallel one between Ustinov and Jaruzelski provide the only references to discussion between the political leaders regarding joint military maneuvers. Kania has said that Brezhnev, after obtaining promises that the Poles would use their forces to crush the Solidarity movement, said that the Soviets would not enter Poland. Brezhnev added, according to Kania, that "if there are complications, we will go in." The Soviet interpreter at the meeting has given much the same version, recalling Brezhnev as saying "okay, there will be no maneuvers. But if we see that they are overthrowing you we will go in."[19]

One significant point on which the new information differs from the earlier interpretations concerns the circumstances under which the Moscow summit was called. CIA said in its December 1980 analysis that the Soviets "probably did not make the decision to defer military action *and to summon Pact leaders to Moscow* until 4 December"[20] (emphasis added). Most accounts in the immediate aftermath described the meeting as "sudden," and a "surprise," and this is still a fairly widely held impression.

---

[19] Dobbs, *Down With Big Brother*, pp. 63-64, 462.
[20] "Approaching the Brink," p. 7. For other examples of the "surprise/sudden" characterizations, see Cynkin, *Soviet and American Signaling*, p. 63; Garton Ash, *The Polish Revolution*, p. 99, and "Soviet Bloc Nations Meet Unexpectedly," *The New York Times*, 6 December 1980, p. A1.

The information now available, however, shows that in the last week of November, the planning for the meeting and the planning for the military maneuvers were taking place in parallel. East German archives have turned up a letter from Honecker to Brezhnev dated 26 November "proposing" that a meeting of Warsaw Pact party leaders be convened in Moscow. He recommended that the meeting be held following the upcoming plenum of the Polish party Central Committee slated to take place from 1 to 3 December. In this letter, Honecker said he was aware that Hungarian party leader Husak and Bulgarian party leader Zhivkov had already been making such proposals.[21] (By the rules of conduct among the Soviet Bloc party leaders, unanimous recommendations from the East European party chiefs usually were in response to signals from Moscow that certain proposals would be welcomed.)

These plans for a meeting of party leaders were thus being discussed at the same time that Kuklinski has said Jaruzelski was involved in discussions of "joint maneuvers" with the Soviets. The East German records indicate that they received their invitation on 28 or 29 November to the 1 December Moscow session to go over the plans for joint maneuvers.[22] The establishment of a temporary restricted area on the East German-Polish border was announced on 29 November. The reports that military preparations were to be completed by 8 December, and that the restricted area on the border was to last through 9 December, suggest that the timing for the military maneuvers was directly linked to the timing and outcome of the high-level political meeting being set up for the end of the first week of December.

Interpreting the Evidence

The evidence clearly shows that the Soviets had not readied a force of the order of magnitude CIA had estimated they would prepare if they were to undertake an externally imposed military suppression of the Polish labor movement. At the same time, however, it is clear that they had prepared for the introduction of at least some forces into Poland. On balance, the evidence is fairly persuasive that—as was concluded in the retrospective intelligence assessment—Moscow was preparing a joint military exercise to be carried out on Polish territory as part of a pressure campaign to force the Poles to carry out their own military crackdown. Brezhnev reportedly told Indian Prime

---

[21] Mark Kramer's translation of this letter is in the *CWIHP Bulletin 5*, Spring 1995, p. 124.
[22] Kuklinski's comments are in "Suppression of Solidarity," Kostrzewa, *Between East and West*, pp. 82-83. Regarding the East German dates, the chief of the East German general staff sent his message to Moscow on 29 November naming his representatives for the upcoming meeting, indicating he had received his invitation on or before that date. See Kubina and Wilke, *Hart und kompromisslos durchgreifen*, p. 134.

Minister Gandhi in a meeting on 8 December 1980 that the Soviets had planned maneuvers but had "postponed" them because of objections raised by Polish leaders.[23]

Moscow knew that the Polish leaders were actively preparing measures for martial law, but doubted their resolve to carry them out. Soviet political leaders would have seen the exercise as a device to strengthen the incentives for the Poles. For Soviet military planners, it offered the additional benefit of rehearsing an operation they might be ordered to carry out if the threatening postures did not produce desired results.

The extent to which Soviet political leaders were actually committed to carrying out the maneuvers remains unclear and may never be known (or knowable). The fact that the target date for bringing forces to full readiness was set for shortly after the planned political summit suggests that implementation of the maneuvers was still contingent on a final political decision expected to be made no sooner than the summit. In his report on the 1 December Moscow meeting, the Czech Army Chief of Staff said that the Soviet chairman of the meeting had said "at the present time the exercise is merely prepared. Its execution, including the timing...will be determined by the political leadership."[24]

It is likely that the Polish leaders' strong opposition to the maneuvers was driven by concerns that insertion of foreign forces on Polish territory—even if only for maneuvers—would make any efforts to organize an indigenous crackdown all the more difficult. It would galvanize the opposition and alienate some elements that might otherwise be willing to support the use of Polish forces for crushing Solidarity. In effect, premature movement of "fraternal forces" into Poland might result in a self-created need for such assistance.

For Kania and Jaruzelski, ordering the use of force carried considerable political risks, but being seen as carrying this out for Moscow would have been even more damaging. It would have undermined whatever hopes they had of portraying themselves as acting in Poland's best interests by implementing a less undesirable solution, which is the justification Jaruzelski used for the implementation of martial law a year later. As noted above, this was alluded to by Gromyko in the 29 October meeting of the Soviet Politburo, and Brezhnev indicated that it had come up in his 30 October discussions with Kania.

---

[23] "Approaching the Brink," p. 5.
[24] "Report of the Chief of Staff of the Czechoslovak Army," *op. cit.*

A major catalyst in the preparations for the military maneuvers and the political pressures that led up to the Moscow denouement appears to have been the brokered Polish Supreme Court ruling on 10 November. Other Warsaw Pact regimes viewed this as the capitulation to Solidarity that Kania had vowed in his meeting with Brezhnev barely a week earlier he would not permit. Both Brezhnev and Honecker cited this in their statements at the 5 December Moscow summit. They said their understanding of the meeting that had taken place between Kania and Brezhnev at the end of October had been that the Poles agreed, in Brezhnev's words, "that there was no room for retreat." Both characterized the ensuing events, particularly the Supreme Court action, as a broken promise—in Honecker's words, "a major setback."[25]

CIA's reporting shows that two of the three divisions observed at full readiness in mid-December began their mobilization within about a week of the Supreme Court action. By the latter part of the month, discussions were under way between Jaruzelski and the Soviets on the plans for joint maneuvers to be held in Poland in early December. On 26 November, the same date as the Honecker letter proposing a summit of political leaders in Moscow, the Polish Politburo stepped up its martial law preparations. Kania directed that draft legislation for a "state of emergency be prepared for submission to the Polish Parliament, and that unilateral government decrees banning strikes and assemblies and tightening censorship also be drawn up."[26]

This was at the height of the Narozniak affair; the same day, Solidarity's Warsaw chapter set the date for a regional general strike and the union's National Commission announced its endorsement of the Warsaw chapter's position. The martial law actions taken by the party Politburo can plausibly be attributed to the acute political crisis at the time. At the same time, however, Jaruzelski's discussions with the Soviets concerning military maneuvers clearly would have added to the motivation of Polish leaders to demonstrate willingness to take aggressive measures on their own.

The martial law initiatives taken by the Polish leadership were reported to Berlin on 28 November by the East German military attaché in Warsaw, albeit in a somewhat exaggerated description. (His report said he had obtained the information the previous day.) The KGB would have been at least as well informed. Kuklinski has in fact reported that Moscow was kept abreast of all the martial law planning. By 29 November, the East Germans had received their invitations to Moscow to discuss the finished plans for the exercise and

---

[25] Kubina and Wilke, *Hart und kompromisslos durchgreifen*, pp. 166–167, Honecker; and pp. 181-191, Brezhnev.
[26] The Polish Politburo minutes are in PZPR Protocol No. 51 (26 November 1980), described in the chronology included in *Poland 1980-82: Compendium*. The text is in Wlodek, *Tajne Dokumenty*, pp. 180-188.

cabled back their acknowledgment.[27] (The same was probably true for the senior military officers of other Warsaw Pact states, but documents are not available.)

On 1-2 December, the Polish party plenum was held, and at the same time, Polish military officers were delivering the detailed plans for the maneuvers being set up by Moscow. The desire to persuade Moscow to defer these maneuvers was presumably a major factor in the strong public statements issued the day after the plenum by the Polish party Central Committee and the Military Council of the Defense Ministry. For the Military Council to make any public statement was itself a noteworthy rarity.[28]

Polish Politburo member Olszowski flew to Moscow the night before the summit convened, presumably to lay the groundwork for the arguments Kania and Jaruzelski would present when they arrived the next day. As noted above, the US Embassy in Moscow reported signs of high-level meetings taking place on the eve of the summit.[29] Normal Soviet Bloc practice would have called for the summit session itself to be scripted in accordance with preparatory discussions. Olszowski's credentials as a hardliner favoring a crackdown would have added credibility to the assurances Kania would give the next day regarding the Polish leadership's intention ultimately to impose a crackdown on Solidarity.

In sum, by the time of the Moscow meeting, the Soviets had received a variety of indications that pressure on the Polish leadership had begun to show results. The Soviets apparently concluded that while they needed to continue to exert pressure on the Poles to implement martial law, they could for the time being accede to Polish requests for more time to prepare, and defer the potential costs and risks that would have accompanied movement of forces into Poland—even if only for an exercise. In what turned out to be an accurate forecast, CIA said that Polish acquiescence—however grudging—in the exercise that had been planned for December would have given the Soviets grounds for believing they could revive the exercise proposal at a later date if necessary. This is exactly what happened three months later.[30]

---

[27] The military attaché report is described in Kubina, Wilke, and Gutche, *Die SED-Fuerhrung*, p. 124. The timing of the East German response to the Moscow invitation is described above, p. 42.

[28] Cynkin, *Soviet and American Signaling*, p. 63; "Leaders in Poland Make Urgent Plea for End of Unrest," *The New York Times*, 4 December 1980, p. A1; "Approaching the Brink," *The New York Times*, 4 December 1980, p. 7; and Garton Ash, *The Polish Revolution*, p. 95. The content of these public statements is summarized above, pp. 33-35.

[29] Declassified State Department cable 19252, 12/5/80, *Poland: 1980-82: Compendium*.

[30] "Approaching the Brink," p. 7.

Meanwhile, taking advantage of the preparatory deployments of various headquarters and communications elements they had already carried out, the Soviet military on 8 December went ahead with a command staff and communications exercise. This provided a means for rehearsing at least part of their plan—and the exercise was extended through the first quarter of the next year as a device to maintain pressure on the Polish leadership.[31]

Alternative Readings

The possibility cannot be ruled out that the Soviets intended to use the Warsaw Pact troops, once in Poland, to support a crackdown on Solidarity. CIA made this point in its retrospective analysis. The evidence suggests that during the initial stages of military preparations (about mid-November) the ultimate mission may have been left open, with plans for deployment of the larger Soviet force of 15 divisions worked out and coordinated on the understanding that, depending on how political events played out, they could be scaled back to an exercise.

The only step needed in December to bring the Soviet forces up to the 15-division level reported by Kuklinski was to implement the mobilization plan prepared by the Soviet Ministry of Defense in August. As had been reported by CIA, and as indicated by the Soviet Defense Ministry plan, Moscow had undertaken preparatory measures to enable this to be carried out in a few days. But there seems no reason why the Soviet military planners would have left themselves dependent on a crash mobilization if they had time to be fully prepared, which the evidence shows they clearly did.

Moreover, if the Polish leaders were uncertain at that time of their ability to deal with the volatility of maneuvers, they almost certainly would not have been able—even if they had wanted to—to assure Moscow of the military cooperation that formed the basis for the Soviet intervention plan. Conversely, the Soviets had ample evidence that use of their own forces could be minimized, if not avoided altogether, if the Poles could be pushed into executing the martial law plans the Soviets knew were being readied. Given the indications that their pressure on Warsaw to take its own forceful measures seemed to be working, the Soviets would have had good reason to avoid committing their force in a risky venture until they had better prepared the playing field.

---

[31] See Ustinov's remarks in the record of the CPSU CC Politburo Meeting of 22 January 1981, in Kramer, "Soviet Deliberations During the Polish Crisis," Document 8 and Translator's Note No. 102 giving the background of those remarks. For other information on the exercise known as *Soyuz '81*, see Cynkin, *Soviet and American Signaling*, pp. 98-103; Garton Ash, *The Polish Revolution*, pp. 153, 158; "Haig is Troubled by Troop Moves on Polish Border," *The New York Times*, 30 March 1981, p. A1; "US Aides Say Build-Up Needn't Signal Move on Poland." *The New York Times*, 5 April 1981, p. 4. The exercises in the spring of 1981 are discussed in more detail below, pp. 102ff.

At the time of the 5 December meeting, Brezhnev already was scheduled to begin a state visit to India on 8 December. A joint exercise in Poland would not cause any significant problems during such a trip. It is highly unlikely, however, that the Soviet leader would have subjected himself to a media-covered event in a foreign capital outside the Warsaw Pact at the same time Soviet military forces were helping crush a workers' movement. He almost certainly would have had to confront accusations of an "invasion." At a minimum his schedule would indicate that, if anything more than "maneuvers" was planned, it was not slated to take place until sometime later.

An alternative at the opposite end of the spectrum is that the Soviets had no intention of carrying out even an exercise on Polish territory, and that the preparations were merely a bluff as part of the coercion. Part of the difficulty in ruling this out is that any evidence that would seem to support the argument that the exercise was really intended can be explained as a successfully implemented part of a deception conspiracy.

Had the Soviets been engaged only in a bluff, however, they could have mounted a more threatening posture by deploying more divisions out of garrison, without adding the cost of actually calling up the full complement of reservists for any one division. Conversely, many of the preparations they did take—such as setting up command structures and preliminary steps in the logistics chain—would not have been readily apparent to the Poles without access to the same kinds of technical collection available to the United States. These measures were mainly used for the command staff and communications exercise that took place on 8 December.

One argument is that the Soviets deliberately undertook such less apparent preparatory measures in the expectation that the US would detect them and warn the Poles, thus lending credibility to the threat. Soviet *disinformatsia* practices lend some plausibility to this argument, but given the US record with Czechoslovakia in 1968 and Afghanistan in 1979, the Soviets would have had to have some uncertainty whether the United States would warn the Poles or simply protest through diplomatic channels. (The justification for such uncertainty would be amply demonstrated a year later.)

CHAPTER 5
Intelligence and Policy

If Moscow did intend to carry out some military action in December of 1980—whether an exercise or something more—the evidence now available leaves little doubt that it had been called off by the end of the Moscow summit and probably sooner. This means that, taking account of the time zone differences, it had already been called off by the time Brzezinski received Turner's call describing the plan reported by Kuklinksi.[1] The White House meetings over the following weekend, the President's diplomatic communiqués and public statement, and the associated White House press briefings actually came after the fact. The possible impact of the actions taken in Washington a few days earlier cannot be dismissed, but any attempt to evaluate this is impeded by the uncertainties concerning what really was planned and about the motivations of the participants in the Moscow Summit.

That said, it is hard to find fault with the vigorous action the Carter Administration took. The ambiguity that continues to exist nearly two decades later illustrates forcefully the uncertainties that were confronted in assessing and forecasting the dynamics of the situation at the time.

The record of the meeting between President Carter and his national security advisors on 7 December describes the President's summation of the discussion as "[W]e did not know whether the Soviets would go in. Our first goal is to keep them out." The text of the President's letter dispatched to Allied leaders following that meeting said that "[W]e cannot be confident that [intervention is in fact intended, but]...the probability is sufficiently high that in my view Western nations should take whatever steps they can to affect Soviet decision making."[2] A phrase that could have been inserted, and which was clearly implicit, would have been "and the stakes are sufficiently high."

---

[1] The East German stenographic record says the 5 December meeting of Warsaw Pact leaders concluded at 3:30 p.m Moscow time, (Kubina and Wilke, *Hart und kompromisslos*, p. 195) which would have been 7:30 a.m. in US Eastern Standard Time. Brzezinski has said that he received the call from Turner describing the Kuklinski report at 9:10 a.m. that day ("White House Diary," p. 38).

[2] Declassified minutes, "Special Coordination Committee and National Security Council Meeting," 7 December 1980, *Poland 1980-82: Compendium*.

With this principle as a basis for action, the available intelligence clearly merited the administration's moves. The United States had received, from one of its most well-placed and proven human source assets of the entire Cold War period, a report that strongly indicated military intervention was about to occur. Intelligence analysts also had been seeing indications for some time that the Soviets were, at a minimum, increasing their readiness for such a contingency. As has been described by Robert Gates, much of the western USSR was obscured by weather during the critical time frame in late November and early December. The analysts were thus confronted with the problem that the small amount of force preparations they could confirm might be the tip of a much larger iceberg.

All this was taking place just one year after the Soviets had intervened militarily in Afghanistan. This factor gets at most only passing reference in the various meeting records, but its influence on the intelligence components' tendency to lean towards the worse case—and on the aggressive approach taken by the policy officials—cannot be discounted. There was a clear inclination among senior intelligence officials to "err on the high side."

An aspect of the administration's policy that might be vulnerable to criticism involves not the actions taken, but rather that those actions were taken late in the game—and then only after receiving intelligence that seemingly indicated intervention was certain. US officials meeting on the afternoon of 6 December possessed information that, if true, meant the challenge they faced was not deterring a decision under consideration, but reversing a decision already made. According to the DCI's initial briefing, Soviet forces would be ready to carry out the operation within 48 hours, and he previously had said the plan called for Soviet forces to enter Poland as early as the next 36 hours.[3] Months of clear indications that Soviet forces had been increasing their preparedness for just such an action preceded this information.

Nonetheless, the participants concluded their meeting by agreeing to recommend to the President that no action be taken until they were "fairly certain in their own minds that this was about to happen."[4] According to Brzezinski's account, the participants in the meeting had uncertainties about the accuracy of the intelligence, and their skepticism was most pronounced on the reporting that indicated Polish collusion in the intervention. By the time the President's letter to Allied leaders was sent the following afternoon and his public state-

---

[3] In informing Brzezinski of the report from Kuklinski, Turner had said the Soviet troops were to enter Poland on "Monday morning" (8 December). Allowing for the six-hour time difference between Washington and Warsaw, this would have been a few hours after midnight, Washington time, on 8 December. The 6 December meeting in Washington began at 4:00 p.m., according to Brzezinski, "White House Diary," *Orbis*, p. 39.

[4] Brzezinski, "White House Diary," p. 40.

ment was released, it was 10:00 p.m. in Warsaw, the night before Soviet forces reportedly were to enter Poland. By then, if the reporting was correct, the intervention units probably would have been deploying toward the border. Even the relatively late US public and diplomatic actions appear to have required the direct intervention of the President. These were buttressed by late-breaking information from the DCI and a wire service report that seemed clear that Soviet forces would enter Poland on the morning of 8 December. (Both pieces of information, as described above, turned out to be misrepresented.)

This demonstrates that the declared principle of "not certain, but enough evidence to warrant action," can be difficult to implement in practice. As illustrated in the account of the 6 December meeting, those responsible for policy decisions are understandably reluctant to act until they are "fairly certain." Intelligence producers face the challenge of forecasting decisions by foreign actors before those decisions have been made, and usually when the actors are themselves not certain what their decisions will be.

Waiting for certainty, however, requires waiting until a decision has been made, and reversing decisions is much more difficult than influencing them beforehand. Once the players become certain, the policy question usually moves from prevention to reaction. To adapt a metaphor, if certainty requires a "smoking gun," it means waiting until the "bullet" has been fired. This is a systemic tension between intelligence and policy that cannot be eliminated, only blunted. There is no single formula for achieving this, but a fundamental ingredient is the explicit recognition and continuing consciousness of its potential impact on the effectiveness of intelligence in supporting policy. The danger for the intelligence producers is that it causes them to become fixed on a "bottom line," and to narrow the analytic options.

The critical role played by intelligence in generating the vigorous US diplomatic and public policy measures on the Polish situation was manifest from the early stages of the civil turmoil there. Declassified White House documents show that intelligence reporting prompted the meeting on 23 September to develop responses to a potential Soviet intervention. Brzezinski's notes describe his actions and the President's initiatives in the first few days of December as responses to the picture painted in the daily intelligence reports and the Alert Memoranda from the DCI. The spurt of meetings and escalation of the administration's offensive on the weekend of 6-7 December were a direct result of the pivotal report from the CIA's crucial human asset in Poland.

The degree of certainty with which the intervention was portrayed in the late stages can be justifiably criticized. To some degree, however, this was the flip side of the problem of the policy arm's reluctance to act in the face of ambiguous evidence. In this case, the record raises a legitimate question of whether the administration would have acted as forcefully as it did without such expressions of certainty from intelligence. It is likely that, to some extent, intelligence officials were reacting to the criticism that had been leveled at the Intelligence Community for equivocating on warnings of a Soviet intervention in Afghanistan.

The analysis can be faulted for the extent to which it was dominated by a single premise: that Polish leaders would not impose force on their own, would not cooperate with, and, in fact, be likely to actively combat, a Soviet imposition of force. As a consequence, the threshold of Soviet military preparations the analysts were looking for to indicate a looming military crackdown—however triggered—far exceeded what the Soviets appear to have actually contemplated. This put the analysts at risk of misinterpreting the signs, and may have contributed to the policymakers' decision at the 6 December to defer prominent public actions.

In any case, it would have been difficult, solely based on physical evidence, to interpret preparations for the collaborative imposition of force described by Kuklinski. By comparison, mobilizing some 30 divisions and accompanying logistical support would be a strong indication that a military operation was intended. This led to the DCI's initial estimate that the Intelligence Community would be able to give two to three weeks' warning of Soviet intervention. Detection of only a few mobilized divisions, on the other hand, especially in the western USSR (where they would constitute only a small fraction of the divisions based in the region), could be variously interpreted. Examples would include annual reservist training call up, or perhaps contingency measures for commitment of a large force in response to a future decision yet to be made—which is how the preparations were being interpreted prior to receiving information about a different scenario. Under these circumstances, tactical warning would have been far more uncertain.

Once a hierarchy of expectations becomes an analytic framework, it tends to narrow the use of empirical evidence. In describing the limited mobilization and scant logistic preparations observed by 1 December, CIA said "available evidence does not yet suggest that the extensive mobilization and logistics buildup that would be needed to support a *large scale invasion* has been initiated." This report also said that the measures that had been completed would make it possible for the Soviets "*under urgent circumstances* [to] carry out their final preparations [for such an invasion] in less than a week." (emphasis added).[5] The report did *not* go on to state that the preparations *had* put the Soviets in position, if they obtained Polish cooperation, to immediately move a few divisions into Poland for a joint imposition of force. The assessment of

---

[5] Declassified CIA Situation Report 1 December 1980 (European Brief), p. 3.

the readiness posture of the Soviet forces was confined to predicting how soon the scenario judged most likely could occur, not whether that judgment was still valid.

This trap is not unique to intelligence; it is inherent to all fields of analysis.[6] The "key premise" vulnerability is particularly acute when the premise deals with perceptions and future decisions of political leaders—in this case, the views of Polish leaders on the use of force and decisions they would make in future. This is a process of judging what decision a player will make before that player has made the decision. It normally means relying on inferentially developed assumptions. The principal danger comes from the frequent tendency to allow such assumptions to become accepted constants in the day-to-day analysis of incoming information.

This "key premise" hazard cannot be avoided, only contained. In practice, this means explicitly highlighting the premise or premises that bind together the analytic equations, and the potential impact that a change in one of these premises could have on the overall conclusions. Making these factors an explicit part of the analytic product can help focus collection on those key premises upon which the analysis rests most heavily, and raise sensitivity to any contradictory information.

In the case of Poland in late 1980, the premise that the Polish leadership probably would not employ or cooperate with the Soviets in the use of force was so central to the outcome that it warranted continuous scrutiny. One reason it did not get more attention was probably the fact that it was so widely shared. As the meeting records indicate, a majority of the policy officials and other western experts shared the intelligence judgment.[7]

Perhaps more important to the analytic process was the judgment that even if some Polish leaders were willing to cooperate with the Soviets, any effort to use force would encounter such strong resistance in Poland that a major Soviet intervention would ultimately follow. Information now available shows that this judgment may well have been initially correct. As their own records show, both the Soviet and Polish leaders were concerned about how the Polish army might react to any use of force against Solidarity. They clearly shared the US intelligence view that some segments of the Polish Army might rebel against

---

[6] An exceptional contribution to understanding how this, as well as other aspects of the way humans intellectually process information, can impede effective analysis is a recent work by Richards J. Heuer, Jr., *Psychology of Intelligence Analysis* (Washington, DC: Center for the Study of Intelligence, 1999).

[7] See "Summary and Conclusions," SCC Meeting, Tuesday, 23 September 1980, National Security Archives, and Ash, *The Polish Revolution*, p. 69.

such force. They even considered the risk of some soldiers actually joining Solidarity in active resistance.[8] It was to deal with this problem that Moscow was pressing its offers of military backing.

But in offering military backup the Soviets were acting more in line with the perception Brzezinski had outlined to the DCI on 30 October—that the Polish military would offer organized resistance only if directed from the top, which the Soviets apparently believed it could control. The records of Soviet meetings show that Polish leaders' willingness to at least develop plans for martial law was the central factor in Soviet planning. These records show that Moscow still believed its preferred option of having the Poles carry out their own suppressive action was feasible, and the Polish leadership was giving signs that encouraged Moscow to continue.

The main contention between Moscow and Warsaw was not over justifying force, but whether the Poles would be willing to carry it out, when, under what circumstances, and what role, if any, there would be for Soviet backup forces. As Kuklinski described, this was a major point of contention in Soviet-Polish exercise planning in late November, and in the decision to "postpone" the maneuvers in December.[9]

The Polish leadership's approach to the use of force was central to all interpretations of the physical evidence and to any ability to anticipate the form that a Soviet military intervention might take. The assumption that the Poles would not or could not collaborate led to the belief that military suppression would be presaged by mobilizing a 30-division Soviet invasion force. The Polish regime's stance on the use of force was also central to formulating US policy initiatives for deterring possible action. And CIA had received information indicating that its key conclusion about the willingness of Polish leaders to support the use of force was quite possibly in error—that martial law plans were being developed under the supervision of several top Polish leaders, including the Prime Minister and a deputy prime minister, the Minister of Defense, the Chief of Staff of the Polish armed forces, and the Minister of Internal Affairs. This was different from the 1968 "Prague Spring," in which the Czechoslovak party leadership was leading the liberalization movement.

---

[8] See for example the records of CPSU Politburo discussions on 3 September 1980, Translator's Note No. 9, and 29 October 1980, with Translator's Note No. 16, in Kramer, "Soviet Deliberations on the Polish Crisis," Documents 1 and 2.
[9] Records of the CPSU Politburo Discussions of 13 September 1980, Translator's Note No. 12, and 29 October 1980, Translators Note No. 16, in Kramer, "Soviet Deliberations During the Polish Crisis," Documents 1 and 2. Kuklinski, "Suppression of Solidarity," Kostrzewa, *Between East and West*, pp. 82-83.

The apparent lack of more vigorous efforts to probe this question, especially given the exceptional human intelligence access CIA had in this case, clearly was a shortcoming of the analytic process during this period. As events played out, this shortcoming probably had little effect on the outcome of the events at the time. But the issue of how intelligence on this subject was used would become even more pronounced a year later, when the Polish government imposed martial law.

Finally, this also demonstrates the complementary nature of the diverse sources of intelligence information. Throughout the period leading up to the December US policy offensive, interpreting observed, physical evidence was shaped by beliefs about the intentions of Polish and Soviet leaders. It is hard to know what people think. In theory, intentions can be inferred from physical actions. In practice, however, the process is too often reversed— actions are interpreted on the basis of existing beliefs about intentions. Experience has repeatedly demonstrated that getting inside human thought processes is best done by a human source, with the caveat that this can vary widely depending on the human sources available. Accurate information from a reliable human source can be a major factor in the ability to interpret a massive amount of physical evidence.

This impact is illustrated in CIA assessments after mid-December. After acquiring persuasive human source information showing more Polish willingness to cooperate in the use of force than had been previously assumed, CIA's interpretation of the physical evidence was a very close fit with what later information has shown to have actually been intended and contemplated. Physical preparations that were assessed in CIA reporting of 1 December in terms of their implications for readying a large-scale intervention were interpreted in a later assessment as indications that the Soviets had prepared to carry out an exercise with Polish cooperation. The same physical preparations were also seen as indicating that the operation may have been intended as a Polish-implemented, Soviet-backed imposition of force, a scenario which until then had been treated as highly unlikely.

Chapter 6

Escalating Challenges to the Polish Regime

The 5 December meeting of the Warsaw Pact party chiefs in Moscow had a sobering impact on Solidarity's national leadership. The circumstances of the meeting itself and the public alarms sounded in the West conveyed a clear warning that the union had pushed party authorities both in Warsaw and in Moscow closer to the brink of some form of draconian measures. On the day of the Moscow summit meeting, Solidarity's National Coordinating Commission issued a statement pointing out that there were no strikes in Poland and that none were planned. Polish party officials responded shortly after their return from Moscow with an appeal for restraint, declaring their willingness to negotiate and seek compromise. In an effort to portray an atmosphere of truce, party and government officials appeared with Solidarity leaders and church representatives at a 16 December ceremony to commemorate the 1970 shootings at the Lenin Shipyard in Gdansk.

On the surface this seemed to signal a respite from confrontation and offer at least the possibility of an accommodation between the growing civil movement and the Polish party. The underlying volatility of the situation, however, became quickly evident in confrontations that erupted on two major issues within a month of the Moscow summit. One was the effort by Poland's private farmers to organize and legally register their own independent union modeled after Solidarity. This dramatically expanded the civil opposition movement. The other confrontation was over the issue of work-free Saturdays and a five-day work week, and was part of the continuing struggle over implementing the provisions of agreements reached in the strike settlements at the end of the previous summer.

A Farmers' Gdansk[1]

This confrontation had been percolating for a long time. In autumn 1978, three "Farmers' Self-Defense Committees" had been set up with the assistance of (and on the model of) the Committee for the Defense of Workers (KOR)—the organization of dissident intellectuals created in 1976 to support the factory workers' movement. After Solidarity emerged in September 1980, a group from the Farmers' Self-Defense Committees sought to set up Rural Solidarity as a farmers' union parallel to Solidarity. Similar unions were piloted under the titles "Peasants' Solidarity" and "Union of Agricultural Producers Solidarity." Their fundamental objectives were recognition of private farming's role in the national economy, and legal protection for the inheritance of land.

On 24 September 1980, the same day that Solidarity submitted its documents to the Warsaw Provincial Court for formal registration as an "Independent Self-Governing Trade Union" (NSZZ), the private farmers submitted their own papers for registration as "NSZZ–Rural Solidarity." At the end of October, the Warsaw court ruled that private farmers were "self-employed" and thus not entitled to organize as a labor union. Like the factory workers of Solidarity, the farmers appealed this ruling to the Polish Supreme Court.[2]

The factory workers lined up in support of the farmers. Lech Walesa had attended the court session at which the Warsaw court issued its ruling against registration of the farmers' union. When Solidarity threatened a nationwide strike in the struggle over its own legal registration, its demands included the formal registration of Rural Solidarity.

On 14 December, while the farmers were waiting for the ruling on their appeal, they went ahead with an all-Poland founding congress for their independent union. One thousand delegates claiming to represent 600,000 private farmers met in Warsaw to establish Rural Solidarity. They called for formal registration, guarantees for private ownership with rights for sales and

---

[1] An extensive description of the conflict over formation of the independent farmers union is given in Garton Ash, *The Polish Revolution*, pp. 110-134. Mr. Garton Ash "camped in" with the protesters for a period, and in the third chapter of his book he gives an intimate account of events. He notes (on p. 112) that the stronghold of independent farmers in southeast Poland was the result of efforts by the Polish Communists after WWII to buy the allegiance of farmers in what had once been Austrian–ruled Galicia. This involved redistributing some 15 million acres of land in private plots averaging about 12 acres. Other, less intimate but informative treatments are Andrews, *Poland 1980-81*, pp. 105-107; and Peter Raina, *Poland 1981: Toward Social Renewal* (London: George Allen and Unwin, 1985), pp. 57-59.

[2] Raina, *Poland 1981*, p. 56, gives the date of the court "ruling" as 29 October. Garton Ash, *The Polish Revolution*, p. 111, gives the date of the court "hearing" as 22 October.

purchases of land, an end to subsidies to the state agricultural sector, increased pensions for private farmers, an end to press censorship, and restoration of a religious curriculum to state schools.[3]

The day after Christmas, a group of farmers occupied a public building in Ustrzyli Dolne (in the southeast corner of Poland near the border with Ukraine), to protest the diversion of roughly 150,000 acres and large monetary sums to a resort there reserved for party functionaries.[4] A few days after that, farmers' delegates gathered again in Warsaw for the long-awaited Supreme Court ruling on their union's registration. On 30 December, however, the court again postponed it on a flimsy pretext.

In early January, a group of independent farmers and workers in Rzeszow, also in the southeastern corner of Poland about 60 miles above Ustrzyli Dorne, occupied the headquarters of the government-sanctioned provincial trade union. Their initial purpose was to protest the government's presumptive appropriation of the funds of what was, by then, the defunct government union. In a sequence reminiscent of the events in Gdansk five months earlier, a protest initially directed at a local issue quickly escalated to a confrontation with national civil and political implications.

Almost immediately after the protesters in Rzeszow began their occupation, they demanded anew the registration of a Rural Solidarity for independent farmers. They increased their demands in the ensuing two weeks to include the return of state-requisitioned land to private hands; guarantees of private ownership and inheritance of property; access to fuel, machinery, building materials and improvement grants that were then being exclusively channeled to the public sector; free elections to self-governing organizations at the local level; permission for school children to choose what languages they would study (e.g. English, German, or French instead of Russian), and truthful history books. One observer on the scene has described the events at Rzeszow as the "farmers' Lenin Shipyard," with farmers there seeking a "Gdansk agreement for the countryside."[5]

As this farmers' protest blossomed into a confrontation with national resonance, Solidarity's factory workers launched the first of their nationwide work boycotts in their battle over a five-day work week.

---

[3] Raina, *Poland 1981*, p. 57
[4] The protesters were evicted from the building by police on 12 January but continued their protests for more than another month. See declassified Situation Report, "Poland," 12 January 1981, and Garton Ash, *The Polish Revolution*, p. 111.
[5] Garton Ash, *The Polish Revolution*, p. 114.

Work-Free Saturdays

The struggle for a five-day, 40-hour work week in Poland also had deep roots. Polish workers' considered it to be nothing more than a demand for the same conditions enjoyed by workers not only in Western Europe but in Eastern Bloc countries such as East Germany and Hungary. The shorter work week had been promised to them at the beginning of the Gierek regime 10 years earlier, and they were still waiting for it to be delivered. The Gdansk accord signed on 31 August 1980 included a provision stating that the government would present by year's end a program for more work-free Saturdays, or other ways of shortening what was then a 46-hour work week—eight hours each week day and six hours on Saturday. The agreement signed with the miners at Jastrzebie three days after the Gdansk settlement went further, with a government commitment to make all Saturdays work free in 1981.[6]

The government subsequently made the not-unreasonable argument that because of the state of the Polish economy, it would be damaging to try to move too quickly to a 40-hour week, and that two work-free Saturdays per month were all the economy could afford.[7] The government also correctly pointed out that its specific commitment for *all* Saturdays to be work free had been made only to the miners at Jastrzebie. In early November, the government floated (in its controlled media) the alternatives of either a five-day week with longer work days amounting to a 42.5-hour week, or a mix of five- and six-day work weeks with pre-designated work-free Saturdays.

Solidarity rejected both alternatives, insisting that the government was obligated to make all Saturdays in 1981 work free. Solidarity's reaction was driven mostly by distrust of government intentions among the union's increasingly radicalized rank and file. Even though the government had some legitimate arguments in this case, the workers looked upon the latest offer as just one more instance of the government evading its commitments in the Gdansk agreement. Whether there was room for negotiation is difficult to discern, because the regime did not try.

After a prolonged period of non-communication, the government unilaterally declared in late December that there would only be 25 work-free Saturdays in 1981. Then, on 2 January, this was modified to grant work-free

---

[6] Detailed accounts of the struggle over work-free Saturdays are in Andrews, *Poland 1980-81*, pp. 103-105; Ascherson, *The Polish August*, pp. 235-236; Garton Ash, *The Polish Revolution*, pp. 135-137; and Raina, *Poland 1981*, pp. 30-37. (Ascherson provides, on p. 237, an English translation of the passage in the Gdansk agreement dealing with work-free Saturdays.)

[7] Garton Ash, *The Polish Revolution*, p. 135, cites a *London Times* article of 10 January 1981 that agreed that "it was unreasonable of the workers to demand shorter working hours until productivity improved."

Saturdays on alternative weekends throughout 1981, with a commitment to gradually increase the number of work-free Saturdays each year to achieve a 40-hour week by 1985. This in effect meant there would be two working Saturdays per month through 1981, beginning with 10 and 24 January. Solidarity responded on 7 January by resolving to observe a five-day, 40-hour work week until the government came up with an acceptable proposal. The Intelligence Community's reporting on these events referred to Solidarity's reaction as "setting the stage for a confrontation...."[8]

Massive work boycotts were carried out on both government-designated work Saturdays in January, despite the regime's announcement that those who did not work would not be paid. The full number of workers who participated in the boycotts was subject to dispute. Solidarity claimed the figures were about 70 percent on 10 January and some 70 to 90 percent on 24 January. The government claimed that only 35 percent of the workforce observed the boycott on the first Saturday and that only about 40 percent did so on the second one.[9]

The Intelligence Community reporting did not attempt to resolve the competing claims on specific numbers, but it did describe the participation on 10 January as an impressive demonstration of strength, and said the number participating on 24 January was even larger. The intelligence reporting pointed out that the boycotts idled many of Poland's industrial centers.[10] Even the government's lower percentages would produce numbers into the millions. By any measurement, the boycotts dramatically demonstrated Solidarity's power to galvanize workers nationwide in defiance of the regime.

Reflecting sensitivity to charges that its actions were contrary to the national economic interest, Solidarity insisted that what it was seeking was the government's agreement to the *principle* that all Saturdays would be work free. The union declared that once there was agreement on this principle, there could be discussions on postponing full implementation out of concern for the national interest. In what some observers regarded as a further effort to deflect charges that its boycott was for a self-serving provision that was not in the national economic interest, Solidarity also declared the 24 January boycott a

---

[8] Declassified CIA Situation Reports on Poland, 3 January and 8 January 1981. Additional background is in Raina, *Poland 1981*, pp. 30-31.
[9] The numbers used here are from Raina, *Poland 1981*, p. 32. Garton Ash, *The Polish Revolution*, p. 136, describes a somewhat lower participation on 10 January, while Andrews, *Poland: 1980-81*, p. 104 describes it as "most workers," which would put it at the order of magnitude claimed by Solidarity.
[10] Declassified CIA Situation Reports on Poland, 12 January and 26 January 1981.

protest for a broader range of previously contested issues.[11] These included implementation of the demands the factory workers had been pressing since the Gdansk agreement—e.g., access to Polish media, easing of censorship, release of political prisoners, official codification in law of the status of independent unions—and the registration of Rural Solidarity.

The inclusion of an independent farmers' union in the list of demands attached to the nationwide work boycott was viewed by both the Polish and Soviet leaderships as indicating a growing alliance between workers and peasants. Solidarity's National Coordinating Commission had already made a public declaration of support for the protesting farmers in Rzeszow on 8 January, just before the first Saturday work boycott by the factory workers, and Solidarity representatives began joining the farmers' sit-in there. On 19 January, workers at the Szczecin shipyard, one of the three main sites of the confrontations back in August 1980, said they would launch a sympathy strike. The next day, Solidarity's National Commission passed resolutions declaring that 28 January would be a "Day of Solidarity" with the farmers. Worker committees around the country were asked to send delegates to Rzeszow, and Walesa showed up there on that "Day of Solidarity" to deliver another of his crowd-rousing oratories. The government began direct negotiations with the farmers there the next day.[12]

Meanwhile, in the heady atmosphere of union power following the Saturday work boycotts, wildcat strikes broke out at various regional centers throughout Poland. Solidarity's National Commission, partly as an effort to regain control over its increasingly belligerent rank and file, announced on 28 January that it would impose a one-hour national demonstration strike on 3 February if the government had not met the demands for work-free Saturdays by then, registered Rural Solidarity, and provided free access to the media. The union also tentatively agreed to consider declaring a longer strike on 18 February if negotiations with the government did not progress.[13]

---

[11] Declassified Situation Report on Poland, 24 January 1981. The perception that the broadening of issues was a tactic to deflect the "national interest" criticism was also described in "10 Cities in Poland Swept by Work Stoppages," *The New York Times,* 23 January 1981, p. A1, and "Walesa Urges Poles to Stage Boycott of Their Jobs Today," *The New York Times,* 24 January, p. A1.

[12] Declassified Situation Report on Poland, 8 January 1981, and "Poland," decl. *NID* article, 21 January 1981. A day-to-day account of these developments is in Garton Ash, *The Polish Revolution,* ch. 3., pp. 110-134. See also Andrews, *Poland 1980-81,* pp. 104-106. For Soviet reactions, see Cynkin, *Soviet and American Signaling,* pp. 79-84. The talks were initiated by the Provincial Governor and Minister of Trade Unions, and taken over a few days later by the Deputy Minister of Agriculture.

[13] "Poland," (re wildcat strikes) and Situation Report-Poland, 29 January 1981, (re strike threats). decl. *NID* article, 16 January 1981. Also "Wildcat Strikes Continue in Poland," *The New York Times* 29 January 1981, p. A7.

Assessing the Prospects

These new confrontations were burgeoning in Poland at the same time the US was undergoing a change in administrations. In his final message to Congress, President Carter had highlighted the turmoil in Poland as a critical policy challenge for the United States and its NATO allies. The first interagency policy meeting on Poland under President Ronald Reagan was held 23 January, just three days after the inauguration. By this time, the occupation strikes by independent farmers in southeast Poland were already underway, a sit-in by student protesters was beginning southwest of Warsaw in the town of Lodz, the first Saturday boycott had already taken place, and the second one was slated for the next day.[14]

This growing confrontation in Poland immediately revived concerns over the possibility of Soviet military intervention. An intelligence report in mid-January said that while the Soviets may not have set specific guidelines for Kania at the 5 December summit meeting, Moscow would probably see capitulation to the workers' political demands as evidence that he was losing ground. On the same day the new administration held its first policy meeting on Poland, the State Department issued a public statement that the US had seen no indications of Soviet preparation for military action in Poland. The next day, incoming Secretary of State Alexander Haig, responding to Soviet Foreign Minister Gromyko's perfunctory congratulatory note, reaffirmed former President Carter's warning of the major consequences for East-West relations if the USSR intervened militarily in Poland.[15]

The first National Intelligence Estimate (NIE) on Poland, disseminated by the new administration in late January, presented a stark outlook. It described the situation as a "protracted crisis" with "no prospect for resolution of the basic tensions between workers and the regime in the months ahead." The Estimate pointed out that at the 5 December Moscow meeting, Polish party First Secretary Kania had received a clear message that he had little room for maneuver. The Estimate said he would "feel compelled in the interests of pre-

---

[14] Gates, *From the Shadows*, p. 227; "Walesa Urges Poles to Stage a Boycott of Their Jobs Today," *The New York Times*, 24 January 1981, p. 1.
[15] "USSR-Poland: Moscow's Position," decl. *NID*, 12 January 1981. The State Department statement appears in "Walesa Urges Poles to Stage Boycott...," *The New York Times*, 24 January 1981, p. 1. The Haig letter stirred a mini dust-up in the media when it was leaked (reportedly by the Soviets) on 28 January, the day before Dobrynin delivered Gromeyko's response "reaffirming" the Joint Communiqué from the 5 December Warsaw Pact Summit in Moscow, and later on 11 February when Moscow publicized the text of Gromyko's reply. See "President Sharply Assails Kremlin: Haig Warning on Poland Disclosed," *The New York Times*, 30 January 1981, p. A1; and "Soviets Disclose Gromyko Letter to Haig," *The New York Times*, 12 February 1981, p. A1, and text of reply, p. A12.

serving his own position to initiate more forceful measures to quell domestic turmoil and to head off conservative criticism that his 'leniency' is perpetuating instability."[16] Reining in hardliners in these conditions would be difficult.

At the same time, the union rank and file continued to push Solidarity's leadership to continue pressing for full implementation of the provisions of the accords that ostensibly had settled the wave of strikes in late 1980. Most Polish workers considered the party's walk-back efforts in the union registration crisis, the provocative tactics in the Narozniak affair, and the continued obstructionism of local party officials as clear demonstrations that confrontation was the only way to get the regime to act on its promises.

The Intelligence Estimate also described how these tensions were being exacerbated by the inability of both the party and Solidarity to exert effective control over the activities of their regional components. In the provinces, party officials as well as labor organizations interpreted national agreements and compromises in terms of their local concerns. Regional government and party authorities, in fact, frequently refused to deal with local union branches and ignored national agreements, continuing instead to function in their long-established opaque, arbitrary and self-serving manner.

Local union organizations often used their newfound powers of strikes and sit-ins to address local complaints, and in some cases to redress past grievances. They demanded the removal of officials accused of corruption and misuse of office. Solidarity's leaders felt compelled to support their regional constituents, to avoid exacerbating the divisions already beginning to appear in the workers' movement. This provided additional fuel for local confrontations to escalate.

The Polish party was experiencing its own increasing pressures for decentralization of power, led mainly by local party chapters and lower-echelon members in what became known as the "Horizontal Movement." The demands included new party statutes for electing party officials to fixed terms by secret ballot, barring party officials from simultaneously holding government positions, initiating binding policies from below, and holding top leadership accountable for its performance. Some local party bodies had already begun to defy directives from higher echelons.

---

[16] Declassified National Intelligence Estimate (NIE) 12.6-81, "Poland's Prospects Over the Next Six Months," p. 1, National Security Archive. The remainder of this section is a description of the picture presented in this NIE and the perceptions of intelligence analysts at the time. There is a striking similarity, however, in the descriptions given by intelligence analysts at the time and the portrayals by Andrews, *Poland 1980-81*, pp. 97-103, and Garton Ash, *The Polish Revolution*: pp. 101-109, authors who were in Poland at the time. (The first edition of Garton Ash's book was published in 1983, Andrews's in 1985).

Moscow perceived yet another challenge to the central authority of the Polish United Workers Party. It also was a clear validation of warnings from several Warsaw Pact capitals about the "contagion" potential of the Polish labor movement and civil opposition. The PZPR's "Horizontal Movement" quickly became the target of Soviet media attacks of the same kind that had been launched at Solidarity, adding steam to Soviet efforts to push the Polish leadership into reasserting its control.[17]

Underlying these destabilizing factors was the miserable state of the Polish economy. Its condition was the result of systemic flaws exacerbated by ten years of incompetent direction under the Gierek regime. The economic stresses had prompted the clumsily implemented price increases in mid-1980, which set off the wave of strikes that catalyzed the labor and civil opposition movement embodied in Solidarity. Those events in turn exerted a further depression on the economy. For example, the mining and ship-building strikes and the terms of their settlement reduced output in both industries, and both produced critical exports for Poland. Hard-currency earnings therefore went down even further and the debt level went higher. The loss of hard-currency earnings caused some factories dependent on materials or components from the West to shut down, further reducing output. Similarly, the increased wages paid to placate strikers simply resulted in more money chasing fewer goods and ratcheted up inflation. This economic dilemma increased pressures on the Solidarity leadership to continue to push its demands on wages, benefits and working hours. The same economic conditions made it more difficult for the government to respond to those demands.[18]

These factors led the US Intelligence Community, at the end of January 1981, to assign a higher probability for Polish-imposed martial law than had been the case in earlier assessments. It said that "in comparison with the October-November 1980 period, the chances are greater that the Polish regime will respond with force, probably at Soviet urging, if faced with a major confrontation such as a prolonged general strike or the threat of such a major confrontation." In presenting this judgment the NIE drew on the growing evidence of Polish martial law planning, and the belief that Moscow was reluctant to incur the high political and economic costs of carrying out a military intervention. The Estimate pointed out that the Soviets had a number of options for pushing the Poles to take stronger measures, including engineering another change in Polish leadership, increasing political pressure, and engaging in demonstrative military posturing to heighten the specter of intervention.[19]

---

[17] The Intelligence Community's view of the situation within the party and Solidarity is presented in detail on pp. 7-9 of NIE 12.6-81.
[18] A detailed description of the economic despair of Poland at this time is in NIE 12.6-81, pp. 5-7.
[19] NIE 12.6-81, pp. 2-3, 10, and 12. The quotation appears both on p. 3 of the Key Judgments and p. 12 of the main text.

Intelligence analysts believed they had already seen an indication of such a strategy in the mid-January visit to Warsaw by a large contingent of senior Soviet military officers, headed by the commander-in-chief of Warsaw Pact Forces, Soviet Marshal Kulikov, and his deputy commander, Army-General Gribkov. For public consumption, the Soviet story was that the officers had come to attend the anniversary celebrations of the 1945 Soviet liberation of Warsaw. Western media reported speculation that the visit was connected to the ongoing crisis in Poland. US intelligence analysts believed the delegation also had the mission of assessing the loyalty of the Polish military. A delegation led by Soviet Central Committee member Leonid Zamyatin also carried out a week-long visit to Poland at the same time, and the interpretation by intelligence analysts was that he was there to perform the same task with the Polish political leadership.[20]

But while the January NIE described increased chances that the Polish leaders might attempt to impose martial law, intelligence analysts saw little increase in the Polish Army's dependability in enforcing it. The Estimate said that if large-scale violence erupted, the Polish army was unlikely to be able on its own to contain it, and that the most likely outcome would be disintegration of the armed forces. As a consequence, "[T]he introduction of Polish military forces under such circumstances would run a high risk of bringing about the intervention of Soviet forces."[21]

The intelligence analysts also concluded that "[W]hatever the Soviet perception of the costs of intervention, they would quickly fade into secondary considerations if the Soviets see their vital interests threatened." The Estimate said that while the Soviets probably had not set a specific timetable when they granted Kania more time to bring the situation under control, they would "not allow the present deterioration to continue indefinitely...." Among the developments listed as likely to provoke "one or another form of Soviet military intervention" was "a general strike of some duration to which the regime did not respond decisively." (This judgment was recorded the day before Solidarity announced its threat of a general strike for 3 February.)[22]

---

[20] Re military delegation, see "Russian Alliance Chiefs Turn Up In Poland," *The New York Times*, 14 January 1981, p. A3. Subsequent information from Kuklinski and most recently Gribkov's own account have confirmed these interpretations. See Kuklinski, "The Suppression of Solidarity," in Kostrzewa, *Between East and West*, p. 87. Re Gribkov's account see Kramer, "Soviet Deliberations on the Polish Crisis," Document 8, Translator's Note No. 112, and Document 11, Translator's Note No. 131. Re Zamyatin, see Cynkin, *Soviet and American Signaling*, p. 82. Zamyatin's visit was also reported in Moscow in *Pravda*, 21 January 1981.
[21] NIE 12.6-81, p. 3 of the Key Judgments and p. 13 of the text.
[22] *Ibid.*, p. 2 of the Key Judgments, and pp. 10-11 of the main text.

The concluding paragraph of the Estimate stated:

> We believe that Soviet military activities in November and December demonstrate that the Soviets are in fact willing to intervene militarily. As time passes and if the regime shows no convincing progress in consolidating the party and gaining control of events, the Soviets are likely to conclude that nonintervention options are insufficient.... We believe that Soviet pressure on the Polish regime will increase and that, if the pattern of domestic confrontation continues, the trend is toward ultimate intervention.[23]

More Government Concessions and New Confrontations

On 30 January 1981, as this NIE was being distributed to US policy agencies, a Solidarity delegation headed by Lech Walesa met in the Council of Ministers building in Warsaw with a delegation led by Prime Minister Pinkowski. Walesa had met with the Prime Minister on 19 and 21 January in an attempt to resolve the work week issue, but achieved nothing. On this day, however, Solidarity and the government reached a compromise agreement.

The government offered a commitment to the goal of establishing a 40-hour week, while the union agreed that movement toward this goal would be gradual and would take economic stresses into account. The parties agreed that for the remainder of 1981, every fourth Saturday would be an eight-hour work day, resulting in an average work week of 42 hours. The government also agreed (in writing) to the weekly publication of a Solidarity national journal, although commitments regarding Solidarity's access to radio and TV were unclear. Rural Solidarity issues remained unresolved, but Western observers nonetheless viewed the outcome as "a substantial victory for the union."[24]

On its face, the difference between the regime proposal floated in November and the agreement reached on 30 January seemed small relative to the level of confrontation. The confrontation, however, was at least as much over the regime's tactics as it was over the terms of its plan—mainly the failure of the government to bring Solidarity into consultations on issues in which workers had a major stake. In a rare public acknowledgment, a Polish deputy

---

[23] *Ibid.*, p. 3 and p. 15 respectively. Detailed discussions are on pp. 12-15.
[24] "Strike Threat Eases As Talks In Poland Produce Agreement," *The New York Times,* 1 February 1981, p.1; Andrews, *Poland 1980-81*, p. 105; Garton Ash, *The Polish Revolution*, pp. 136-137; Raina, *Poland 1981*, pp. 36–39 (which includes the text of the public declaration of what was agreed). The "substantial victory" quote is from *The New York Times*.

minister stated at a news conference two months later that the government had erred in not submitting its initial proposals for public discussion, and in not sending them to the heads of the unions for comment and negotiation.[25]

From this perspective the real measure of Solidarity's "win" was the union's demonstration of its place at the decision table for issues that affected workers' jobs and well being. US intelligence analysts concluded that both the Polish populace and the Soviet leadership would see it this way.[26]

Nonetheless, the agreement provoked a stormy debate in Solidarity's National Coordinating Commission, reflecting the fractiousness in the union's leadership and the growing militancy of its rank and file. Again, criticism was provoked as much by process as content. Walesa was charged with taking too much authority on himself to conduct negotiations and make commitments. Some union representatives argued that because Rural Solidarity's registration remained unresolved, the threatened general strike on 3 February should be carried out. Walesa and other moderates ultimately prevailed in having the strike "suspended."[27]

Meanwhile, the farmers at Rzeszow and Ustrzyki Dolne continued their sit-ins, and regional wildcat strikes continued to erupt. The student sit-in at Lodz also was sparking sympathy strikes at other academic centers. The students were demanding university reforms and recognition of their own nationwide Independent Students Union.

One of the more prominent regional strikes was in the province of Bielsko-Biala, in south-central Poland. Without consulting the union's national leadership, Solidarity's Inter-Factory Committee in that province launched a sit-in on 26 January at 110 industrial plants in the province. The strikers demanded the removal from office of several regional government officials on charges of abusing local government funds and failing to implement agreements that had been reached with the union. Walesa sought to contain the confrontation and enlisted intervention by the church, but he also felt compelled to threaten a national strike if force was employed against the strikers.[28]

---

[25] Andrews, *Poland 1980-81*, p. 105, citing an article in the Polish *Trybuna Ludu*, 23 February 1983.
[26] "Poland," decl. Situation Report, 3 February 1981.
[27] "Polish Labor Union Calls Off Strike Set For Tomorrow," *The New York Times,* 2 February 1981, p. A1, and Garton Ash, *The Polish Revolution*, pp. 140-142.
[28] "Workers in Poland Alerted For Sit-In If Any Force Used," *The New York Times*, 5 February 1981, p. A1; "Strike in Southern Poland Ends As Government Yields;" *The New York Times*, 6 February, p. A1; Andrews *Poland 1980-81*, pp. 109-110; Garton Ash, *The Polish Revolution*, pp. 141-142, and Ascherson, *The Polish August*, p. 261.

On 6 February, a settlement was announced: the Prime Minister had accepted the resignation of the regional governor of Belsko-Biela and two deputy governors. An intelligence report pointed out that the regime had reversed itself in yielding to strikers' demands. The report said these concessions would "provide more ammunition for hard-liners' criticism of...Kania's moderate policies...." Three days later, another regional general strike began in the southwestern province of Jelenia Gora. Again, the issues were local—the ouster of the regional Minister of Trade Union Affairs (who had been an unpopular provincial party secretary), and the transfer to public use of a local Ministry of Internal Affairs health facility mainly used by security forces. Intelligence analysts thought this added more fuel to the fire as a highly charged party Central Committee meeting opened that day.[29]

---

[29] Declassified Situation Reports on Poland, 7 and 9 February 1981. For more background on Jelenia Gora see Andrews, *Poland 1980-81*, pp. 113-114; Garton Ash, *The Polish Revolution*, p. 142; and Ascherson, *The Polish August*, p. 261.

CHAPTER 7

Jaruzelski Takes the Government Reins

On 9 February 1981, at the end of the first day of a party Central Committee plenum, Polish authorities announced that Prime Minister Pinkowski had resigned, and that Defense Minister Jaruzelski had been named his successor. In the existing cauldron of confrontation and concession, a change in the Polish leadership seemed a natural consequence. Even before the government concessions at Bielsko Biala, the Intelligence Community had concluded that a debate was brewing in the party leadership, with both hard-liners and moderates criticizing Kania's overall policies. Intelligence reports said speculation was spreading that Prime Minister Pinkowski—who had overseen and sometimes directly participated in the recent compromises—would be replaced. Moscow also was engaged in vitriolic public criticism of Solidarity and was maneuvering behind the scenes to help Polish hardliners prevail at the upcoming Central Committee meeting in naming a new Prime Minister and establishing a tougher policy line.[1]

A Moscow-engineered leadership change had been one of the prospects described in the National Intelligence Estimate distributed 10 days earlier, and Soviet actions just before the change reinforced this view. An intelligence assessment said that the Poles had almost certainly obtained Moscow's approval before naming Jaruzelski, and may have discussed the matter directly with Soviet Defense Minister Ustinov. A congratulatory letter to Jaruzelski from Brezhnev and Tikhonov was printed in *Pravda* the day after the appointment was formally confirmed by the Polish Sejm. Many analysts also believed

---

[1] Declassified Situation Reports on Poland, 5 February, 6 February, 7 February, and 9 February 1981.

that the Soviets were not likely to endorse a successor whom they did not believe would be willing to take the forceful measures they deemed necessary.[2]

Nonetheless, to both the Polish population and Western observers, Jaruzelski represented a mixed picture.[3] From one standpoint he was an "orthodox Marxist...trusted by Moscow," a soldier completely committed to Communist ideology and loyal to the Soviet Union, where he had trained in Soviet officer schools. He had been a member of the Soviet-organized Polish Army that fought alongside the Soviets on the eastern front in World War II and crushed the anticommunist Polish resistance. He had become Minister of Defense in 1968 in time to oversee the participation of Polish armed forces in the Warsaw Pact military intervention in Czechoslovakia. He also had been a member of the party Politburo for more than ten years, selected as a candidate member in December 1970 and full member in December 1971.

The party plenum at which Jaruzelski was named Prime Minister featured harsh rhetoric. Prominent hardliner Grabski opened the session by presenting a report—printed in the party-controlled media the next day—purporting to describe the party's views on how to deal with the trade unions. The report leveled its strongest criticism at the KOR, the dissident intelligentsia supporting Solidarity. Attacking KOR leaders by name, the Grabski diatribe accused the organization of having an "anti-socialist orientation" and of seeking to maintain tensions to undercut the government's efforts to resolve the problems

---

[2] Intelligence Community views of Jaruzelski's accession are in declassified Situation Reports on Poland, 10 February and 12 February 1981. Examples of public speculation on the Soviet connection to Jaruzelski's accession are in "Polish Court Denies Appeal by Farmers...," *The New York Times*, 11 February 1981, p. A1; and "New Polish Peril Seen in Moscow," *The New York Times, op.cit.*, p. A11. A summary of Soviet media coverage in this period is in Cynkin, *Soviet and American Signaling*, pp. 85-89, and the text of the congratulatory letter is described on p. 93. See also "Soviet Army Paper Says NATO is Wooing Solidarity," *The New York Times*, 29 January 1981, p. A6.

[3] For the diverse perceptions of Jaruzelski at the time, see "Polish Premier Ousted," *The New York Times*, 10 February 1981, p. A1; "Poland's Four Star Premier," *The New York Times*, 11 February 1981, p. A8. Andrews, *Poland 1980-81*, pp. 114-118; Ascherson, *The Polish August*, p. 261; Garton Ash, *The Polish Revolution*, pp. 143-146; and Dobbs, *Down With Big Brother*, pp. 68-72. The quoted passage is from Dobbs, p. 68.

of the economy and society. (A judicial investigation of the KOR had in fact been announced the previous day, under accusations of "anti-state activity.") The Grabski report also criticized the party for "capitulation."[4]

Polish First Secretary Kania gave a combative presentation, characterizing Poland's problems as the result of "counterrevolution efforts," pointedly noting that "the patient understanding" shown by the USSR and "other friends" could run out. Virtually all speakers at the plenum rejected the idea of allowing farmers to register as an independent union. At the conclusion of the plenum a resolution was issued listing three levels of action the party was to pursue: isolating and containing groups "hostile to socialist rule; strengthening government power and authority; and instituting a program of "socialist renewal." Against this background, most observers saw Jaruzelski's selection for Prime Minister as a move intended to show that the Polish leadership meant business.[5]

The unprecedented choice of a current military officer as Prime Minister was seen by some Western observers as increasing the influence of the military in political affairs and moving the government closer to a crackdown. Jaruzelski's declaration that he would retain the position of Defense Minister was described by CIA analysts as meant to underscore regime hints that martial law would be declared if necessary. The analysts said that while the regime probably still regarded martial law as a last resort, Jaruzelski's dual role would avoid some of the problems involved in a transfer of authority from civilian to military hands.[6]

Within Poland, however, Jaruzelski's military status was viewed more positively. The army as an institution was held in high regard by the Polish citizenry, a view reinforced by its having so far refrained from involvement in the internal political conflicts of the past year. Jaruzelski was seen as an outstanding professional army officer under whose leadership the military had been organizationally improved and modernized. He also had—deservedly—a "clean" image, having abstained from the corruption and material aggrandizement that was common practice among the party elite. One occasional

---

[4] The Grabski report appeared in *Trybuna Ludu*, 10 February 1981, pp. 2–3, and is described in Andrews, *Poland 1980-81*, p. 114, and Garton Ash, *The Polish Revolution*, p. 145. The investigation of the KOR was reported in "Warsaw Announces Plan to Investigate Dissident Group," *The New York Times*, 9 February 1981, p. A1. By this time the group had expanded its formal title to "Social Self-Defense Committee-Workers Defense Committee" (Komitet Samoobrony Spolecznej-Komitet Obrony Robotnikow) but most references continued to use either the old acronym of KOR, or an abbreviated title "Social Self-Defense Committee."
[5] Kania's plenum speech was described in "Polish Court Denies Appeal by Farmers...," *The New York Times*, 11 February 1981, *op. cit*. For the resolution see Raina, *Poland 1981*, p. 50.
[6] Declassified Situation Report on Poland, 12 February 1981.

criticism by his supporters was that he could be "indecisive," although as future events would show it could be argued that this was really a manifestation of his meticulous care in preparing his moves.

Jaruzelski was also generally considered one of the party moderates, and his selection as Prime Minister was interpreted as indicating that the moderates were still in control. He was widely reputed—including in the Western media—to have opposed the use of force to suppress strikes and demonstrations. He was said to have opposed Gomulka's order for using the army in the crackdown on protesting workers at Gdansk and Gdynia in December 1970, and to have withdrawn his support for Gomulka after force was used. He also was reported to have vetoed using the army in the 1976 confrontation, and to have opposed its use to quell the strikes in the Gdansk region in August 1980. The validity of this portrait was and remains a matter of some debate, particularly in the aftermath of the actions he would impose by the end of the year. Nonetheless, its currency at the time is illustrated by the fact that among the sources cited for this moderate picture in Western media accounts were "US intelligence analyst[s]."[7]

Jaruzelski's actions and statements at the time he took over as Prime Minister also contributed to the mixed picture. In his acceptance speech before the Sejm on 12 February he echoed the tough talk voiced at the party plenum. Referring to "evil and hostile political forces...expanding their activities opposed to socialism," he said the situation "could not be allowed to go on" and that "the time has come to arrest a creeping process that has undermined the stability of the country's public life. There is no room for two systems of authority in the state. Such a situation would inevitably lead to a collision with disastrous consequences for the country and the nation."[8]

---

[7] See footnote 33. Re "indecisiveness," see Garton Ash, *The Polish Revolution*, p. 144. For contrary information on his alleged objection to the use of force in 1970, see Tina Rosenberg, *The Haunted Land* (New York, Random House, 1995), p. 211. Another version of the story (Andrews, *Poland 1980-81*, p. 115) is that the party bypassed Jaruzelski in ordering the Army's actions. Since Jaruzelski was Defense Minister at the time, and had just been made a candidate member of the Politburo, this account, if true, raises questions of its own about his political maneuvering. Polish archives also show that he signed a secret directive declaring that the army would cooperate with the Ministry of Internal Affairs in suppressing the turmoil. See Kramer, "Soviet Deliberations on the Polish Crisis," p. 6. Regarding the statements attributed to him in 1976 and 1980, some have concluded that he actually was not referring to his own principles but his judgment of the reliability of the army. See PZPR Protocol No. 28, of 29 August 1980, in Woldek, *Tajne Documenty*, pp. 84-90. For an example of media citations of statements from a "US intelligence analyst," see "Poland's Four Star Premier," *The New York Times*, 11 February 1981, p. A8.

[8] "Polish Leader Asks 90 Strike Free Days...," *The New York Times*, 13 February 1981, p. A1; Andrews, *Poland 1980-81*, pp. 115-117; and Garton Ash, *The Polish Revolution*, p. 145.

On the other hand, Jaruzelski exhibited a pragmatic willingness to engage Solidarity, and expressed determination to introduce a "comprehensive social dialog." He proposed a 90-day moratorium on strikes—"90 days of peace"—urging that "[W]e could use that time to put in order the most fundamental problems of our economy, to take account of both positive and negative aspects [of public life], to undertake the most urgent social programs, to take the first steps toward the introduction of a program of economic stability, and to prepare for wide-ranging reforms of the country." As an instrument for cooperation, Jaruzelski announced the creation of a "permanent committee" for government and union relations, appointing as its head with the rank of deputy prime minister a reputed party "reformist," Mieczyslaw Rakowski, editor of the party journal *Polityka*. Jaruzelski also announced a number of reform laws he intended to introduce to the Sejm. He remained unyielding, however, on the existing censorship laws and was non-committal on the question of Solidarity's access to mass media.[9]

Official reactions in Washington were initially somewhat ambiguous. The day after Jaruzelski's appointment was announced in Warsaw, a State Department spokesperson said in an official, on the record press briefing that as regards the change in Polish leadership, "[W]e see no development [to change] our assessment that the Poles are perfectly capable of handling their internal affairs without outside interference." The spokesperson also said that "if Polish forces intervened to establish order we would consider that an internal matter." Later that day, in what clearly reflected a realization that this could be seen as giving a green light to martial law, the State Department put out an amendment, saying that "[I]n no way did [we] intend to suggest that such a development would not be a matter of grave concern to us."

An official statement released two days later leaned a little more toward cautious optimism, saying the US Government was "looking forward to a constructive relationship with the new Polish Prime Minister." Other press accounts, citing unnamed "Western analysts" and "intelligence sources," said that a crackdown was not expected. These sources reportedly believed that Jaruzelski had opposed the past use of force and that he was still opposed to it. The same sources were quoted as believing the Polish Army would oppose the use of force for party goals.[10]

---

[9] *Ibid.*, "State Department Briefing...," *The New York Times*, 12 February 1981, p. A13, described Jaruzelski's actions in his first days as "zig-zagging."

[10] "US Aides See Pole's Promotion as Bid by Warsaw to Look Firm," *The New York Times*, 10 February 1981, p. A12; "US Doubts Moscow Will Invade Poland," *The New York Times*, 11 February 1981, p. A1; "Poland's Four Star Premier," *The New York Times*, 11 February 1981, p. A8; and "US Vows to Keep Hands Off Poland," *The New York Times*, 13 February 1981, p. A5. The 11 February 1981 article, "US Doubts..." described the US statements as reflecting "some confusion."

Grounds for Hope

On balance, Jaruzelski's elevation to Prime Minister was taken by Solidarity as offering a strong leader who could bring needed order and discipline to the government. While expected to be tough on some issues, he also was seen as having the ability and determination to live up to commitments—which to Solidarity was a welcome contrast to commitments that lasted only as long as it took to calm the latest confrontation. A commonly used characterization was that Jaruzelski was the "last chance" or "last card" for resolving the tumult in Poland without resorting to force.[11]

On 10 February, even before Jaruzelski's accession was confirmed by the parliament, the government agreed to the demands of the strikers at Jelenia Gora and handed over the contested health facility to the local public health service. On this same day, the Polish Supreme Court finally issued its ruling on Rural Solidarity's registration. It said that because Rural Solidarity members were self-employed rather than employees, the organization could not register as a "union," but could register as an independent "association."

Walesa reportedly called this a draw, and urged the farmers to register as prescribed in the court decision. The farmers, however, agreed only to "suspend" their demands until a law on trade unions was taken up by the Sejm. The other two aspirant farmers' unions—Peasants Solidarity and the Union of Agriculture Producers—had recently merged with Rural Solidarity, and there was no inclination in this unified farmers' organization to settle for anything less than their own legally registered and recognized "independent self-governing union" equivalent to Solidarity.[12]

Adopting a cautiously optimistic stance, Solidarity declared its willingness to refrain from actions affecting industries if the regime kept its promises—in effect, conditionally agreeing to Jaruzelski's appeal for a 90-day strike moratorium. On the same day that Jaruzelski made his acceptance speech to the Sejm, Solidarity's National Coordinating Commission (KKP) issued a resolution against wildcat strikes. It admonished that:

> the plethora of local and regional strikes pursuing disparate aims without consent of the National Commission—and often against its advice—not only make little impact, they have sometimes been

---

[11] "Polish Union Chief Indicates He Backs 90 Strike Free Days," *The New York Times*, 15 February 1980, p. A1; Andrews, *Poland 1980-81*, p. 115, on the "last chance;" and Garton Ash, *The Polish Revolution*, p.145, on the "last card."

[12] Declassified Situation Report on Poland, 11 February 1981; "Polish Court Dismisses Appeal By Farmers for Trade Union," *The New York Times*, 11 February 1981, p. A1; Garton Ash, *The Polish Revolution*, p. 132; and Andrews, *Poland 1980-81*, p. 118. The "draw' expression was quoted in *The New York Times*, and is also cited by Garton Ash.

provoked by advocates of confrontation among those in authority as a means to disrupt our unity. As a result we are threatened with dismemberment into 50 regional organizations. This would mean the destruction of our movement.

The resolution concluded by forbidding regional strikes without prior approval by the union's National Commission, and said the commission would "publicly disavow any action undertaken in disregard of this appeal."[13]

Also on that day, in an attempt to prevent some of the friction that recently had been experienced among its leadership, Solidarity's National Commission created a "permanent presidium." Until then, there had been no permanent union executive that functioned between the periodic meetings of the National Commission. The newly created "presidium" was commissioned to represent the union at the national level between National Commission meetings, thus providing a national body to take up government negotiations for the regional chapters.[14]

The promising outlook was reinforced by the accomplishments of the following week. On 16 February, the Polish Government accepted the registration of the Independent Student Union, on the condition that its statutes include a clause obligating it to abide by the Polish constitution. The next day, a general agreement was reached ending the student strikes, which had by then spread from Lodz to several large cities. The government made a commitment to grant more autonomy to universities and agreed that students would no longer be required to study the Russian language.

One day later, an agreement was signed in Rzeszow by representatives of the government, Solidarity, and the Farmers, Strike Committee. The government agreed to guarantee the inviolability of peasants' private property, their rights to inheritance, and recognition of private farming as a lasting and equal element in the Polish national economy. Prohibitive restrictions on sale and purchase of private farmland were to be lifted. The Rzeszow Farmers Strike Committee made its acceptance of this agreement conditional on an agreement being reached at Ustrzyki Dolne. This was achieved two days later, when the government agreed with the Ustrzyki Dolne hill farmers to return to local residents the land that had been set aside as a resort for party officials.[15]

---

[13] Declassified Situation Report on Poland, 13 February 1981. The full text of the declaration is in Raina, *Poland 1981*, pp. 52-54. (The wording could be interpreted as allowing exceptions for a need to respond to "a direct attack by authorities upon members or collaborators of Solidarity or on union chapters."

[14] Garton Ash, *The Polish Revolution*, p. 143.

[15] Andrews, *Poland 1980-81*, pp. 106-109; and Garton Ash, *The Polish Revolution*, pp. 132-134, 147. Andrews appears to describe the Ustrzyki Dolne and the Rszeszow agreements as having been reached in reverse order, but this may simply be a presentational interpretation. The full texts of the agreements are in Raina, *Poland 1981*, pp. 59-74 (Rszeszow and Ustrzyki Dolne) and pp. 77-80 (Lodz Students).

A week earlier, after Jaruzelski's confirmation by the Polish parliament, an intelligence assessment had said the Soviets would give Warsaw's "new tack" a chance. The analysis said "Moscow still appears reluctant to adopt the alternative course—intervention without collaboration by the Polish government...[but] should the [strike] moratorium break down or require significant concessions to Solidarity, the Soviets are likely to demand that the Polish party implement martial law."[16]

If this assessment was correct, Moscow could not have seen the first week of Jaruzelski's tenure as a promising start. A Polish regime that was supposed to be striving for the model of Soviet socialism had in effect endorsed, in a written agreement subsequently published in its official party press, the private ownership and market trade of agricultural property. The Soviets had other information, however, that cast the new leadership in a somewhat less conciliatory light. So did the CIA.

Grounds for Concern

At the same time Jaruzelski's public actions seemed to be reflecting accommodation, the CIA was receiving information that the regime was stepping up its martial law preparations. As Jaruzelski's appointment was being confirmed by the Polish parliament, CIA reported to the President and senior national security officials that the Polish General Staff and Internal Security Forces were about to test the martial law plans in a command and staff "war game" simulation. This CIA report was based on recent information from Ryszard Kuklinski, who continued to be intimately involved in the preparation and testing of the martial law procedures. According to Kuklinski, the simulation game took place the following week. The plans then were adjusted and passed to Jaruzelski on 20 February. Jaruzelski passed the plans to the Soviets on 3 March in Moscow, at a meeting with Soviet Prime Minister Tikhonov, at the conclusion of the 26th Soviet Party Congress.[17]

According to Gates, the intelligence report sent to the President said that Moscow and Warsaw still regarded martial law as a last resort because of the great risk of confrontation and widespread violence. Nonetheless, the report presented clear evidence that refinement of the martial law plans was advancing at the same time Jaruzelski was promoting his public policy of "social dialogue." As Defense Minister, he had already played a key role in the "Party-State Leadership [Crisis] Staff" which had been established at the time of the

---

[16] Declassified Situation Report on Poland, 13 February 1981.
[17] Gates, *From the Shadows*, p. 229. Gates describes the interpretation of the reporting at the time as indicating the "game" was planned for 13-14 February. Kuklinski in his public interview says it was actually held on 16-18 February. See "The Suppression of Solidarity," Kostrzewa, ed., *Between East and West*, pp. 84-85.

Gdansk strikes in August 1980 to formulate recommendations on martial law decisions. He also commanded the armed forces that would be responsible for much of the implementation of martial law. Now, with his dual positions of Prime Minster and Defense Minster, he was both chairman and deputy chairman of the National Defense Committee,[18] which was responsible for fleshing out the plans and preparations for martial law. In the event martial law was declared, the National Defense Committee would control the military, police, and internal security forces. In sum, Jaruzelski now had full control over the planning process and the forces that would carry out the plans.

Intelligence reporting at the time showed a somewhat peculiar schedule for the Polish leaders' attendance at the Soviet party congress. They arrived for the opening, and Kania was the first East European party leader to give a presentation, in which he reiterated his promises to bring everything under control. A day later, both he and Jaruzelski returned to Warsaw; it was most unusual for a Soviet party congress not to have one of the top party officials from each of the Warsaw Pact states present throughout the session. Intelligence analysts speculated that this might have been at the Poles' initiative because they felt that, given the situation in Poland, they couldn't be out of the country for the nearly two-week period of the Soviet party congress. The analysts also suggested, however, that after presenting their case, the Poles absented themselves to give the other Warsaw Pact leaders an opportunity to discuss the situation in Poland. In any event, they returned to Moscow on 3 March and Jaruzelski's meeting with Tikhonov that evening was reported in the Soviet media, although not all the details.[19]

The next day Kania, Jaruzelski, and two other members of the Polish delegation to the Soviet party congress met with several Soviet Politburo heavyweights. The purpose clearly was to provide yet another forum for Soviet authorities to deliver an on-the-record verbal drubbing of the Polish leaders for not taking forceful measures, and for the Polish leaders to make their on-the-record promise to do so as soon as conditions were right. Soviet official media described the discussions at this meeting as having affirmed that the "socialist commonwealth [read Warsaw Pact] is indissoluble," and that its defense "is the affair not only of each state but of the entire socialist coalition as well."

---

[18] Komitet Obrony Kraju or KOK, sometimes translated literally as "Homeland Defense Committee." See Mark Kramer, "Soviet Deliberations on the Polish Crisis," Translator's Note Nos. 3 and 17.

[19] "Poland," decl. *NID*, 27 February 1981, and "Situation Report: Poland," 4 March 1981. It is now known that Kania met with Brezhnev on the same evening. See Kramer, "Soviet Deliberations During the Polish Crisis," Translator's Note No. 108 to Document 9, regarding accounts by Kania and Jaruzelski.

Intelligence analysts saw this as an unequivocal statement of what had been known after the 1968 intervention in Czechoslovakia as "the Brezhnev Doctrine." The statement also expressed "the conviction ... that the Polish communists have the ability and strength to reverse the course of events and to liquidate the dangers that threaten the socialist gains of the Polish people." This was a fairly unambiguous message that the Poles were expected to assert their authority and that Moscow stood ready to "assist." The statements were ominous enough by themselves, but carried extra weight for those who had been informed of the status and sharing of martial law plans.[20]

The previous day, the Soviets had informally put out word that joint Warsaw Pact exercises would be held "in the second half of March," and would include forces of Poland, Czechoslovakia, East Germany, and the USSR. Over the next few days, US intelligence agencies tracked preparations that included movement of vehicles and troop units out of barracks and deployment of mobile communications stations. On 10 March, the USSR, Poland, and East Germany all made formal announcements confirming intelligence information that the exercises would begin 17 March. The announcements described the exercises as "command staff exercises," which intelligence analysts interpreted as an effort to play down the size of the maneuvers and avoid accusations of violating the Helsinki Accord requirement for three weeks' advance notification of field maneuvers involving more than 25,000 troops. All the preparations the intelligence analysts were detecting pointed to maneuvers of considerably more that 25,000 troops.[21]

Major Warsaw Pact joint exercises were fairly routine for the spring, a point that had been made in the NIE disseminated at the end of January. The Intelligence Community had reported a month earlier that exercises of substantial dimension would be held in the western USSR and Poland in March. Nonetheless, the background of recent events, and the fact that the exercises were occurring just as the martial law planning seemed to be reaching a new level, generated substantial uneasiness among intelligence analysts. The exercises seemed to be shaping up very much along the lines of the maneuvers intelligence sources had described being prepared in December 1980, but which were then "postponed"—maneuvers that could provide a cover for putting in

---

[20] Declassified Situation Report on Poland, 5 March 1981. For further text, see Cynkin, *Soviet and US Signaling*, p. 97, citing Radio Liberty Summary for 5 March 1981, and *Pravda*, 5 March 1981. Many scholars are under the impression that it was at this 4 March meeting that the martial law plans were passed. Kuklinski's statement that they were passed over on 3 March, however, has since been reinforced by the accounts by Kania and Jaruzelski cited above. Both also describe the "drubbing" on 4 March.

[21] Declassified Situation Reports on Poland for 4, 6, 9, 11, and 13 March 1981; "Warsaw Pact Games Arouse US Concerns," *The New York Times*, 16 March 1981.

place the Soviet forces assigned to support a Polish-led military crackdown. The US Government made it known the exercises would be given "extra scrutiny."[22]

This "scrutiny" produced public exchanges in which both the President and the Secretary of State accused Moscow of violating the provision of the Helsinki Agreement on Security and Cooperation in Europe.[23] Moscow felt compelled to issue a public denial, repeating that the scheduled activities were only "command and communications" exercises in which the number of participating troops would be less that 25,000. The US administration appeared to backtrack the next day, putting out the word that "intelligence and Soviet assurances had reduced concern about possible military intervention." At least one media account described the State Department as worried about the appearance of "crying wolf." The Intelligence Community had reported shortly before the exercises began, however, that there were no signs of the preparations expected in the western USSR if the Soviets were planning to use the exercises as a cover for a large-scale military intervention in Poland.[24]

---

[22] Declassified Situation Report on Poland, 4 February 1981; "US-Soviet Parley Linked To Poland," *The New York Times,* 11 March 1981, p. A8.

[23] Haig radio statement of 13 March 1981 on the Public Broadcasting System; "US-Soviet Differences Imperil Peace, Haig Says," *The New York Times,* 14 March 1981, p. 3. See also "Reagan Lifts Aid Freeze on Two City Projects," *The New York Times,* 15 March 1981, p. 1; "State Department Accuses Soviet of Ignoring US Appeals on Ending Hijacking," *The New York Times,* 17 March 1981, p. A1; and declassified Situation Report of 14 March 1981.

[24] "US Now Voices Reduced Concern That Russians May Invade Poland," *The New York Times,* 18 March 1981, p. A1.

CHAPTER 8
A Setup for Military Crackdown

By the time the Warsaw Pact military exercise *Soyuz '81* began in the third week of March, the image of a "honeymoon" period for the new Polish Prime Minister was already proving to be an illusion. On 8-9 March, less than a week after the meeting of Polish and Soviet leaders in Moscow, Rural Solidarity held its first national congress in Poznan. Some 500 private farmers elected by an organization that claimed to have 1.8 million members took part in what was described in western media as a "boisterous convention." At the top of the agenda was their demand to be registered as a trade union rather than an association.[1]

At the same time, Solidarity workers in the city of Lodz were threatening to shut down the city for one hour on 10 March to protest the firing of five hospital employees who had caught the director of the hospital siphoning off government-funded supplies. Walesa appealed to the workers to call off the strike, pointing out that it would coincide with his first meeting with new Prime Minister Jaruzelski. The Lodz workers went ahead with their one-hour strike anyway, illustrating the tenuous ability of Solidarity's leadership to control the actions of its lower-echelon components. And the fact that this strike did indeed result in the reinstatement of the five hospital employees only reinforced the views of the union's more radical elements that confrontation was the only way to get results.[2]

Meanwhile, workers at Radom, an industrial site near Warsaw, were also threatening a general strike. Their billboard demand was the dismissal of the local officials responsible for the violent repression of 1976. Adding impetus to the simmering animosity was what appeared to be an increasing pattern of

---

[1] "Boisterous Convention of Polish Farmers Tries Democracy," *The New York Times*, 10 March 1981, p. A8.
[2] "Union Calls on Poles...," *The New York Times*, 10 March 1981, p. A8; "Workers in Lodz Stage 1 Hour Warning Strike," *The New York Times*, 11 March 1981, p. A8; and Garton Ash, *The Polish Revolution*, p. 149.

harassment by police and security components. The regional union was persuaded to call off the strike on 16 March after direct appeals by Walesa, Jacek Kuron of the KOR, and a representative of the Polish Catholic Church—*and after the accused government officials agreed to resign.*[3]

That same day, representatives of Rural Solidarity in Bydgoszcz occupied the offices there of the United Peasant Party, a front organization formerly—and still, theoretically—responsible for representing the Polish private farmers. The issue sparking the sit-in was the farmers' demand for recognition of their organization and their protest over the local governing body's refusal to recognize their right to elect their own representatives to the local agricultural forums. The farmers were joined by representatives of Solidarity, including the regional representative on Solidarity's National Coordinating Commission, Jan Rulewski, who had a reputation as a militant.[4]

Three days later, on 19 March, uniformed police physically evicted a group of farmers and Solidarity representatives from a meeting hall of the Bydgoszcz Peoples Council, the body that passed for a regional legislature. As the protesters were pushed outside the building, a gang in civilian clothes (later reported to have been plainclothes militia) physically assaulted them. Twenty seven people were injured, and three—one of whom was Rulewski—were injured severely and hospitalized.

Protest strikes erupted the next day across the country. Walesa called for calm, but he and the entire Solidarity national leadership had no choice but to support the protests. Solidarity's National Coordinating Commission announced suspension of all talks with the government on all other issues until the regime promised to hold the perpetrators of the violence accountable. A nationwide strike alert was declared. A date for carrying out the general strike was to be set after discussions by the National Coordinating Commission, but workers were instructed to be ready by 23 March. Jaruzelski immediately appointed a deputy prosecutor general to carry out an investigation of the incident, and followed up by creating an investigative commission headed by the Justice Minister.[5]

---

[3] "Polish Workers Threaten Strike at 1976 Clash Site," *The New York Times,* 12 March 1981, p. A2; "Polish Bishops Request Calm...," *The New York Times,* 14 March 1981, p. 3; *The New York Times,* "Poles Call Odd Plans for Walkout...," 17 March 1981, p. A3; Garton Ash, *The Polish Revolution,* p. 151; and Cynkin, *Soviet and American Signaling,* p. 100.

[4] Detailed accounts of the Bydgoszcz affair are in Andrews, *Poland 1980-81,* pp. 120–126; Garton Ash, *The Polish Revolution,* pp. 151–160; and Raina, *Poland 1981,* pp. 81–101. Daily articles in *The New York Times* from 20 through 31 March 1981 covered events as they unfolded.

[5] "Polish Police Break Up Farmers Protest," *The New York Times,* 20 March 1981, p. A3; "Scattered Strikes in Poland Protest Attack on Unionists," *The New York Times,* 21 March 1981, p. A1; Andrews, *Poland 1980-81,* p. 121; and Raina, *Poland 1981,* p. 84.

Official Polish media initially said the police were merely doing their duty to restore order. The story given was that after the Regional Peoples Council session in Bydgoszcz adjourned, dissident private farmers and Solidarity representatives occupied the meeting hall. According to this version, when the protesters refused to leave despite appeals by the mayor and deputy provincial governor, there was no choice but to call on the militia. The information on beatings was characterized as "claims" by Solidarity sources.[6]

The Intelligence Community warned that the clash at Bydgoszcz had "raised political tension to its highest level since last November." This assessment said that if a nationwide strike took place, the Polish regime would come under great pressure from its own hardliners and Moscow to declare martial law. "In the current atmosphere, such an action could lead to a breakdown of civil order. Should this occur, Moscow almost certainly would intervene militarily."[7]

On Sunday, 22 March, the party Politburo issued a statement characterizing the occupation of the council hall in Bydgoszcz as a "flagrant violation of law," and a deliberate provocation by "some forces" in an effort to create new tensions. Two of the most unabashed party advocates of a crackdown, Olszowski (by this time no longer viewed as a reformer) and Grabski, reportedly tried to exploit the incident and the resulting strikes to justify immediate imposition of martial law.[8]

Two days later, on 24 March, Solidarity's National Coordinating Commission announced that a four-hour nationwide warning strike would be carried out on 27 March, and that a general strike would begin on 31 March if the following demands were not met:

- Immediate punishment of those responsible for the Bydgoszcz incident;

- Registration of Rural Solidarity;

- Guarantees of security for all union members;

- Annulment of a government directive giving only half-pay to strikers;

- Closure of all cases pending against people arrested for opposition activity between 1976 and 1980 (in effect, between the founding of the KOR and Solidarity).

---

[6] *Trybuna Ludu*, 20 March 1981, p. 2, cited in Andrews, *Poland 1980-81*, p. 120.
[7] "Poland: Political Tension High," decl. *NID*, 21 March 1981.
[8] "Poland: Situation Remains Tense," decl. *NID*, 23 March 1981; "Polish Regime Ends Parley With Union Without Agreement," *The New York Times,* 23 March 1981, p. A1; Andrews, *Poland 1980-81*, p. 122; and Garton Ash, *The Polish Revolution*, p. 153.

An indication of the belligerent feelings in Solidarity was the fact that this ultimatum was the "moderate" position, for which Walesa was able to get agreement only after an all-night session in which he threatened to walk out. At the outset of the debate a majority of the worker delegates favored a general strike with no prior warning.[9]

The ensuing preparations for a national strike reflected an unprecedented level of planning and coordination for civil opposition in Poland. Each of the regional Inter-Factory Founding Committees (MKZs) moved into a large factory where they decided to remain for the duration of the strike. Many individual Factory Commissions of Solidarity did the same. Around-the-clock guards were set up at each factory site. The countryside became dotted with worker "fortresses". A Solidarity radio station transmitted news and instructions each morning, and printing presses spun out pamphlets for nationwide distribution, all aimed at ensuring nationwide coordination and synchronization. Intelligence reporting on these developments described them as an attempt by the union to deny the regime its ultimate weapon of a declaration of martial law.[10]

A meeting on 25 March between Walesa and Deputy Prime Minister Rakowski proved fruitless. The warning strike took place from 8:00 a.m. to 12:00 p.m. on 27 March. It was the largest strike in the 36-year history of the Soviet Bloc. The discipline was demonstrated by the fact that a clear demarcation was set and observed; essential services such as health facilities, national oil pipelines, armaments factories, and national rail lines were kept in operation. Such day-to-day services as local transportation, however, were shut down. Of particular affront to the regime, a sizable number of party members who also belonged to Solidarity participated in the strike. The union had dramatically demonstrated what it was prepared to carry out on a sustained basis four days later if its demands were not satisfied.[11]

While Solidarity demonstrated its ability to coordinate action on a national scale, the Polish party seemed on the verge of coming apart. A party plenum was set for Sunday, 29 March, amid rumors that it would be acrimonious and probably include a challenge to Kania's leadership. It lived up to expectations, lasting well into the next morning, and by all accounts was dominated by bitter recriminations. At one point, the prominent hardliners Olszowski and

---

[9] "Poland: Pivotal Meeting Today," decl. *NID*, 26 March 1981; and "Poland: Further Talks Slated,: decl. *NID*, 25 March 1981; "Polish Union Divided On New Strike Action," *The New York Times*, 24 March 1981, p. A3; "Polish Strike Set If Meeting Today Brings No Gains," *The New York Times*, 25 March 1981, p. A1; Andrews, *Poland 1980-81*, pp. 123-125; and Garton Ash, *The Polish Revolution*, p. 154-155.

[10] "Poland: Possible Turning Point," decl. Special Analysis, 25 March 1981, and Garton Ash, *The Polish Revolution*, p. 156.

[11] "Polish Workers Stage Nationwide Strike," *The New York Times*, 27 March 1981, p. A1; "Millions in Poland Go on 4-Hour Strike to Protest Violence," *The New York Times*, 28 March 1981, p.1; Andrews, *Poland 1980-81*, pp. 125-126; Garton Ash, *The Polish Revolution*, p. 157; and Ascherson, *The Polish August*, p. 265.

Grabski, along with one other Central Committee member, offered to resign. By the session's end, the resignations had been withdrawn, but there were credible reports that it had taken intervention from Moscow to save their posts. In any event, on the eve of the threatened nationwide general strike, it was Solidarity rather than the regime that appeared to hold the strength—except in one category: armed force.[12]

A Staged Provocation?

The consensus of Solidarity's leadership, Western media, and US intelligence analysts and policy officials was that the Bydgoszcz incident had been a setup by Polish hard-liners for the specific purpose of provoking a Solidarity reaction that could be exploited to justify martial law. The attempts by Olszowski and Grabski to invoke martial law at the 22 March party meeting appeared to confirm that view. The National Intelligence Estimate on "Poland's Prospects" for the first half of 1981 had concluded that one of the potential events most likely to precipitate a Soviet military intervention would be "a general strike of some duration to which the Polish regime did not respond decisively."[13] This was, in effect, a forecast that a full-blown general strike would compel the Polish regime to choose between imposing its own forces or being subjected to Soviet intervention. The Bydgoszcz incident led many to believe that some Polish hardliners shared this judgment, and had staged the incident to force Kania and Jaruzelski into exactly that position.[14]

The same views were expressed even by moderates within the Polish party. One, the chairman of the Polish Journalists' Association, charged on 23 March in an "open letter" to his party: "Our hardliners stand for no program except the concept of confrontation and disinformation.... They are try-

---

[12] "Polish Leaders Continue Meetings in 'Good' Climate," *The New York Times,* 29 March 1981, p. 1; "Polish Ruling Body Reaches An Impasse On Averting Strikes," *The New York Times,* 30 March 1981, p. A1; Andrews, *Poland 1980-81*, pp. 128-132; Ascherson, *The Polish August*, pp. 265-266; and Garton Ash, *The Polish Revolution*, p. 158. For the allegations of Moscow's intervention see *The New York Times,* 14 April 1981, p. A1, "Brezhnev Phone Call Said to Have Protected Hard-Liners in Poland," and Weschler, *The Passion of Poland*, p. 183.

[13] "Poland's Prospects Over the Next Six Months," NIE 12.6-81, p. 2.

[14] For the views of Western observers and reporters see articles by John Darnton in "Scattered Strikes In Poland Protest Attacks on Unionists;" *The New York Times*, 21 March 1981, p. 1; "Warsaw Talks Set For Today On Crisis Over Police Attack," *The New York Times,* 22 March 1981, p. 1; and "Sense of Despair Over Poland," *The New York Times*, 24 March 1981, p. A3. Also see Andrews, *Poland 1980-81*, p. 138; Garton Ash, *The Polish Revolution*, pp.152-154; and Ascherson, *The Polish August*, p. 264. For the Intelligence Community view, see Gates, *From the Shadows*, p. 229.

ing to involve the whole party leadership and government in a clash with the entire society. With incalculable consequences, *they are trying to provoke society to behavior justifying the use of force.*" (emphasis added) [15]

The details that emerged over the next few days as to what actually transpired at the meeting hall in Bydgoszcz certainly seemed consistent with the provocation theory.

- The farmers and Solidarity representatives did not *intrude* into the Provincial Council Hall, they were *invited* to send a delegation of six representatives to the meeting on 19 March at which—they were told—their grievances would be addressed. While these grievances were not listed on the formal agenda for the council meeting, the farmers and solidarity representatives were told the issues would be raised under "other business" to provide the protesters an opportunity to argue their case.

- The council meeting abruptly adjourned, however, with no reference to the Rural Solidarity issues, and no call for tabling "other business." The presiding officials departed the hall. Then the protesters declared their intent to stage a sit-in. A large contingent of regular council delegates remained behind to talk with the protesters. When these councilors learned why the Rural Solidarity group was there, they persuaded the group not to stage the sit-in by agreeing to work out a joint statement calling for a special meeting of the Council to address the farmers' complaints.

- While negotiations on the wording of this joint statement were still under way (and according to most accounts, nearing agreement) a large force of police entered the hall, ordered the premises vacated and threatened to use force. The farmers and their Solidarity supporters instinctively resisted, and then the violence occurred.

- All of the events *inside the hall*, beginning with the politely expressed initial order to depart and all the ensuing contentious reactions of the protesters, were conveniently recorded on tape.

- During the time that negotiations were in process between the farmers' representatives and the councilors, the telephone lines to those inside the building were cut off. Thus anyone trying to find out

---

[15] Open Letter to the PZPR by Stefan Bratkowski, 23 March 1981; full text in Raina, *Poland 1981*, pp. 210-212.

what was happening—one of whom was Walesa—and who might have counseled safer conduct, was unable to get through.[16]

The fact that these events took place while Jaruzelski and Kania were not on the scene (Jaruzelski was at the *Soyuz '81* exercises and Kania was visiting Budapest) added credence to the theory that the incident was rigged to force their hand. There has been some speculation about various schemes and who might have played a role in them. But to date, no evidence has been released by intelligence agencies or obtained from the records of former Warsaw Pact countries to confirm or disprove definitively the judgment of a deliberately contrived provocation.

Whatever its origins, the Bydgoszcz incident and the reactions it provoked did indeed appear to intelligence analysts at the time to have completed setting the stage for the use of force:

- Martial law plans already had been tested, updated, and passed to the Soviets.

- Preparatory deployments of command, communication, and logistic measures to facilitate introduction of outside forces were in the process of being put in place through the *Soyuz '81* exercises.

- And now, an excuse for implementing the martial law plans had been provided.

The scheme also appeared to have achieved its intent of putting Jaruzelski into a trap with little wiggle room. The Intelligence Community saw little prospect that he could accede to all of Solidarity's demands—identify and punish those responsible for the Bydgoszcz incident and, at the same time, close all pending legal actions against political dissidents. If he did not accede, and Solidarity did not budge, the strike seemed unavoidable. If the strike occurred, it was hard to see any other regime option except force or martial law. The American press reported the widespread perception that "Western diplomats believe that if talks fail and the strike goes ahead on 31 March, the Polish Government will declare a state of emergency [martial law]."[17]

The Intelligence Community agreed, summing up this dilemma with the conclusion that "the chances have increased markedly that the regime will impose martial law, even though doing so [lacking any element of surprise]

---

[16] Andrews, *Poland 1980-81*, p. 122; and Garton Ash, *The Polish Revolution*, pp. 151-152. This description was for the most part eventually acknowledged, albeit in terms less indicative of culpability, in the report of the Minister of Justice assigned to investigate the events, and broadcast on Polish television on 28 March 1981. The full text of the minister's report is presented in Raina, *Poland 1981*, pp. 86-98.

[17] "Millions in Poland Go on 4-Hour Strike...," *The New York Times,* 28 March 1981, *op. cit.*

risks provoking widespread disorder and a military intervention by the Soviets." It was precisely because of the likely disastrous outcome of a martial law attempt, however, that the Intelligence Community did not completely rule out "another capitulation by the government." It said "some in the regime may be prepared for greater compromise, believing the Soviets still want to avoid military intervention."[18]

Positioning the Military Forces?

For intelligence analysts, actions that made the *Soyuz '81* exercises look increasingly like a cover for positioning Soviet and other Warsaw Pact military units to support martial law reinforced the gloomy outlook for Poland's political dynamics. By 26 March, it had become clear that the exercise had been extended for an indefinite period. A command and communications network had been activated that could be used for directing military operations in Poland while by-passing normal Polish military communications networks. Three Soviet General Staff operations groups—the type of group that would employ these networks—were moved into Poland. There were also signs that Soviet, East German, and Czechoslovak units carrying out maneuvers near the Polish borders were receiving fresh troops (although US intelligence showed that—contrary to some public accounts—these forces had not crossed into Poland.)[19]

On 27 March, the US Defense Attaché in Bonn reported that a knowledgeable source—probably from the Polish military attaché mission—said he had reason to believe "a state of emergency [martial law] would be declared by Prime Minister Jaruzelski over the weekend of 28-29 March." Some of the source's reasoning reflected questionable perspectives—for example, that Solidarity was in a weakened state and that momentum was with the party. On the other hand, the source confirmed that there was a consensus among Warsaw Pact military liaison officers expecting the imposition of force, and that some Soviet military contacts reportedly were saying they expected their forces to be called upon to actively support the Polish effort. The report also quoted

---

[18] "Poland: Possible Turning Point," decl. *NID* Special Analysis, 25 March 1981.

[19] Initial reporting of the extension of *Soyuz '81* is described in "Poland: Further Talks Slated," decl. *NID* article of 26 March 1981. For the other activities, see Gates, *From the Shadows*, p. 230; also "US Warns Russians and Poles on Force Against Union," *The New York Times*, 27 March 1981, p. A1; "Haig Is Troubled By Soviet Moves On Polish Border," *The New York Times*, 30 March 1981, p. A1; and "US Asserts Soviet Steps Up Readiness to Move on Poland," *The New York Times*, 4 April 1981, p.1. Kuklinski subsequently described these preparations in his 1987 interview. See "Suppression of Solidarity," Kostrzewa, *Between East and West*, pp. 88-89.

another Warsaw Pact military representative—one who had accurately dismissed US public warnings of a military crackdown in December 1980—now saying that such a move "is coming and is coming fast."[20]

At the end of March, the Intelligence Community repeated its earlier warning that "[T]he deepening crisis in Poland has markedly increased chances that the Polish Government will impose martial law and that the Soviets might subsequently intervene militarily. ..." Photography revealed four Soviet divisions in the western USSR (one in the Baltic district and three in Carpathia) being fleshed out with reservists. Some preparations for the movement of tanks, armored personnel carriers, and field artillery also were observed at a nearby railroad trans-loading yard. Intelligence reporting said that "if the Poles request immediate Soviet assistance...a limited Soviet force could participate with little or no warning." This force was described as consisting of about 12 divisions, including some drawn from the fully manned Soviet forces based in East Germany and perhaps Czechoslovakia.[21]

These activities could be rationalized as part of the *Soyuz '81* exercises, but the forces involved also seemed to match up with the descriptions of the intervention forces for the scenario last December. And compared to the situation in December, the readiness of Soviet forces for movement—with the command, communications and logistic infrastructure already in place because of the ongoing exercises—was significantly higher.[22]

At the same time, however, CIA also said—as it had during the December confrontation—that "[T]he risks to the Soviets [of such a move] would be high ... because a small force might not be able to cope with potentially rebellious elements in the Polish Army and an aroused population." The intelligence analysts continued to estimate that a Soviet force designed to contend with such risks would contain 30 or more divisions. The analysis said that a major intervention by such a force, whether "at the request of the Polish regime or solely at Moscow's initiative would require large scale preparations lasting 10-14 days. ...Preparations for [such] a major intervention would exceed those of last December and would include an extensive mobilization of reservists and civilian vehicles and other large scale logistical activity." No signs of such a buildup had yet been reported.[23]

---

[20] USDAO Bonn, 271138Z Mar 81, Bonn GE 06212, "Weekend of 28-29 March Ominous For Poland," *Poland 1980-82: Compendium.* For speculation as to the source, see Mark Kramer, "Colonel Kuklinski and the Polish Crisis, 1980-81," *CWIHP Bulletin 11*, Winter 1998, p. 48, regarding the Polish Defense Attaché to West Germany.
[21] "Poland: Warning of Intervention," decl. *NID*, 28 March 1981; "Poland: Concessions Cause Tensions," decl. *NID*, 31 March 1981; "Photographic Summary," CIA Memorandum of 30 March 1981.
[22] *Ibid.*
[23] Declassified *NID* article, 28 March 1981, *op. cit.*

Most of this intelligence was publicized in late March and early April in a steady stream of US warnings to Warsaw and Moscow of the consequences of introducing force. The day before Solidarity's warning strike, the US Administration—having learned that the *Soyuz '81* exercises had been extended indefinitely—released a statement saying "The United States has watched with growing concern indications that Polish authorities may be preparing to use force to deal with continuing differences in that country. We are similarly concerned that the Soviet Union may intend to undertake repressive action in Poland...any external intervention or any measures aimed as suppressing the Polish people...could have a grave effect on the whole course of East-West relations." A State Department official was quoted at saying "all signs are bad...the Warsaw Pact exercises have been extended and the Russians have the infrastructure to move into Poland very, very quickly."[24]

On the day of the warning strike, Secretary of State Haig publicly described the potential for martial law, while Secretary of Defense Weinberger warned of Soviet military intervention. Weinberger declared that "...if the Russians go into Poland, that would end any possibility of any useful or effective disarmament or arms limitation talks." On 29 March, Haig referred in a television interview to intelligence reporting on the movement of fresh Soviet troops, and the establishment of a command and communications structure by the Soviets in collaboration with the Polish leaders to circumscribe potential opposition within the Polish military.[25]

The United States soon learned from Kuklinski that on 27 March—the day of Solidarity's four-hour warning strike—a group of about 30 senior Soviet military officers and KGB officials had flown into Warsaw to review the martial law plans with the Polish leadership. Marshal Kulikov, who had already been in Poland for the *Soyuz '81* exercises, headed the military delegation. Leading the KGB delegation was then-Deputy Director Vladimir Kruchkov, head of the First Chief Directorate, responsible for foreign intelligence. A group from the Soviet State Planning Commission (Gosplan) also arrived, led by its chairman, Nikolai Baibakov.

The Soviets pushed for changes in the plans Jaruzelski had passed to them in early March. They argued that when martial law was declared, the Polish constitution should be suspended and supreme authority transferred to the military. They also sought changes in the timing and procedures for the arrests and internments that would precede the formal declaration of martial law, and insisted that Soviet military and security officers be placed as "advisors" in all components of the national and regional commands charged with implement-

---

[24] State Department statement, see "US Warns Russians and Poles on Force Against Union," *The New York Times,* 27 March 1981, p. A1; and "Statement on Poland," *The New York Times,* 27 March 1981, p. A9.
[25] "Allies Said to Agree With US On Poland," *The New York Times,* 28 March 1981, p. A5; and "Haig is Troubled..." *The New York Times,* 30 March 1981.

ing martial law. In effect, Moscow seemed to be seeking to impose a forceful crackdown using Polish forces under Soviet direction, and to use the crackdown as a cover for introducing at least some additional Soviet forces into Poland. The Soviet delegation pressed Kania and Jaruzelski to set a date for implementing the plans.[26]

The Poles, not surprisingly, resisted many of the proposed changes. But agreement was finally reached on the text of three joint planning documents, which the Polish leaders and the Soviet representatives then signed. With so little of the intelligence from this period declassified, there remains some ambiguity as to how much the United States knew about the contents in the three documents.[27] What is a matter of public record is that Kuklinksi was involved in preparing the plans and that he reported the discussions to Washington intelligence agencies. Knowledge of those discussions added to the emerging picture of impending martial law.

A Respite?

On the evening of 30 March, Polish television broadcast a joint announcement by the government and Solidarity that an agreement had been reached and that the threatened strike had been suspended. The government acknowledged that the police actions at Bydgoszcz constituted a violation of legal rights, agreed to carry out a full investigation, to suspend those under investigation until a decision was reached on responsibility, and to place before a tribunal those who were found to be responsible. The government also made a commitment to expedite the passage through parliament of the law governing free trade unions, and to submit to the parliament a draft law for registering the private farmers' union. Rural Solidarity would be permitted to function as a de facto union until the law was officially passed. (This law finally went into effect on 10 May.) Workers who participated in the four-hour warning strike on 27 March were granted full pay for the time they were on strike, although no general commitments were made regarding wage payments to participants in past or future strikes.

The agreement was more ambiguous on Solidarity's demand for implementing the Gdansk provisions on security and rights of free speech for union members, saying only that the matter would be submitted to a parliamentary

---

[26] The arrival and composition of the Soviet delegations and the nature of the discussions are described by Kuklinski, "The Suppression of Solidarity," Kostrzewa, *Between East and West*, pp. 87-88. The fact that Kuklinski reported this to CIA at the time is described by Gates, *From the Shadows*, p. 230.

[27] Much of what was in these three planning documents is now known from the Polish Archives. See Kramer, "Soviet Deliberations During the Polish Crisis," Document No. 11, Translator's Note No. 121.

commission for debate. And it was silent on Solidarity's demand for closure of cases pending against political prisoners arrested between 1976 and 1980. Walesa was said to have claimed that Solidarity got "70 percent" of what it sought in the agreement.[28]

Over the next two days (31 March–1 April) a fierce debate took place within Solidarity's National Coordinating Commission. The terms of the agreement were criticized for being too vague on what the government would do in investigating the Bydgoszcz incident, and offering nothing on the release of political prisoners and on a standing policy for wage payments to strikers. Once again, however, the most strident criticism was levied not at the substance of the agreement but the means by which it was negotiated. Walesa again was accused of arrogating too much authority to himself, this time with the added dimension that he had taken it upon himself to speak for the farmers. Some Commission members tendered their resignations; some were later withdrawn, while others followed through.[29]

Anger notwithstanding, Solidarity's National Commission ratified the cancellation of the strike by a vote of 25-4, with six abstentions. The vote seemed to reflect the commission's belief that whatever its unhappiness with the terms of the agreement, re-instituting the strike call would be extremely difficult, and even if it were somehow successful it would leave Kania and Jaruzelski no room to avoid turning to martial law. Indeed, throughout the negotiations the regime had used multiple channels to convey the message that if a way could not be found to head off the strike, martial law would be the regime's only recourse. On the eve of the decisive round of talks, Walesa received this same message from representatives of the Catholic church, and from some of his own advisors.[30]

---

[28] The full text of the joint agreement is given in Raina, *Poland 1981*, pp. 99-101. A description of how it was reported at the time is in "Polish Strike In Abeyance as Pact is Signed," *The New York Times*, 31 March 1981, p. A9, including the Walesa "70 percent" remark. This article says a commission was ordered to look into the issue of political prisoners, but no such provision is in the actual agreement text.

[29] "Divisions Over Polish Agreement," *The New York Times*, 2 April 1981, p. A1; "Workers Criticizing Polish Party Chief," *The New York Times*, 4 April 1981, p. 5; Andrews, *Poland 1980-81*, p. 127; and Garton Ash, *The Polish Revolution*, pp. 160-162.

[30] Andrews, *Poland 1980-81*, p. 127, and especially note 32 on p. 316; and Garton Ash, *The Polish Revolution*, p. 159. For a unique perspective on the Church's interventions, see also Gates, *From the Shadows*, p. 231.

Kania and Jaruzelski may also have seen themselves being pushed into a situation in which they would be forced to impose a crackdown. Their reluctance to be pushed into such action probably was reinforced by the evidence that the Bydgoszcz incident had been staged for the precise purpose of forcing their hand. While they did not yield on all of Solidarity's demands, they did concede more than many observers thought they would or could. In a preemptive move to head off grumbling over the concessions, Jaruzelski circulated a written "commentary" explaining why they were not as significant as they appeared. (Many of the terms he cites in defense of the agreement are the same ones that were criticized by Solidarity members who wanted to reject the agreement.)[31] There seems little question, nonetheless, that Kania and Jaruzelski shared with Walesa the concern that they would not be able to control events once the general strike had begun.

The US Government's immediate reaction seemed to signal its belief that the crisis had passed. A State Department spokesman said on 31 March that the fresh Warsaw Pact troops whose deployment in the exercise had earlier prompted alarm did not appear to be moving toward Poland, and that the US expected tensions to ease. The next day, an administration spokesman said the Soviets were not expected to enter Poland. The press was also informed that the United States was examining options for rewarding the Polish Government for continued restraint. Among the options mentioned were extending $200 million of additional commodity credits in addition to the $670 million already granted for the year; supplying Poland with surplus dairy stocks; emergency donations of wheat under food-for-peace legislation, and a further rescheduling of Polish debt.[32]

False Alarm

Just as the US administration was conveying its perception that the crisis appeared to be receding, the Intelligence Community suddenly escalated its warning of a Soviet military intervention. An Alert Memorandum disseminated on 3 April stated:

> We believe that the Soviet leaders have become *convinced* by the evident impotence of the Polish party and government leaders *that military intervention is necessary.* They have set preparations in motion and would have the capability to move in a *considerable force* within 48 hours. We believe it likely that they would want to

---

[31] "Commentary to the Joint Statement of 30 March 1981," Cde. Jaruzelski to Politburo Members, 2 April 1981, National Security Archive, Document 48 of Jachranka materials.
[32] "US Expects Tensions in Poland to Ease," *The New York Times,* 31 March 1981, p. A9; and "No Sign Russians Will Exploit Reagan Shooting to Enter Poland," *The New York Times,* 1 April 1981, p. A1.

have stronger forces than they could move that quickly and that it would take about another seven days to have the 30 or so divisions needed if the Poles were to resist. We do not know whether they have reached a final decision to act, but this decision could come at any time and the decision could be to take the Poles by surprise. If this should be the case, *there could be a move this weekend.*[33] (emphasis added)

The resonance of this Alert Memorandum with policy officials was enough to cause Secretary of State Haig to consider postponing his departure that evening for a trip to the Middle East. According to Haig, he and his advisors—at the end of what he has described as a "long day" tracking the evidence through the State Department Operations Center—concluded that "whatever Moscow's purpose...it did not include on this Friday an invasion of Poland." Late that evening, he boarded a plane for Cairo.[34]

Some CIA analysts contested the judgments in this Alert Memorandum as it was being drafted. There was no evidence that additional divisions had been mobilized beyond the four reported a few days earlier. The Soviet "considerable force" that the 3 April Alert Memo said was ready to move in 48 hours, was essentially the same one that had been described as recently as 31 March as a "limited force," which the Soviets could introduce with little or no warning. The earlier reports had described this force as consisting of about 12 divisions—including the four that had been mobilized in the western USSR. (Secretary Haig refers to this 12-division force in his account of the Alert Memorandum.) The 3 April Alert Memorandum described the force as 12 to 20 divisions, but the high side of this range was based on a larger input drawn from the Soviet forces in East Germany, which did not require mobilizing reservists.[35]

The issue was not whether the Soviets were positioned to introduce such a force suddenly. They were prepared to rapidly move the forces they had already mobilized. Additional preparatory steps the Alert Memorandum cited as increasing readiness included: logistic enhancements, movement of helicopters and other transport into Poland using what appeared to be flight patterns to evade Polish radar, and movement of various formations toward Poland's borders. The continued operational status of the special command and communications system was also cited. There were even reports that

---

[33] "Poland," DCI Alert Memorandum, 3 April 1981.
[34] Alexander Haig, *Caveat: Realism, Reagan, and Foreign Policy* (New York: MacMillan, 1994), pp. 243-244.
[35] CIA documents of 28 and 31 March and 3 April 1981, *op. cit.* The "12 division" statement was one of the few unredacted portions of the 31 March memo. Haig refers to the 12-division force in his description of the 3 April Alert Memorandum in *Caveat*, p. 244.

Soviet forces permanently based in Poland had sent detachments to Warsaw to provide increased security for the Soviet Embassy and residential compounds there.[36]

The key issue was whether the Soviets were willing to inject a force of this size without Polish military collaboration. All the preparations were consistent with Soviet anticipation of martial law, as described in the warning issued a few days earlier. Conversely, the absence of preparations for a larger force suggested a unilateral invasion was unlikely. Previous analysis had come to the same conclusion regarding the risks of committing a force of only 12 to 20 divisions without assured collaboration. Even then it was viewed as risky. The new consideration for an imminent Soviet invasion given in the 3 April Alert Memorandum rested on the concept of taking the Poles by surprise, but conditions in Poland then seemed to rule that out.

The lack of force preparations led the same analysts to question the Alert Memorandum's judgment that the Soviets had been "convinced...that military intervention is necessary." Virtually all analysts acknowledged that—leaving aside the issue of when—it was entirely plausible that Moscow now believed military intervention was necessary. This conclusion would have been a natural product of the propositions in the National Intelligence Estimate on Poland two months earlier. That Estimate concluded that Moscow would not allow the present situation in Poland to continue indefinitely, and that if the regime was unable to regain control of events, the Soviets would conclude intervention was necessary and would accept the costs.[37]

There was reason to conclude that the Polish party's control over events had continued to deteriorate and that the regime was showing no signs of being willing to implement the forceful crackdown Moscow deemed necessary. The case for a Soviet decision that intervention was necessary was thus logically sustainable. Nonetheless, in the views of some analysts, the lack of physical evidence left far more room for uncertainty on the Soviet outlook than was reflected in the Alert Memorandum.

---

[36] Many of the details regarding military activities have been redacted from the declassified intelligence documents from this time frame. The descriptions given here benefit from the author's participation in the meeting at which the text of the Alert Memorandum was debated. Moreover, former Secretary of State Haig, who received it, gives the same description in *Caveat*, pp. 243-244. The same description of Soviet moves is given by Gates, *From the Shadows*, p. 230, although, unlike Haig, he does not specifically reference a report of 3 April. Kuklinski also described these steps in his 1987 interview; see "Suppression of Solidarity," Kostrzewa, *Between East and West*, p. 88.

[37] See pp. 78-79, above.

The Alert Memorandum's divergence from preceding intelligence assessments was reflected in the media during the next few days. The day after the 3 April Alert Memorandum was disseminated, press accounts citing "US officials" described "new preparations" that would enable the Soviets to intervene with military forces "at a moment's notice." Some of the same articles, however, cited other sources within the administration that said intelligence showed the Soviets were not mobilizing more divisions in the western USSR, and that "there was no evidence" a decision had been made to intervene. One article presenting the diverse views referred to a "late night meeting" on 3 April, which sounds very much like Secretary Haig's "long day."

Conflicting stories continued to appear in the press through the weekend, with increasing detail. On 5 April, the press reported that the President had sent a letter to Brezhnev admonishing him against turning the Warsaw Pact exercises into an invasion of Poland. "Government officials" were quoted as saying that a force of "12 to 20 divisions" could be inserted quickly. One article even gave a breakdown of Soviet divisions in East Germany, Czechoslovakia, Poland and the western USSR that could make up a rapid insertion force of this size. At the same time, however, other US officials said this force was sufficient only to support martial law, not invade. The press also reported the intelligence assessment that the Soviets would require about 30 divisions to intervene unilaterally, and that another 10 days or so would be necessary to mobilize a force of that size.[38]

By Monday, 6 April, CIA analysis had returned to describing Polish martial law as the near-term threat, although there was still concern about the high state of Soviet readiness. Intelligence information on 6 and 7 April showed that readiness was sustained, but reported no mobilization of additional forces. On 7 April, the Soviets announced the end of the *Soyuz '81* exercises.[39]

For another few days, intelligence reporting and official public statements voiced concern over various forms of a military crackdown. Defense Secretary Weinberger continued to warn of a possible Soviet invasion, and NATO defense ministers issued a statement warning Moscow of the consequences of

---

[38] Samples of press reports where this information can be found include "US Asserts Soviet Steps Up Readiness...," *The New York Times*, 4 April 1981, p. 1; "Preparedness for Movement Into Poland Now Complete," *The New York Times*, 4 April 1981, p. 5; "US Weighing Aid to China if Russians Act Against Poland," *The New York Times*, 5 April 1981, p. 1; "Russians in Poland: Signs of Alertness," *The New York Times*, 5 April 1981, p. 3; and "US Aides Say Buildup Needn't Signal Move on Poland," *The New York Times*, 5 April 1981, p. 4; "Reagan Note to Brezhnev Tells of Concern About Poland," *The New York Times*, 6 April 1981, p. A1.

[39] "Poland: Increased Preparedness," decl. *NID*, 6 April 1981; "Poland: Martial Law Under Consideration," decl. *NID*, 7 April 1981; and "Continued State of Readiness," decl. *NID*, 8 April 1981.

such action. But by then, concerns were abating, and Secretary Haig said he was "relieved." On 8 April, press articles began to offer speculation about what had transpired, e.g.: An intervention had been planned but called off? Forces had been positioned for a contingency? The Soviets had been engaging in a bluff to force the Poles to act? Some Western experts outside the government were described as believing that a forceful crackdown was still the likely long-term outcome.[40]

On 9 April, the President received a CIA assessment that essentially reversed the judgment of the 3 April Alert Memorandum. Drawing on Kuklinski's reporting, the new assessment described Moscow's intense pressure on the Poles to declare martial law, and the successful Polish resistance so far. The DCI attached a note pointing out Moscow's dilemma. He said it was clear the Soviets knew of the immense costs of a unilateral intervention, but faced a threat to the entire Soviet system and military alliance if they did not act forcefully. Given these bleak choices, the DCI's memo concluded that "before sending divisions in, they will move heaven and earth to get the Poles to crack down themselves."[41]

---

[40] "Reagan Note to Brezhnev Tells of Concern About Poland," *The New York Times,* 6 April 1981, p. A1; and "Brezhnev Has Talks in Prague as Crisis Deepens in Poland," *The New York Times,* 7 April 1981, p. A1; "Weinberger Sees Poles Threatened With Invasion 'By Osmosis;'" *The New York Times,* 8 April 1981, p. A1; "Brezhnev Expresses View That Poland Can Solve Its Crisis;" "Soviet Intentions In Poland: What Happened?;" "Former Officials Gloomier Than Reagan;" and "NATO Defense Aides Issue Joint Warning to Soviets on Poland," *The New York Times,* 9 April 1981, p. A1.

[41] Gates, *From the Shadows,* p. 231.

CHAPTER 9

A Close Call?

Officially released documents from Soviet and Warsaw Pact archives include records of deliberations about using force in Poland in spring 1981. Accounts by both Polish and Soviet participants have also been made public. These sources confirm judgments based on the evidence available at the time that Moscow was going all out to push the Polish regime into implementing martial law.

Soviet Prodding

Exploiting the March exercises to pressure the Poles was discussed at a Soviet Politburo session in mid-January 1981, two months before the exercises were slated to begin. Soviet Defense Minister Ustinov stated that "we need to apply constant pressure on the Polish leadership...," and recommended to his Politburo colleagues that the planned exercises be "boosted" (*"pripodnyat"*) to make clear to the Poles that Moscow had "forces ready to act." Ustinov's recommendation came during a discussion of an assessment of the Polish situation held a week earlier by the visiting Soviet political and military officials. Their assessment accused the Polish leaders of continuing to resist Moscow's demands for adopting "emergency measures" (the euphemism for martial law). Ustinov recommended using the *Soyuz '81* exercises to "apply constant pressure on the Polish leadership and constantly get after them." The same tactic of pushing the Poles "to resort to more decisive measures" was discussed by Brezhnev and East German Party First Secretary Honecker during the CPSU 26th Congress held at the end of February.[1]

Several sources describe direct, intimate Soviet involvement in the preparation of the Polish martial law plans. This included participation by senior Soviet military and KGB officers in the Polish martial law test game conducted 16–18 February. The Soviet military participants were led by Army-General Anatoly Gribkov, who was First Deputy Commander and Chief of

---

[1] CPSU Central Committee Politburo Sessions for 22 January 1981 and 12 March 1981 (when Brezhnev described the Honecker conversation to the Politburo), in Kramer, "Soviet Deliberations on the Polish Crisis," Documents 8 and 9.

Staff of the Combined Warsaw Pact Forces (i.e., Kulikov's principal deputy). KGB Deputy Director Vladimir Kruchkov headed his organizations delegation. Whether Soviet participation consisted of "advising" or "overseeing" depends on whose account is accepted.[2]

This appears to have been essentially the same contingent of Soviet military and KGB officials who returned to Warsaw on 27 March to discuss refinements to the martial law plans with Polish leaders, and who demanded an expanded role for Soviet "advisors" in implementing the plans. The size and apparent composition of this combined Soviet delegation (about 30 officers, according to Kuklinski) suggests Moscow was seeking to insert its advisors immediately. Kania told the Polish Politburo that Brezhnev had telephoned him that same day to urge him to exploit the Bydgoszcz incident to impose martial law.[3]

This delegation of senior Soviet military and KGB officers remained in Warsaw for at least another week. Marshal Kulikov told East German Defense Minister Hoffman on 7 April—the day the *Soyuz '81* exercises officially concluded—that the Soviets had "placed an array of specialists" from the General Staff and KGB in Warsaw since mid-March. Kulikov said that although the *Soyuz '81* exercises had formally ended, no order was to be given "for now" to withdraw the staff of the combined forces and "other organs of the Soviet Union...[because]...one should not relinquish the seized positions."

Kuklinski has said that the command and communications system the Soviets set up for the contingency intervention to support martial law remained in place until the end of 1981.[4]

Indicating their hopes for martial law, the Soviets tried to get the Poles to postpone the semi-annual turnover of conscripts scheduled for 12 April. Some 52,000 conscripts who had completed their two-year mandatory service were due to be released and replaced by a new draft. Ustinov considered this to be important enough to raise it at the 2 April Soviet Politburo meeting. Kulikov

---

[2] Kramer, "Soviet Deliberations During the Polish Crisis," Translator's Note No. 149 to Document 12. This description is based on Gribkov's account in "Doctrina Brezhnev: I pol'skii krizis nacha 80-kh godov," published in *Voeno-istoricheskii shurnal*, Moscow 1992, pp. 48-49. Kramer cites Kuklinski, and accounts by Kania and by Vitali Pavlov, who was KGB station chief in Warsaw at the time.

[3] Kania's report of this phone call is given in PZPR Protocol 83, 27 March 1981, in Wlodek, ed., *Tajne Dokumenty*, p. 320. See also Kramer, "Soviet Deliberations on the Polish Crisis," Translator's Note No. 121.

[4] "Record of conversation between Kulikov and DDR Chief of General Staff Hoffman on 7 April 1981 in Legnica, Poland," Document from DDR archives, Militaerishches Zwischenarchiv Potsdam, ANZ 32642, translation in *Poland 1980-82: Compendium*; and Kuklinski, "Suppression of Solidarity," Kostrzewa, *Between East and West*, p. 89. The fact that these senior Soviet officials were still in Poland a week later is indicated by Ustinov's comment at the 2 April Politburo session that they were to meet with the Polish military leaders at 8:00 p.m. that night. See Kramer, "Soviet Deliberations on the Polish Crisis," Document 11.

told East German Defense Minister Hoffman that the Soviets had tried to persuade Jaruzelski to put the conscription off until 27 April. It is difficult to explain why a two-week extension of the two-year active duty service of the lowest-ranking Polish soldiers would receive such high-level Soviet attention, except as a contingency for some action in early April.[5]

The frustration expressed by Soviet officials after the Polish leadership's agreement with Solidarity on March is itself an indication that Moscow was expecting a forceful crackdown of some kind. On 2 April, for example, Brezhnev began a Politburo session by angrily asserting that "the [Polish leaders] listen and agree with our recommendations, but in practice do nothing." He said that in a phone conversation with Kania on 30 March, he told the Polish leader "how many times have we insisted...that you need to take decisive measures,...you can't keep making endless concessions to Solidarity." He called avoiding a general strike "capitulation to the opposition." At the same meeting, Gromyko stated that "the [Polish] leaders went back on their word in what they had promised us." And at a 9 April Soviet Politburo meeting, Ustinov said *"[A]s you know*, they did not want to back down on the Bydgoszcz conflict, but then they did..." (emphasis added).[6]

The Clandestine Meeting

On the evening of 3 April, a Soviet aircraft transported Kania and Jaruzelski to a meeting with Andropov and Ustinov in a rail car near Brest, in the Western USSR. The meeting began at 9:00 p.m. and lasted until 3:00 a.m. the next day. Stories about such a meeting had circulated at the time, but the details were kept secret. When Kuklinski gave his first public interview in 1987, he still thought that the Polish leaders had flown to meet with Brezhnev.[7]

Subsequent accounts of the meeting have drawn on Jaruzelski's description in his memoirs, and thus have tended to portray it as a Soviet initiative to administer a verbal thrashing to exhort the Poles to go ahead with martial law. Unless the minutes of the 2 April Soviet Politburo session have been completely doctored, however, the Polish leaders requested the meeting. Three participants in that Politburo meeting (Brezhnev, Ustinov, and Gromyko)

---

[5] Record of Conversation between Kulikov and Hoffman, 7 April 1981, *Poland 1980-1982: Compendium.*
[6] Kramer, "Soviet Deliberations on the Polish Crisis," Documents 11 and 12; Record of conversation between Kulikov and Hoffman, 7 April 1981.
[7] See Kuklinski, "Suppression of Solidarity," Kostrzewa, *Between East and West*, p. 88. For rumors in Warsaw about Jaruzelski's "travel to meet with other Communist leaders," see "Poles Put Off Special Session of Parliament," *The New York Times,* 5 April 1981, p. 3.

made separate references to the Polish request to meet. The record concludes: "[A] decision is made...to approve the request of the Polish comrades to hold a meeting..."[8]

Kania and Jaruzelski at the time were under fire both from their own hardliners and from Moscow for backing down from the expected imposition of martial law—and for having "capitulated" to Solidarity. The Soviets already had set up the military structure to support a Polish military crackdown, and, if necessary, to insert backup forces. The Soviet military and KGB "advisors," led by the Warsaw Pact commander in chief and the chief of the KGB foreign intelligence directorate, were at the time still in Warsaw applying pressure on the Polish leaders.

Under these circumstances, it would have been understandable for the Polish leaders to request a meeting with higher-ups in Moscow—in effect, going over the heads of the senior Soviet officials in Warsaw. At the same time, it also is not surprising that the two Polish leaders would have undertaken the trip with great trepidation. They knew how much the Soviets were counting on them to do something they were going to try to justify *not* doing. At a minimum, they would have anticipated a verbal drubbing. Soviet entrapments and arrests of Hungarian and Czechoslovakian leaders in 1956 and 1968 could have called up even worse images.[9]

Why the Soviets agreed to the meeting is clear from the discussion at the 2 April Politburo session. Andropov, for example, pointed out the need "to find some way of exerting greater influence on the [Polish] leadership." In recommending that the Poles' request for a meeting be accepted, he said "we can urge them to adopt severe measures and not to be afraid of what might result, possibly even bloodshed." Gromyko pointed out the value of the opportunity "to convey everything to the Polish [leaders] on a personal basis." Several participants in the Politburo discussion advocated the meeting as an opportunity to gauge the intentions and commitment of the Polish leaders. Brezhnev and Ustinov raised the possibility, depending on the outcome of the meeting with Kania and Jaruzelski, of convening another Warsaw Pact summit—"a meeting of the Seven at the highest level"—presumably along the lines of the 5 December Moscow summit.[10]

---

[8] Kramer, "Soviet Deliberations on the Polish Crisis," Document 11. Regarding interpretations of Jaruzelski's version in *Les Chaines et Le Refuge*, see Rosenberg, *The Haunted Land*, p. 192, and Dobbs, *Down With Big Brother*, p. 65.

[9] Soviet General Gribkov accompanied the two Polish leaders as they boarded the plane for their trip to the meeting. His account of their trepidation is described in Kramer, "Soviet Deliberations on the Polish Crisis," Document 12, Translator's Note No. 143.

[10] Session of CPSU CC Politburo, 2 April 1981, Kramer, "Soviet Deliberations on the Polish Crisis," Document 12.

The account of the Brest meeting given by Andropov and Ustinov at a follow-up Politburo session on 9 April fully substantiates Jaruzelski's version of the verbal pounding that was administered. The Soviets harangued the Poles for constantly backing down and making concessions to Solidarity. They said that martial law would enable the Polish party to "smash the...counterrevolutionary forces...put an end once and for all to the strikes and anarchy in economic life," and asserted that it could have been implemented long ago.

The Poles countered that it was "impossible to introduce martial law" in the existing circumstances, and that the introduction of troops from the outside to assist was "absolutely impossible." They indicated that they could not rely on their armed forces, especially if foreign troops were introduced. Ustinov said that in response to his question "Why they had changed their decision on [the] Bydgoszcz [incident]..., they asserted that the threat of a general strike was hanging over them." Kania, according to Andropov, said "recent events, particularly the warning strike and the events in Bydgoszcz, had shown that the counterrevolution is stronger than we [the Polish party] are."[11]

This was not the first time the Soviets were hearing this argument. The Polish leaders had tried to make the same case to Marshal Kulikov in the days following the contentious Polish party session on 29–30 March. Kulikov told the East German Defense Minister that both Kania and Jaruzelski had separately told him they could not rely on their army and security forces in the kind of critical situation that could erupt in the existing circumstances. Kulikov said the Poles had "subtly" indicated to him that "it could even be possible, in the event of an invasion by other Warsaw Pact troops, certain [Polish army] units might rebel."[12]

At the meeting in Brest, Andropov and Ustinov presented the Polish leaders with documents that were essentially implementing directives for the martial law measures set out in the planning documents already agreed upon and signed at the Warsaw meeting a few days earlier. These directives included blanks for dates to be filled in when the documents were signed, and the Soviets were demanding that the Poles sign them and fill in the dates. Moscow clearly was trying to lock the Polish leaders into a commitment from which

---

[11] Session of the CPSU Politburo, 9 April 1981, in Kramer, "Soviet Deliberations on the Polish Crisis," Document 12. Jaruzelski's version is in *Les Chaines et Le Refuge* (Paris: Jean-Claude Lattes, 1992), pp. 253-257.

[12] Record of conversation between Kulikov and Hoffman, 7 April 1981. One occasion when Kulikov could have heard this from Jaruzelski was the meeting he was to have had with the Polish military leaders on the evening of 2 April.

they could not—or so the Soviets apparently hoped—back down. According to Andropov, the Poles, after some bobbing and weaving, agreed to "look over and sign [the] document[s]" on 11 April.[13]

A week later, Marshal Kulikov (who had returned to the USSR after the *Soyuz '81* exercises ended) was back in Poland to meet with Jaruzelski on 11 April, as was agreed at Brest, to get the signed and dated implementing documents. Jaruzelski put him off for two days, claiming an overloaded schedule. He was depressed over the prospect that he might yet be forced to impose some scaled-back version of martial law, according to Kuklinski, and was considering short-term detentions of extremists as a middle ground between capitulation and the drastic steps Moscow wanted. The US Intelligence Community also reported at this time that Jaruzelski was preparing to declare some limited form of martial law.[14]

By the time Jaruzelski met with Kulikov on 13 April, however, his confidence had been bolstered by reactions to a speech he had made to the parliament on 10 April calling for a two-month moratorium on strikes. The parliament had passed a resolution calling for the moratorium, and much of the Polish populace had reacted favorably. Solidarity had reserved the right to strike where its "fundamental interests were threatened," but clearly indicated that the union's leadership wanted to comply with the two-month moratorium and would discourage strikes. At the meeting with Kulikov (apparently Kania attended as well), the Polish leaders refused to sign and date the documents. According to Kuklinski, no dates were affixed to them until late 1981.[15]

The Polish Sidestep

Even before he turned over the plans in Moscow in early March, Jaruzelski had assured the Soviets of his resolve to impose martial law, according to Kuklinski. Jaruzelski had tried to convince the Soviet leaders, however, that it was necessary to wait until the "ratio of forces" improved somewhat—until Solidarity lost some of its popularity and the government gained some support. He also insisted on the need to deal with weaknesses in the military and security forces who would impose the crackdown. Kuklinski has said the

---

[13] "Soviet Deliberations on the Polish Crisis," Document 12. The references in the discussions of what was to be signed shift back and forth between singular and plural, "document" or "documents." This may simply reflect difficulties inherent in written records of oral accounts. Kuklinski used the plural.

[14] Kuklinski, "Suppression of Solidarity," Kostrzewa, *Between East and West*, p. 89; Also "Poland: Increased Preparedness," decl. *NID*, 6 April 1981, and "Poland: Martial Law Under Consideration," decl. *NID*, 7 April 1981.

[15] Kuklinski, p. 89; Andrews, *Poland 1980-81*, p. 151.

Soviets dismissed this argument by asserting that they were prepared to "alter the unfavorable ratio of forces by sending in their divisions and even Czech and East German divisions."[16]

The evidence from Kuklinski and the Soviet records support Kania's and Jarzelski's accounts that they saw themselves being squeezed into a trap by a combination of Soviet pressure, the Bydgoszcz provocation, and Solidarity's reaction. They believed that if the threatened nationwide general strike was launched, they had no real alternative to calling a state of emergency and attempting to impose a forceful solution. It is also clear that they feared a violent outcome that could include rebellious splits in the army and security forces, all of which would result in the insertion of sizable forces from the USSR and other Warsaw Pact "allies." Slipping out of this trap was viewed at the time as a close call. The information in records that are now available provides glimpses of the maneuvers the Polish leaders resorted to in this escape.

At the time, the general perception from the outside was that Moscow had prolonged the *Soyuz '81* exercises, originally due to end on 23 March. According to what Marshal Kulikov told East German Defense Minister Hoffman on 7 April, however, the exercises had been prolonged at the specific request of the Polish leaders. He said they wanted "to show Solidarity and the KOR that the Warsaw Pact countries were prepared to render Poland help." He also said that Kania and Jaruzelski had even tried to have the exercises extended beyond 7 April, but the Soviets had turned them down because of the negative international attention already evident.[17] (One could speculate that the "negative attention" became a factor after Moscow finally accepted that Kania and Jaruzelski were not going to undertake martial law, at least not at that time.)

Jaruzelski and Kania had every reason to play up the threatening image fostered by the prolonged exercises. Faced with the likely costs of the martial law if a general strike took place, they were willing to offer more concessions to Solidarity than most had expected. They could not, however, accede to all of Solidarity's demands; they needed to show they had drawn a line. For that, they had to convince Walesa and other Solidarity leaders that the union also needed a way out of the looming collision, and that it was worth giving some ground to find the way out. By all accounts, the regime's ability

---

[16] Kuklinski, pp. 86-87. Kuklinski was directly engaged in preparing materials for these exchanges.

[17] Record of discussion, Kulikov and Hoffman, *op. cit.* For examples of the commonly held view see Andrews, *Poland 1980-81*, p. 148. Also "US Warns Russians and Poles on Use of Force," *The New York Times*, 27 March 1981, p. A1; "Millions in Poland Go on 4 Hour Strike," *The New York Times*, 28 March 1981, p. 1; and "US Weighing Aid to China If Russians Act Against Poland," *The New York Times*, 5 April 1981, p. 1, regarding Weinberger remarks.

to convincingly portray martial law accompanied by Soviet intervention as the likely alternative to compromise was a decisive factor in producing the agreement on 30 March that averted the strike.

Even after that compromise was achieved and the strike was called off, the specter of a Soviet invasion would have strengthened Jaruzelski's hand in getting Solidarity to tacitly sign on to his parliamentary initiative for a strike moratorium. He needed this breathing space to gain time to work on correcting the "unfavorable ratio of forces." This could have been why he and probably Kania sought to have the exercises extended further, at least until after his initiative with the parliament.

The threat of unilateral military intervention appears to have been—then, at least—more bark than bite. In addition to the intelligence on the status of Soviet forces, the records of Soviet meetings contain no hint that the Soviets were prepared at that time to undertake an invasion if the Poles failed to launch a crackdown. On the contrary, Marshal Kulikov told the Polish leaders that the Soviets assumed "that unless the Polish security organs and army would be deployed, outside help cannot be expected, for otherwise considerable international complications would result." According to the East German record of Kulikov's account of his discussions with Kania and Jaruzelski, he told them that "their common goal should be to solve the problems without the deployment of allied armies into Poland." He said he "emphatically brought it to the attention of the Polish comrades that they have to try first to solve their problems by themselves. If they cannot do so alone and then ask for help, the situation is different from one in which [outside] troops had been deployed from the outset."[18]

This record of Kulikov's conversation has received a fair amount of attention in various post-Cold War discussions of what Jaruzelski was given to believe the Soviets *would* be willing to do if he needed assistance.[19] The flip side, however, is what it seems to say about what they were *not* prepared to do, at least at that time. With due caution regarding the uncertainties about Kulikov's statement, it would seem on its face to have also informed Jaruzelski that he had some leverage to fend off Moscow. If the Soviets were averse to unilateral military intervention, they probably were willing to grant Jaruzelski more time in the hope of getting him to enforce his own crackdown, for which they would continue to harangue him.

---

[18] Record of conversation between Marshal Kulikov and East German Defense Minster Hoffman, *op. cit.*

[19] See, for example, Mark Kramer, "Jaruzelski, the Soviet Union, and the Imposition of Martial Law in Poland: New Light on the Mystery of December 1981," *CWIHP Bulletin 11*, Winter 1998, p. 8.

It seems quite plausible that this helped stiffen Jaruzelski's stance during the confrontation in the rail car at Brest. It also could have contributed to his willingness, after seeing signs that he was going to get some breathing space in the domestic confrontations, to stonewall on signing and dating the implementing documents for martial law. This refusal reversed what the Soviets considered to be a commitment given by the Polish leaders at Brest to sign the documents.

During in the Brest meeting, according to the Soviet records, Jaruzelski "again" offered to step down as Prime Minister. The Soviets told him it was "essential for him to remain...." Jaruzelski's offers to step down have been interpreted by many as indicating his wish to be relieved of a job in which he might find himself compelled to employ Polish forces against Polish citizens. An equally plausible explanation, however, especially in view of his actions over the longer term, is that he was in effect challenging the Soviets. He had repeatedly promised to carry out the martial law measures, but at a time and in a way he judged would be most likely to succeed with the least risk of violent confrontations that could leave permanent scars. He offered the Soviets the choice of allowing him latitude to follow the course he thought best—to produce a result they both wanted—or to replace him.

At that point the Soviets had no credible alternative to Jaruzelski to implement their preferred solution: Polish martial law. His stature as leader of the Polish military was unrivaled. He had been Defense Minister for 13 years, and a member of the Politburo for more than a decade. His departure as Prime Minister almost certainly would have been seen as a result of his refusal to comply with Moscow's insistence on the use of force. The Soviets may have been indulging in some self-deception about the reliability of the Polish military, but they could have had no illusions over the negative impact Jaruzelski's removal would have on the cohesiveness of those forces. And if Jaruzelski left the Prime Minister's post because of open opposition to the use of force, it is hard to see how he could be kept on as Defense Minister. Removing him from the latter post because of opposition to Soviet pressure for the use of force could result in open divisions within the military.

Jaruzelski was not opposing the Soviets on the issue of whether martial law should be imposed. He was insisting that attempting it just then could be disastrous, and that it would take time to create the necessary circumstances and cohesion among the military to carry it off successfully. For Moscow, the other options would have been to find someone to replace Jaruzelski and then try to go through the process of rebuilding a cohesive force for martial law, or to mount their own invasion. Conceding some time for Jaruzelski to live up to his promises would have been the least undesirable option.

Soviet deliberations in the aftermath of the Brest meeting reflect this attitude. On 9 April, after hearing members of the Soviet Politburo muse about other possible Polish leaders, Ustinov said that, problems notwithstanding, "we still need this pair—Kania and Jaruzelski—to stick together and strengthen their relations." At another session a week later, Brezhnev said that it was important in dealing with the Poles not to "badger them without need." He said "we should avoid making them so nervous that they throw up their hands in despair. On the other hand, we should exert constant pressure and tactfully draw their attention to the errors and weaknesses in their policy..." He also suggested preparing a "broader...strategic analysis, which will permit us to stand back from the daily flow of events and take a longer-term perspective..." When this "strategic analysis" was presented to the Politburo a week later, it included the conclusion that with regard to Kania and Jaruzelski, "both of them, especially Jaruzelski, enjoy authority in the country. At present, there are in fact no other officials who might take over the party and state leadership." The evidence suggests that Jaruzelski also sensed this conclusion and played his hand accordingly.[20]

All the evidence now available shows that there was indeed a high risk in late March and early April 1981 of some form of military crackdown in Poland. This evidence shows the risk to have been much closer to occurring than was the case in December 1980. That it did not happen was more than anything a result of the fact that the Polish leaders found a way out of a trap, (with some assistance from Walesa and the Catholic church).

One could even speculate that creating the trap itself ultimately thwarted a Soviet-engineered Polish martial law crackdown. Polish hardliners appear to have overplayed their hand with the Bydgoszcz incident. They probably hoped that it would close off any room for Kania and Jaruzelski to retreat from a crackdown. But instead it inflamed Solidarity to burrow into a fortress posture, seemingly ensuring that the use of force would result in widespread violence and bloodshed. In effect, staging the Bydgoszcz crisis created the very situation in which Kania and Jaruzelski were most determined to avoid resorting to force.

Intelligence in Hindsight

On balance, contemporary intelligence information and analysis holds up well in light of what is now known. The 3 April Alert Memorandum seems to have been an isolated example. And unlike in late 1980, even after the 3 April Memorandum was disseminated, the Intelligence Community did not allow the invasion scenario to lock out equal consideration of others, and the evidence continued to be weighed against the spectrum of possibilities. Less than

---

[20] Kramer, "Soviet Deliberations During the Polish Crisis," Documents 12 and 13 (Politburo sessions of 9 and 16 April).

a week later, the DCI sent another Memorandum to the President that seems to have been right on the mark in describing Soviet motivations and efforts to force the Poles into imposing martial law. Indeed, had martial law occurred in the circumstances then existing, it would have been accurate to characterize it as Soviet intervention—given the planning, execution, and near certain involvement of Soviet troops.

The strongest endorsement of the intelligence assessment seems to come from Jaruzelski and Kania. Their views on the consequences of attempting martial law and the leverage they had with the Soviets are very close to those produced by the Intelligence Community.

Much of this record is unquestionably the result of the insights provided by the astonishingly well-placed human intelligence source, Ryszard Kuklinski. None of the declassified CIA documents identifies information as specifically coming from Kuklinski, but Gates makes clear that much of the reporting on the potential for Polish martial law was based on Kuklinski's information. Many of the Soviet moves and Polish martial law deliberations that Gates and Haig say they learned then are the same ones Kuklinski described later in his public interview. They were mainly the kind of low visibility, covert activities for which human sources provide a unique window.

Aside from secretly acquired intelligence, the circumstances in Poland in March and April were such that the potential for military action was obvious to anyone paying attention. The burgeoning, national-level opposition to the regime by workers, peasants and students, the Bydgoszcz provocation, and the publicly announced Warsaw Pact military maneuvers left no room for questioning the potential dangers. There also is no doubt, however, that intelligence assessments were used by the US administration to brighten the media spotlight. On the general issue of a military crackdown, no one can be accused of crying wolf, because the wolf was indeed in the vicinity. The wolf did not attack, but no one could claim to have been surprised if it had.

What effect US policy had on the outcome is always difficult to determine, even with the benefit of hindsight. What is clear is that Solidarity's preparations for resisting martial law was a deterring factor for Kania and Jaruzelski. Solidarity and the Polish populace certainly did not need the United States to point out the dangers of a military crackdown. Nonetheless, the aggressive public stance by the United States and its Allies kept the issue under a spotlight. Kulikov's comments to Jaruzelski about why Moscow was insisting that the Poles take the initiative also suggest that the message was getting through to Moscow and other Warsaw Pact capitals.

CHAPTER 10

Liberalization Infects the Party

From mid-April to about mid-July of 1981, the level of confrontation between the regime and Solidarity was relatively constrained—certainly by comparison with the preceding nine months. To some extent this was a result of the union's tacit agreement to abide by Jaruzelski's call for a strike moratorium in his 10 April speech to the parliament. It also was a reflection of increased sensitivity on the part of leaders from both sides to the risks that even relatively limited confrontations could erupt with potentially disastrous consequences. Equally important, however, was the fact that both the party and Solidarity were then grappling with internal challenges.

Kania and Jaruzelski were struggling to contain a defiant reform movement in their party's grass roots, while simultaneously preventing party reactionaries from exploiting the struggle for their own hard-line purposes. The status of the Polish United Workers Party and its leaders' authority had already been severely eroded by their inability to rein in Solidarity. But before Kania and Jaruzelski could hope to rebuild the PZPR to undertake decisive measures, they had to stem the damaging centrifugal forces from the party's rebellious reformists and combative reactionaries.

Solidarity, meanwhile, was organizing its own internal structure and preparing for its own elections. Heated debates were underway within the union over how to define its leadership's mandate for negotiating and making commitments for the rank and file. Even more fundamental was the question of how the union would define itself—as a trade union focused on defending workers' concerns, or as an acknowledged political organization with a pro-active role in the formulation of social and economic policy and the management of Poland's economy. The pressures from this latter question would intensify through the summer, as the already dismal economy continued to decline.

The party and Solidarity were preparing for their individual congresses. For the PZPR it was to be an "extraordinary" congress, which had been called for amidst the crisis of late 1980 for the express purpose of addressing the demonstrable failures in party policies and economic performance that had given birth to Solidarity. For Solidarity, it was to be its first national congress, and would be the first occasion for its operating statutes and rules and its identity as a political entity to be debated in such a forum. These congresses would shape the identity and character of the regime and the union that would confront each other again later in the year.

The reform effort within the party was spearheaded by what had become known as the "horizontal movement." Its genesis was the effort by factory level party organizations to replicate the lateral coordination employed by Solidarity's Inter-Factory Strike Committees. A network among lower echelon party groups had begun to coalesce as far back as the fall of 1980, and it had almost immediately begun pressing for a fundamental overhaul of party election statutes. Its principal goal was to enable individual party units to put forward their own nominees and conduct their own elections for leadership posts at each echelon, rather than merely voting their approval of a list of candidates submitted from the top. The reformers wanted the same system applied for electing national party leaders. They argued that party organizations at individual enterprises should be empowered to nominate and elect their own delegates to assemblies at the regional level, which should then follow the same process to select delegates for a national congress. They called for the national congress to conduct open nominations and hold secret votes for electing a Central Committee and the top party leaders.[1]

On 15 April 1981, just as the storm over the *Soyuz '81* exercise was calming, the horizontal movement held a formal meeting to endorse a set of reform proposals for submission to the party's upcoming extraordinary congress. This assembly was held in Torun, and was attended by 750 delegates of Polish party organizations from at least 11 provinces. The delegates agreed on a package that included the earlier proposals for a bottom-up electoral system and horizontal links between party organizations, and also called for all delegates to the upcoming party congress to be elected by secret ballot from a list of nominees put together by the voting organizations. Other recommendations included lifting censorship on grass-roots initiatives, making changes in the Politburo and party Central Committee secretariat, limiting terms of office for

---

[1] For further background on the origins of the "horizontal movement" see Andrews, *Poland 1980-81*, p. 89; Garton Ash, *The Polish Revolution*, pp. 170-171; and Raina, *Poland 1981*, pp. 23-24.

party officials, establishing procedures to enforce accountability, and restricting the practice of allowing individuals to hold offices simultaneously in the party and government.[2]

The same day these proposals were publicized, Kania said publicly that he agreed that there was a need for greater democracy, but he emphasized even more the need to rebuild the party's internal cohesion, and its power and authority for effective action. A party plenum two weeks later provisionally endorsed—subject to ratification at the upcoming party congress—somewhat watered-down versions of many of the horizontal movement's proposals, including free nomination of candidates by lower party echelons and secret ballots. Competing nominations from the top down would continue to be permitted, however.[3]

US intelligence analysts described these developments as indicating the Polish party leadership was moving on a "moderately reformist course in response to growing demands from the rank and file...." The leadership's acceptance of liberalized election laws, according to intelligence analysts, was designed to demonstrate a general commitment to reform and to blunt pressures from lower levels. According to one intelligence assessment, the party leaders may also have believed they could still manipulate the outcome of elections for the higher-level positions. This intelligence analysis also pointed out, however, that rank-and-file reformers were not going to be satisfied with half measures, and would press for greater change and more influence at the party congress. "The pressure has become more intense, more public, and more organized," according to the intelligence analysis, and the reformers believed they could use the new election rules to oust opponents of further reform.[4]

A *New York Times* article on 16 April commented that "should such a democratization movement ever gain significant power, it would be as revolutionary to East European Communism as the work of Copernicus...was

---

[2] "Polish Communist Party Faction Appeals for More Freedom in Party System," *The New York Times*, 16 April 1981, pp. A1-13; "Soviet Commentary," decl. *NID,* 16 April 1981. Other accounts give different numbers—e.g., Garton Ash, *The Polish Revolution,* p. 172, says 13 provinces, and Raina, *Poland 1981*, p. 212, says 14 provinces.
[3] "Poland: Party Plenum," decl. *NID,* 30 Apil 1981: and "Poland: Soviet Treatment of Kania's speech," decl. *NID,* 1 May 1981. The proceedings of this party plenum were published by the Poles. See Andrews, *Poland 1980-81,* p. 319, note 13. Kania's remarks are described in Raina, *Poland 1980*, pp. 212-213, citing *Trybuna Ludu* of 17 April 1981.
[4] Decl. *NID,* 16 April 1981, *op. cit.,* and "Special Analysis: Poland: Reform in the Party." decl. *NID,* 23 April 1981.

to science."[5] What was particularly noteworthy was that this referred not to the democratization movement being pushed by Solidarity, but one driven from within the Communist Party itself. Moscow clearly shared this view.

One week later, a Soviet delegation led by senior ideologue Mikhail Suslov (a Western press account characterized him as a "symbol of Kremlin orthodoxy") arrived in Warsaw to meet with senior Polish leaders. CIA's *National Intelligence Daily* reported that this delegation, led by a "veteran hardliner," was carrying a message to Polish leaders to rein in the budding liberalism within the party. The communiqué issued at the end of the visit did not include the standard line about Soviet "confidence" in the Polish party's ability to control the pace and scope of change, reflecting the mood of the discussions, according to the intelligence report. The same report said Suslov had tried to persuade the Poles to postpone the upcoming party congress, concerned that the reformists might be able to grab significant power. The analysts nonetheless doubted—correctly, as it turned out—that Kania could or would agree to a postponement, although they expected that he probably would use Soviet prodding to strengthen his hand for resisting more radical reforms.[6]

The day after Suslov returned to Moscow, Soviet media ran a tirade charging that "revisionism" threatened the Polish party from within, and labeled the horizontal movement "contrary to democratic centralism." The Soviet news agency TASS said a campaign to discredit the Polish party leadership was being waged by "revisionist elements within party ranks...who would like to paralyze the party of the Polish Communists as the leading force in society." An intelligence report pointed out that the term "revisionist" was "one of the most serious charges the Soviets can level against another Communist regime," and that Moscow had used it to describe Czechoslovak party liberals before the invasion in 1968. US press reports said much the same, characterizing the charge as denoting one of the "gravest ideological heresies" in the Marxist-Leninist dogma.[7] Nonetheless, less than a week later the Polish party affirmed that its congress would begin on 14 July.

Near the end of May, Soviet fears of the potential impact of the "reformed" voting procedures seemed to have been realized. Early results of elections of party Congress delegates showed established apparatchiks were losing to unknowns. Moscow renewed its attacks on the party "revisionists," and for the

---

[5] *The New York Times,* 16 April 1981, *op. cit.* The author was John Darnton.
[6] "Suslov in Poland," decl. *NID,* 24 April 1981. Much the same was in "Suslov Arrives Unexpectedly in Poland for Discussion," *The New York Times,* 24 April 1981, p. A9, (including the quote); and "Suslov, Ending Talks, Silent on Poland," *The New York Times,* 25 April 1981, p. 3.
[7] "Moscow Condemns Revisionists," decl. *NID* article, 27 April 1981; "Kremlin Intensifies Criticism of Poland: Charges Revisionism," *The New York Times,* 26 April 1981, pp. 1, 14.

first time linked them with the "anti-socialist forces" in Solidarity, claiming they had formed a "united front" to undermine the party. Similar media rhetoric in other Warsaw Pact capitals echoed Moscow's attacks.[8]

In a counterproductive move, Soviet media also gave favorable treatment (partly through selective excerpts) to virulent public rhetoric from a fringe reactionary group of Polish party members called the Katowice Forum. These included accusations that the Polish party had lost its direction because of "ideologically alien influences ...[and] right wing opportunism and bourgeois influences within the party ranks themselves." The Soviet media neglected to mention, however, that the Katwotice Forum's diatribe included charges that "revisionist" pressures for horizontal structures were being driven by "Trotskyist-Zionist views."[9]

For too many Polish party members, this smacked of the virulent, nationalistic anti-Semitism they had heard during the intra-party battles of the late Gomulka era. A storm of criticism followed from party members as well as the public, and even hardliner Olszowski had to publicly disassociate himself. The party Politburo issued a public rebuttal on 2 June. Two days later, the Katowice Forum announced a suspension of its activities, although that did not prevent the Soviet media from continuing to cite the validity of the attacks. Western media speculated that the Forum had been created by covert backing (from the Soviets? East Germans? Polish hardliners?) as a mechanism to spearhead a counterattack on the reform faction in the run-up to the party's Extraordinary Congress.[10] No information has been made public to date that would confirm or refute this. If true, it would have been another case of a hand overplayed.

The Intelligence Community concluded that the main impact of all this rhetoric was to galvanize the reformers even more and to "further weaken the already feeble conservative forces in the Polish party." The virulent public attacks by the Soviets and their allies were interpreted by analysts as a reflection of Moscow's increasing fear that the upcoming party congress would ratify a sweeping liberalization of the party, and oust most of its current leaders.

---

[8] See "Criticism of Warsaw," decl. *NID*, 22 May 1981; "Criticism of Polish Party," decl. *NID*, 23 May 1981; "Options in dealing with Poland," decl. *NID*, 29 May 1981; and "More Criticism of Polish Party," decl. *NID*, 3 June 1981.

[9] "USSR-Poland: More Criticism of Polish Party," decl. *NID*, 3 June 1981; "Strike Alert Set at Polish Factory," *The New York Times*, 2 June 1981, p. 1; and "Moscow Publicizing Hard Line Polish Statement," *The New York Times*, 3 June 1981, p. A6.

[10] "Polish Leaders Denounce Hard Line Party Group," *The New York Times*, 4 June 1981, p. A10; For further background on the reactionary groups in Poland, see Andrews, *Poland 1980-81*, pp. 154-156; Garton Ash, *The Polish Revolution*, pp. 174-175; and Raina, *Poland 1981*, pp. 208-210 and 213-216. Regarding the "anti-Zionist" attacks of the late 1960's, see Norman Davies, *God's Playground: A History of Poland, Vol. II* (New York: Columbia University Press, 1982), pp. 588-590.

If the pressures being exerted did not begin to reverse what Moscow apparently saw as a growing trend, intelligence analysts expected the Soviets to make another bid to have the congress postponed.[11] The analysts did not have long to wait.

A Blast From Moscow

On the weekend of 6–7 June, stories began appearing in Polish and other East European media about a Soviet "ultimatum" made in a letter to Polish leaders. A special meeting of the Polish Central Committee was reported to have been scheduled for 9 June, at which the letter clearly was to be the major topic. The letter's contents began to be leaked to Western reporters the day before the meeting. According to various accounts, it arrived on 5 June, and included harshly worded criticisms leveled at Kania and Jaruzelski by name, accusing them of repeatedly backing down from their promises to take action to control the situation. The letter also was said to have declared that the Soviet Bloc countries "would not leave Poland 'at the mercy of counterrevolutionaries,'" a statement the Western press interpreted as another veiled threat of intervention.[12]

The *NID* described the letter as a manifestation of the desire of the Soviets, in concert with Polish hardliners, to provoke a showdown. Intelligence analysts postulated that the Soviet leaders were hoping their letter would encourage Polish conservatives to counter the reformists. The analysts allowed for the possibility, though rating it unlikely, that it might result in Kania's ouster and a postponement of the party congress. At a minimum, according to this intelligence analysis, the letter could provide the Soviets with a device for testing whether the reform process was out of control and whether Kania had the ability to oppose it.[13]

When the Polish party meeting convened on 9 June to discuss the letter, Kania took his usual middle-of-the-road stance. He said Soviet concerns were justified and promised more resolute action, but at the same time he confirmed that the party congress would take place as scheduled and that he supported moderate reforms. The next day the party Central Committee reconvened to address the "problems" described in the letter. This session erupted into an

---

[11] "Poland: Tensions Rising Again," decl. *NID*, 5 June 1981; and "USSR-Poland: Open Polemics," decl. *NID*, 6 June 1981.

[12] "USSR-Poland: Soviet Pressure," decl. *NID*, 8 June 1981; "Amid an Increasing Sense of Crisis, Polish Leaders Call a Meeting, *The New York Times*, 8 June 1981, p. A1; and "We Will Not Let the Poles Alone, Russian Warns," *The New York Times*, 9 June 1981, p. A1. The story first appeared in Warsaw in *Trybuna Ludu* of 6-7 June 1981. See Kramer, "Soviet Deliberations on the Polish Crisis, 1980-1981," Document 15, Translator's Note No. 179.

[13] "Poland: Central Committee Plenum," decl. *NID*, 9 June 1981.

open power confrontation between hardliners and what intelligence analysts and the Western press described as "moderates" grouped around Kania. Grabski led the attack, calling for Kania's removal as party First Secretary. He declared that the present composition of the party leadership led by Kania was not capable of leading the party out of its political crisis.

During the ensuing acrimonious arguments, Kania called a pause to consult with some of the other Politburo members and then proposed that the Central Committee hold a vote of confidence for each of the 11 members of the Politburo (including Grabski and Olszowski). Any member who received less than 50 percent would agree to resign. As he had doubtless anticipated when he made his gamble, the Central Committee backed down from holding the vote. According to press reports, the meeting ended with a swell of support for Kania and Jaruzelski. Intelligence analysts pointed out, however, that although the moderates could justifiably see the outcome as a victory, it also had intensified the polarization in the party.[14]

The same day this confrontational meeting took place, the complete text of the Soviet letter appeared in the French newspaper *Le Monde*, described as an "unattributed report" from Moscow. That evening it was broadcast on Polish TV and a day later it was printed in the Polish media and in the United States. It fully lived up to the descriptions that had been leaked. It also made abundantly clear Moscow's immediate concern over the potential impact the reform movement within the party could have on the upcoming extraordinary party congress:

> Recently the situation within the PZPR itself has become a cause of particular concern...forces hostile to socialism are setting the tone of the election campaign [for the extraordinary congress]... As a result of the many manipulations of revisionists and opportunists—enemies of the PZPR—experienced activists entirely devoted to the party and with irreproachable reputations and morals are being passed over... One cannot rule out the possibility that during the Congress itself an attempt will be made to deal a decisive blow to the Marxist-Leninist forces in order to bring about its [sic] elimination.[15]

---

[14] "Poland: Kania's Speech," decl. *NID*, 10 June 1981; and "Poland: Party Openly Split," decl. *NID*, 11 June 1981. "Polish Leader Says Soviet Bloc Alarm is 'Fully Justified,'" *The New York Times*, 10 June 1981, p. A1; and "Kania Affirms Role as Poland's Leader After Soviet Letter," *The New York Times*, 11 June 1981, p. A1.

[15] "Text of Letter...," *Le Monde*, 10 June 1981, p. 6, available in Foreign Broadcast Information Service, Daily Report for 10 June 1981, "Soviet Union," (FBIS-Sov-81-III). Also "Text of Soviet Letter," *The New York Times*, 11 June 1981, p. A8.

The US Government, in an official statement on 11 June, called the letter "interference in the internal affairs of Poland...[and] inconsistent with the Helsinki Final Act." The US statement noted that no increase in Soviet military activity had been observed around Poland, but added a reminder that Soviet forces in the vicinity "remained in a high state of readiness." State Department officials were quoted unofficially that there was concern military action might be taken to protect Soviet interests in Poland, and that this concern had motivated the US to object publicly. A day later, Secretary of State Haig made the same points in a public statement during a stopover in Hong Kong, saying he feared an intervention ultimately would occur.[16]

Soviet Options: Invade or Accept Liberalization

As this pattern of events unfolded in the Polish party, US intelligence assessments began to say Soviet options were narrowing. A CIA "Special Analysis" on 29 May said the liberalization trend in Poland was likely to continue, and that "the Soviets know that [it] must be brought under control if they are to maintain hegemony in East Europe." "Moscow also realizes," according to this intelligence analysis, "that, at this stage, it would be difficult—if not impossible—to replace Poland's leaders with stalwarts who could impose tougher policies." The intelligence assessment said Soviet options had already been reduced to either "admonishing the Poles...or invading with overwhelming military strength."

The enormous costs and risks of an outright military invasion provided strong disincentives, according to this intelligence analysis, and at least some Soviet leaders were therefore believed to advocate giving the Poles "more time to sort themselves out." This analysis also pointed out, however, that the Soviets already had used political and military pressure tactics without much success, and now confronted a new challenge with liberalization spreading to the Polish Communist Party itself. "The continuing liberalization, which the party Congress may well legitimatize, could force the Soviets to...conclude that failing to act decisively would mean forfeiting their last chance to preserve a Soviet-style Communist system in Poland."[17]

Another Special Analysis, disseminated a day later, said the "Soviet failure to invade" could lead to a politically liberalized Poland in which the principal internal issues would be the difficulties faced by the union, the party and church leaders in achieving economic recovery, with a government made up of

---

[16] "Poland's Crisis...," *The New York Times,* 12 June 1981, p. A1; and "US Charges Soviet is Meddling in Poland," *The New York Times*, 12 June 1981, p. A3; "Haig in Hong Kong, Says Situation in Poland is 'Seriously Deteriorating,'" *The New York Times*, 13 June 1981, p. 4.

[17] "USSR: Options in Dealing With Poland," decl. Special Analysis, *NID*, 29 May 1981.

inexperienced but ambitious individuals. The bulk of this two-and-a-half-page assessment was devoted to the *external* impact of a liberalized Poland, and predicted:

- In other East European societies, contagion—and pressures for their own liberalization;
- In the USSR, a mixture of contagion and recrimination;
- In Western Europe, a boost for détente, arms control, and trade;
- In the Warsaw Pact military alliance, a major blow to the viability of its existing strategy and planning.[18]

Neither assessment gave prospects for the likelihood of martial law. On the contrary, several intelligence assessments in the ensuing weeks explicitly took martial law off the table of options for suppressing the political challenge in Poland. An in-depth CIA Intelligence Assessment disseminated around early June, for example, said:

> There is reason to believe that Soviet leaders may have felt at one time that if Warsaw Pact forces could be inserted into Poland in support of the introduction of martial law by the Polish regime itself, there might be less resistance. ...However, *we believe that by now the Soviets, in contemplating military intervention, no longer see any viable alternative to an outright invasion*—staged, to be sure, with whatever 'invitational' cover could be arranged. Given the Soviets' likely assessment of the substantial resistance that Pact forces would encounter, we believe they would feel compelled to employ a large invasion force of at least 30, and perhaps as many as 45, divisions (emphasis added).[19]

After the failed Soviet effort to engineer Kania's ouster at the party meetings on 9–10 June, some intelligence assessments went even further. Not only was martial law off the table as an option for suppressing the liberalization

---

[18] "Europe: Impact of a Soviet Failure to Invade Poland," decl. Special Analysis, *NID*, 30 May 1981. Another CIA product specifically designed to address the implications of a Soviet failure to invade Poland was disseminated on 18 May 1981. Its text has not been released to date, but its title suggests its assessment of the consequences if Moscow did not invade: "Liberalization in Poland: Impact and Implications." See page 1 of the declassified report cited in footnote 19 below.

[19] "Implications of a Soviet Invasion of Poland," decl. CIA Intelligence Memorandum, p. 2. The date of this document is obscured by spillover from an adjacent redaction. Its description of itself as a "companion paper" to the "recent" Memorandum of 18 May indicates its publication was in late May or early June. Other examples are the declassified Special Analyses from *NID*s of 15 June 1981, "USSR-Poland: Officials Deny Imminent Intervention" and 19 June 1981, "USSR-Poland: Moscow and the Polish Party Congress."

movement, it instead had become an option for fending off Soviet efforts at military suppression. A memorandum from the State Department Bureau of Intelligence and Research (INR) to the Secretary of State said that:

> Poland's first line of defense against Soviet intervention would be to try to deter it with a show of national unity, which would imply maximum resistance. The Poles might resort to *a declaration of martial law* and deploy Army units around key points, *not to suppress the labor movement but to maximize deterrence by preparing defenses against attack.*" (from summary, emphasis added).

> As tensions mount, Jaruzelski might additionally invoke a state of emergency or some variant of martial law in order to gird the nation against a threatened Soviet invasion. In late March, it appeared the Poles were thinking of imposing martial law had Solidarity carried out its threat of a nationwide strike. The Soviets seemed poised to intervene in a supportive role had the Poles proved unable or unwilling to control the situation on their own. *A declaration of martial law now, however, would be different; it would be intended to prevent civil disturbances from developing, thus depriving the Soviets of this pretext for intervention. It would also keep the Polish armed forces in a heightened state of alert, thus enabling them to react more quickly against a Soviet move.*" (emphasis added).[20]

A similar description of Polish objectives for implementing martial law was given in a CIA memorandum disseminated on 30 June. Describing the size and disposition of Polish armed forces that might be used to combat a Soviet invasion, the assessment said: "If the Polish leadership...imposed martial law prior to an invasion, the military would be operationally organized, armed, and better positioned to offer early opposition [to a Soviet invasion]...."[21]

The prospect of military resistance from the top added significantly to what both the INR and CIA memoranda described as the enormous risks of Soviet military intervention. Even so, it still did not provide confidence that Moscow would be deterred. (There was some divergence of views in CIA on this cost assessment.) Intelligence assessments at this time also reaffirmed the standing estimate that, if the Soviets chose to intervene militarily, their uncertainty over

---

[20] *Poland 1980-82: Compendium,* decl. memorandum to the Acting Secretary of State from INR, 15 June 1981.

[21] "Polish Reaction to a Soviet Invasion," decl. CIA Intelligence Memorandum, 30 June 1981, p. 2,. This CIA assessment was re-issued in July in a slightly different format under the title "Probable Polish Reaction to a Soviet Invasion." This version also is in the National Security Archive. Other than the one word added to its title, and a change in the sequence of three paragraphs, the texts are virtually identical.

the reaction of the Polish armed forces would lead them to prepare a force of at least 30 divisions. The daily intelligence reports on Poland through the second half of June clearly reflect a "watch" for signs of Soviet preparations for military intervention. Several articles on the subject also appeared in the US press for the next week or so.[22]

Unlike the earlier speculation on this prospect, however, the Soviet motivation was not attributed to the challenge posed by Solidarity, but to the threat of "revisionist forces" seizing power at the upcoming Polish party congress. Intelligence forecasts said that at the upcoming party congress "the liberalization trend should be ratified and most hard-liners dropped from the Central Committee...." It said the congress "will elect a new and almost certainly more liberal Central Committee, which will in turn choose a new Politburo. This process will give significant additional legitimacy to the reform movement in the party." Kania's success in outmaneuvering the Soviet and Polish hardliners' efforts to replace him, according to this analysis, "created a new situation that puts Kania and the Soviet leadership directly at odds." The intelligence analysis said these were "compelling developments to those in the Kremlin who would urge a prompt military move into Poland."[23]

Intelligence analysts as well as the Western press pointed out that the letter the Soviet leaders sent to the Poles was very similar to one sent to the Czech leadership just before the Soviets invaded to pre-empt an extraordinary congress of the Czech party that threatened a reformist takeover. Now, it was the Polish party that was about to hold an extraordinary party congress that appeared both to intelligence analysts and Western reporters as a potential forum for "irreversible changes." The situation in Poland was said to have "reached the point where the Soviets cannot ignore further Polish defiance." "Soviet persuasion" was assumed to rest with the credibility of its military threat, and the belief expressed that if the Soviets wanted to fend off revisionism, they would have to act before the congress. One of the most

---

[22] Samples include "Poland: Continued Political Pressure," decl. *NID*, 13 June 1981; "USSR-Poland: Officials Deny Imminent Invasion," decl. *NID*, 15 June 1981; "USSR-Poland: Military Activity," decl. *NID*, 19 June 1981; and "Poland: Soviet Pressure Intensifies," decl. *NID*, 22 June 1981. Press descriptions are in "Polish Leader Says Soviet Bloc Alarm is 'Fully Justified,'" *The New York Times,* 10 June 1981, p. A1; "Poland's Crisis: Party Defiant, *The New York Times,* 12 June 1981, p. A1; "US Charges Soviet is Meddling in Poland," *The New York Times,* 12 June 1981, p. A3; "Crisis in Poland: Soviet Forces Formidable," 14 June 1981, p. 3; "Soviets and Poland: Options Dwindling," *The New York Times,* 15 June 1981, p. A3; "Young Polish Moderates Emerge in Party Elections," *The New York Times,* 17 June 1981, p. A10; "Polish Rebels Regret: Party Is Seeking Liberal Lead," *The New York Times,* 25 June 1981, p. A2; and "Vigil in Kremlin: Tension High as Polish Talks Near," *The New York Times,* 27 June 1981, p. 3.

[23] "USSR-Poland: Moscow and the Polish Party Congress," decl. Special Analysis, *NID*, 19 June 1981.

influential dissidents, Jacek Kuron, was quoted as having said the situation in the party had brought things to a "critical threshold" in which Soviet invasion was no longer impossible.[24]

No Soviet preparations for military intervention were detected, however, in the weeks leading up to the party congress. Intelligence analysts concluded that Moscow was resigned to allowing the congress to proceed rather than trying to pre-empt it with military intervention. The reasoning was that the Soviets would prefer first to see if their pressures succeeded in tempering the reform trend at the congress. They would calculate their next move on the basis of what occurred at the congress and the resulting balance of forces in the Polish party.[25]

The Party Congress[26]

The rules that Polish party leaders had finally approved for election of congressional delegates did not completely meet the demands of party reformists for a bottom-up election sequence. The leadership still was permitted to nominate its preferred candidates for election at various lower echelons, and did so. Nonetheless, the lower party cells also were allowed to nominate competing candidates, and all candidates, whether nominated by the leadership or the party cells, were to be elected by secret ballot. The upper powers of the party continued to attempt—sometimes successfully—to intervene to skew the vote in favor of their nominees. But by any comparison with the congresses of the other Soviet bloc parties, the delegate selection process for the Polish party's extraordinary congress represented a dramatic departure in the direction of democracy.

The impact was evident in the results of the delegate elections, which were completed by the end of June. Of 1,964 delegates elected, only about 10 percent had participated in previous party congresses. More than two thirds of the party Central Committee members, including a few Politburo members, failed

---

[24] Extensive reporting and interpretations of these issues are presented in the series of declassified intelligence reports and Western press articles cited in footnote 22. Kuron is quoted in the 25 July article, "Polish Rebels Regret...."

[25] Decl. Special Analysis, *NID*, 15 June 1981, *op. cit.*

[26] Declassified *NID* articles from 19 June through 23 July provide almost day-to-day coverage (except for Sundays and holidays) of the Congress and the events leading up to it. Comprehensive presentations including background on its origins are in Andrews, *Poland 1980-81*, pp. 179-188; Garton Ash, *The Polish Revolution*, pp. 174, and 178-182; and Raina, *Poland 1981*, pp. 229-236. Raina (pp. 237-253) also gives the full text of the party's program produced at the Congress, which was published after the Congress in various vehicles, including *Trybuna Ludu*. The three authors (and the Intelligence Community) give slightly different numbers for the delegate breakdown, but not different enough to affect the interpretation of proportionality. An interpretation of the delegate voting results also was presented in "Kania's Role Buttressed by Polish Party Elections," *The New York Times*, 2 July 1981, p. A2.

to be elected to the congress. Since the congress was to elect a new Central Committee from candidates nominated from its ranks, and the new Central Committee would then elect a new Politburo from its membership, failure to get elected to the congress was a de facto removal from the Central Committee and—for those to whom it applied—the Politburo.

Western media reported that most Western and Polish observers interpreted the delegate election results as an indication that the congress was likely to reaffirm Kania's policies of "moderate change." Press reports noted that the biggest casualties in the delegate elections were among the more strident conservatives and more radical reformers. Stories that Kania was about to be "swept aside" were no longer being heard, according to the press. The Intelligence Community now described his position as "strong—at least for the near term."[27]

This view was reinforced by the announcement that Soviet Foreign Minister Gromyko would visit Warsaw on 3 July. The *NID* pointed out that Gromyko would not be the one to carry a stern message. It also called attention to a new tone of moderation in Soviet commentary on the Congress, and said the communiqué issued in Warsaw at the end of Gromyko's visit had a positive tone. This intelligence analysis also pointed out, however, that Soviet media were continuing to transmit the "Brezhnev doctrine" message that communism in Poland was a legitimate concern for all Warsaw Pact countries. The diplomatic circuit reportedly had concluded that the Soviets were sending a message that they were "grudgingly" willing to accept a congress that seemed likely to return the moderate regime, so long as that regime would staunchly defend Poland's status as a Warsaw Pact ally and a loyal Communist state.[28]

Once the congress got underway on 14 July, a further dramatic cut of veteran *apparatchiks* in the central party organs occurred. Of the less than one third of the Central Committee members who had managed to get elected to the congress, most failed to get re-elected to the new Central Committee—holdovers constituted less than ten percent of the new Central Committee. And that small list included only four members of the former Politburo: Jaruzelski, Kania, Barcikowski and hardliner Olszowski. Politburo members who

---

[27] See "Kania's Role Buttressed...," *The New York Times,* 2 July 1981, p. A2; and "Poland: A Different Party Congress," decl. *NID* Special Analysis, 13 July 1981.

[28] "USSR-Poland: Softer Soviet Line," decl. *NID*, 3 July 1981; and "USSR-Poland: Emphasis on the Positive," decl. *NID*, 6 July 1981. "Gromyko in Warsaw," *The New York Times,* 3 July 1981, p. 3; "Gromyko Confers With Poles Again On Party Congress," *The New York Times,* 5 July 1981, p. 1; "Soviet Intentions in Poland Unclear After 3-Day Talks," *The New York Times,* 6 July 1981, p. A1; and "TV Report Suggests Soviets Will Await Polish Outcome," *The New York Times,* 13 July 1981, p. A7.

did not make the cut included three hardliners—one of whom was Grabski—but also two moderates, including the deputy prime minister who had negotiated the Gdansk agreement.

The new Central Committee then elected Kania as First Secretary with about two-thirds of the vote. His token opponent, Barcikowski, received about 30 percent, and about four percent of the new Central Committee members either voted no or abstained. The last step was the election of the new Politburo, which consisted of the four holdovers and 11 new members. Western media described the election process at the congress, especially submitting the election of a first secretary to a secret vote of the full assembly, as a first for the Soviet Bloc.[29]

The Intelligence Community's initial description of the outcome of the congress was relatively positive. It said Kania—"a moderate favoring incremental reforms with certain bounds"—had been strengthened. It said the Polish party had emerged with "a predominantly new leadership, a greater sense of unity, and a renewed commitment to moderation." Tentative approval had been given to statute changes that went some way toward meeting the demands of reformists. Party officials were limited to two terms in office, individuals were prohibited from simultaneously holding top party and government positions (except in the case of the prime minister), and provision was made for the general use of secret ballots and multiple candidate slates. Final approval of these statutes was subject to review by a commission whose future was left vague.[30]

The Western press pointed out, however, that despite the massive turnovers, the political make-up of the regime had not changed much. The Politburo vote was described as backing the "centrists," but while nearly three fourths of the Politburo was new, it still included three prominent hard liners. One, of course, was the survivor Stefan Olszowski, and another was Alban Siwak, a bullish first secretary from a lower party echelon. The third was Miroslaw Milewski, who had been the Interior Minister, and who was known by US intelligence analysts as a key figure in martial law planning.[31]

---

[29] The day-to-day events at the Congress were described in the *NID*s for 15-20 July 1981, all of which are now declassified, as well as in "Polish Communist Chief May Ask Re-election Vote By Whole Party," *The New York Times*, 11 July 1981, p. 5; "Candidates Listed For Polish Congress," *The New York Times*, 13 July 1981, p. A7; "Polish Party Split Over Voting Rules," *The New York Times*, 15 July 1981, p. A1; "Polish Communists to Select Leader by Secret Ballot," *The New York Times*, 16 July 1981, p. A1; and "Kania Elected By Poles to Head Party," *The New York Times*, 19 July 1981, p. 1.

[30] "Poland: Conclusion of Congress," decl. *NID*, 21 July 1981; "Poland: Beyond the Congress," Special Analysis, *NID*, 23 July 1981.

[31] Special Analysis, *NID*, 23 July 1981, *op. cit.*; "Poland's Premier Says Some Prices Will Rise by 110 Percent," *The New York Times*, 20 July 1981, p. A1.

Shortly after the congress, in accordance with the new party statutes, Milewski gave up the Interior Ministry post. Jaruzelski replaced him with a senior military officer, General Kiszcak, whose former positions included chief of military intelligence and commander of the internal military service. Another military officer, General Hupalowski (who had been the principal deputy chief of the General Staff) was appointed Minister for Administration, Local Economy and Environment.[32] Neither appointment drew any attention at the time, either in the media or intelligence reports, but in hindsight they appear to have been early steps toward positioning the military to run the show if a state of emergency were declared.

---

[32] According to Cynkin, *Soviet and American Signaling*, this information was reported in the international media at the time. His reference is Radio Free Europe Research and Analysis Department, Background Report 32, February 1982.

CHAPTER 11

Solidarity Charges Ahead, and the Regime Digs In

Solidarity completed its own elections for its first national congress at the end of June, about the same time the party finished its delegate elections. Solidarity's congress was not scheduled to take place until September, however, and was to be held in two parts. The first was to begin on 5 September and was intended to be a short, three-day assembly to debate the union's organizational and constitutional statutes. The congress would then take a break to redraft proposals in response to the first session's debates. It would re-convene on 26 September for what was envisaged as about a week-long assembly to enact statutes and a program for the future and to elect the union's leadership. In contrast to the Polish party congress, where the leaders' main challenge was to hold ground, Solidarity's challenge was to reach agreement on how far to go.

A critical factor that would shape this path was the plummeting Polish economy, which was beginning to reach crisis proportions in mid-summer. On 23 July, the government announced that monthly per capita meat rations would be cut by 20 percent. The same day it also published a price list that showed food items such as butter, bread, sugar, and milk had more than tripled in price, and others, such as flour and ham, had more than doubled. By this time, the regime's practice of simply printing money to deal with the wage settlements of the past year had resulted in production costs exceeding retail prices for many consumer items. A week later, the parliamentary budget commission reported that per capita national income for 1981 was expected to be 15 percent lower than the already dismal 1980 level.[1]

---

[1] The price hikes and rationing cut were reported in a declassified *NID* article of 25 July 1981, "Poland: Protests Over Food Shortages." They had been forecast in the economic plan presented at the party congress. See "Poland: First Day of the Congress," decl. *NID*, 15 July 1981. Descriptions of the Polish economic problems are contained in Andrews, *Poland 1980-81*, pp. 189-192, on the immediate issues of the July rationing and price actions, and his entire chapter 13 on the broader programmatic issues. Garton Ash, *The Polish Revolution*, pp. 183-187, gives a vivid presentation of the societal and political impact of the government's actions, and Raina, *Poland 1981*, pp. 298-301, gives a concise but data-rich account.

These announcements acted like a match to tinder. Protests and "hunger marches" erupted almost immediately. Local Solidarity chapters, over the objections of the union's National Coordinating Commission, helped to organize and supervise some of these marches in an effort to channel the anger. The anger among the populace was intensified by stories—in an increasingly open national media—revealing the degree to which the economic suffering was being aggravated by gross incompetence and mismanagement in the distribution of the already limited supplies. Adding still more fuel to the outrage was the ill-disguised corruption and skimming by party and government officials, and rumors of secret hoarding.

Solidarity called a special meeting of its National Coordinating Commission on 24–26 July to come up with a plan for coping with the deepening economic crisis. Such a plan could not, however, be addressed separately from the union's overall vision of its role in shaping national economic and social policies. These July discussions would thus have a powerful impact on the shape of the First National Congress slated for September.

To deal with the immediate problem of shortages and rationing, the union demanded direct access to all government stores and to government data on food and other critical consumer goods. Initially interpreted as a demand for "control," this was later clarified as a demand to audit the data and monitor the distribution, to remove incompetent officials, and to refer for prosecution any corruption that was discovered. In part, the demands put forth by the union leaders were aimed at easing the social ferment generated by the refusal of a distrustful populace to accept explanations from government officials even when they were truthful.

Another issue shaping the backdrop for Solidarity's upcoming congress was the concept of "workers' self-government." The principle of workers' participation in enterprise management was a longstanding myth of the communist system, and with government concurrence it had been included in the Gdansk agreement. Solidarity's efforts to avoid charges of political aspirations, however, had led the Union to avoid actions that would be interpreted as efforts to take over management of the enterprises. Solidarity had instead focused mainly on trying to bring reality to the sham of elected "workers' councils" that were supposed to have a consultative voice in plant decisions and in the appointment and rating of managers. Solidarity had taken this stance in its national program, published in April.[2]

---

[2] It was published on 17 April 1981 in Solidarity's weekly *Tygodnik Solidarnosc*. The full text is in Raina, *Poland 1981*, pp. 172-197.

No more. At the end of July, Solidarity made the establishment of genuine workers' self-government the centerpiece of its program for economic renewal. Workers' councils at enterprises were to be freely elected, and would have the authority to choose and to remove managers. There remained some debates even within Solidarity's leadership over what procedures should be established, and how the authority for appointing and removing managers would be structured. But there was no disagreement within Solidarity that the objective was to assume *authority* for running enterprises, not simply consultative status.

During the first two weeks of August, these demands by Solidarity became the issues of debate in meetings between the union leadership and government representatives. An agreement of sorts was reached on the distribution of food and other consumer goods, once it became understood that by "control" Solidarity meant checking information on all aspects of food supply, and seeking to constrain black market sales. Solidarity also showed some understanding of the need for price increases, as long as these were managed in coordination with the union.

The talks on self-governing enterprises, however, broke down in a confrontation that resulted in a public exchange of accusations. Ostensibly, the principal sticking point had to do with how much authority the workers would have over the appointments of enterprise managers and directors. The government's tactics seemed designed to cause a confrontation, however, in a way suggesting that the real issue was Solidarity's move to share authority in national policy decisions—which the regime obviously considered its exclusive territory.[3]

The tenor of relations between Solidarity and the regime at this juncture was exemplified in a speech Kania delivered to a party plenum, and which was published in full in the Polish media on 4 September, the day before the opening of Solidarity's congress. He said that "our enemies say the authorities will not proclaim a State of Emergency in Poland. I would like to state categorically that the authorities will make use of all essential means to defend the socialist system in Poland." The *NID* reported that this was the first time Kania personally had threatened a "state of emergency." Meanwhile, the Soviets had already announced that on that same day a large exercise would begin,

---

[3] A detailed, day-to-day account of these meetings, along with the various communiqués and competing public statements that accompanied them, is in Raina, *Poland 1981*, pp. 299-318. Garton Ash, *The Polish Revolution*, pp. 187-198, gives a contextual presentation including the social-political dynamics. The events were reported incrementally in the *NID* throughout the month.

with army units in the western USSR and naval units on the Baltic Sea operating all around Poland's borders, including off the coast of Gdansk where the first session of Solidarity's congress was to be held.[4]

Solidarity's First National Congress: The Initial Salvo

A report in the *NID*, previewing the first session of Solidarity's congress, described the fundamental issues to be addressed as including the authority of union leaders, demands for a far-reaching system of worker self-management, and how far the union should go toward being a political party.[5] By all accounts, the congress meetings had all the characteristics of a rival party convention. Debates on the touchy issues of the organization and future goals of the union were open and raucous—anyone could speak, and most did. The daily sessions featured guest speakers from the journalists' association and from West European member unions of the International Labor Organization. (The head of the US AFL-CIO, however, had been denied a visa by the Polish Government). Because the Polish Government insisted that it be allowed to "edit" the segments of the congress shown on Polish television, the union refused to allow Polish television to produce live coverage of the congress. West European TV coverage was thus more extensive than what was presented to the Polish citizenry.[6]

Formal adoption of a union program for economic renewal was to be left to the second segment of the congress, but the first segment nonetheless released a list that it described as its assessment of Poland's "national needs." One was "economic reform through creation of self-management bodies and an efficient economic system through *abolition of the party nomenklatura.*" Another was "safeguarding democracy by holding *free elections to the Sejm* and the peoples' councils" (emphasis added). These statements alone almost certainly would have met the criteria for what the Polish regime would later characterize as "a program of political opposition."[7]

---

[4] "Poland: Kania Continues Tough Line," decl. *NID*, 5 September 1981. The quoted passage from Kania's speech was in the Embassy cable described below in note 16. For the Soviet exercise, see "Poland: More Strikes in the Offing," decl. *NID*, 4 September 1981.

[5] "Poland: Solidarity's First National Congress," decl. Special Analysis, *NID*, September 1981.

[6] Detailed descriptions of the first segment of Solidarity's National Congress are in Andrews, *Poland 1980-81*, pp. 196-199; Garton Ash, *The Polish Revolution*, pp. 208-213; and Raina, *Poland 1981*, pp. 319-323.

[7] "Polish Communists Assert the Union Invites a Tragedy," *The New York Times*, 17 September 1981, p. A1. The full "needs" list is given by Andrews, p.197, and Raina, p. 321. The quotation is from the official Polish government response on 16 September, described below.

The real bombshell from this session, however, was a "message of solidarity" addressed by the Congress to the workers of the USSR and East Europe. It said that:

> As the first independent labor union in Poland's postwar history, we deeply feel a sense of community [with you].... Our goal is to struggle for an improvement in life for all working people. We support those of you who have decided to enter the difficult road of struggle for a free and independent labor movement. We trust that our and your representatives will be able to meet soon to compare union experiences.[8]

Reactions to this message and to the declarations of the Solidarity congress in general were as expected. Moscow's TASS declared that the union had unmasked itself as a rival political movement seeking to usurp the authority of the socialist government. Most of the other East European capitals also weighed in with expressions of outrage at what they described as Solidarity's brazen interference in their internal affairs. The Polish Foreign Ministry called the Solidarity message to other East European workers "a blow against Poland's national interests...[and] demonstrative interference in the internal affairs of the other socialist states." After the first round of Solidartiy's congress ended on 10 September, many Western media commentaries said the union seemed to have gone too far.[9]

Revived Concerns Over Martial Law

In the wake of this eruption, the State Department cabled the US Embassy in Warsaw on 15 September, saying that:

> The increased tension between the [Polish] regime and Solidarity, together with Kania's September 4 warning that the government might use force 'to defend Socialism,' raise the possibility of a government imposition of martial law in the coming weeks or months. Given the importance such an action would have on USG policies toward Poland, we would appreciate the Embassy's evaluation.[10]

---

[8] The full text is given by Garton Ash in *The Polish Revolution*, p. 212, and Raina, *Poland 1981*, pp. 320-321. It originally appeared in Solidarity's weekly publication *Tygodnik Solidarnosc* on 8 September 1981 and an English translation appeared in the 9 September 1981 FBIS *East European Daily*, p. G7. It was reported in now-declassified *NID* articles "Poland: Militant Proposals at Party Congress," 10 September 1981, and "Poland: End of Union Congress," 11 September 1981.
[9] Andrews, *Poland 1980-81*. Page 198 lists a few examples of comments published in various East and West European media.
[10] Declassified State cable 245350, "Martial Law and the Kania Government," 150117Z September 81, *Poland 1980-82: Compendium*. It was sent from Washington on 14 September but was received by the Embassy on 15 September Warsaw time. It gave as the date for Kania's speech the day it was reported in the Polish media, which was a day after the speech was given.

The Embassy was asked to address such issues as the circumstances that might precipitate martial law, modalities by which martial law might be introduced (e.g. total or partial), and the likely reactions of Solidarity and Rural Solidarity, the church, the general populace, the army, and the security organs. The cable also asked for an evaluation of the regime's chances for success in such an effort, including an examination of alternative scenarios for success and failure.

The day after the Embassy received this request, but before it had a chance to respond, the Polish party released what one US press report called "its hardest statement yet" in a pattern of increasing references to its willingness to use force. It characterized Solidarity's letter to the East European unions as a "crazy provocation" and the union's demand for changing parliamentary election procedures as "arrogant." It accused Solidarity of producing a "program of political opposition" that hit at the vital interests of the Polish nation, and which could lead to a national confrontation that "resulted in bloodshed." It asserted that there was "no room and could be no room for such a program in Poland," and that "the State will use for its defense such means as required by the situation."[11]

The increasing tensions prompted a warning in the 18 September *NID* that:

> The Intelligence Community has sensed a qualitative change in the attitudes of Solidarity and the Polish Communist Party. The former has directly challenged the authority of the Polish party and, indirectly, Soviet hegemony. The latter has indicated a determination to confront Solidarity's challenges if necessary with the use of force...
>
> The Polish regime has drawn up a detailed plan of military measures, including curfews, shows of force, total military control of the country, and arrest of Solidarity leaders. The Polish leadership appears to be readying itself for the possible employment of at least some of these measures in the near future...
>
> The chances of a confrontation leading to the regime's use of force have risen considerably unless the more moderate elements of Solidarity manage to tone down those union actions most objectionable to the government.[12]

---

[11] "Poland: Confronting Solidarity," decl. *NID*, 17 September 1981; and "Poland Union Under Pressure," decl. *NID*, 18 September. The "hardest yet" quote is from "Polish Communists Assert the Union Invites a Tragedy," *The New York Times,* 17 September 1981, p. A1. For additional media views see also "Warsaw Declares Union Jeopardizes Nation's Existence," *The New York Times*, 19 September 1981, p. 1.

[12] "Poland: Prospect for Confrontation," decl. Special Analysis, *NID*, 18 September 1981.

This judgment was itself a qualitative change from the assessments conveyed in intelligence products in preceding months, which had allowed little room for outcomes other than Soviet invasion or unchecked liberalism in Poland. It was presented in a Special Analysis that apparently was the product of an interagency group of analysts, which may account for its sharp distinction from the more complacent view that would continue to be reflected in the *NID* in the ensuing weeks.[13]

The same day this intelligence assessment was disseminated, the official Polish media carried the text of yet another letter from the Soviet regime, this time lambasting the Polish leaders for their failure to quell the "anti-Sovietism" being fostered by Solidarity:

> ...any further leniency to any manifestation of anti-Sovietism does immense harm to Polish-Soviet relations...
>
> We expect that the Polish United Workers Party leadership will take determined and radical steps to cut short the...actions hostile to the Soviet Union.

According to a Western press account, "few times since the end of WWII" had such language been seen in communications between the Soviets and one of their Warsaw Pact allies. The letter reportedly had been delivered before—and therefore probably had been the force behind—the statement released by the Polish Politburo on 16 September.[14]

The State Department again accused the Soviets of intervening in Poland's internal affairs. Press reports said US officials believed the Soviet letter was an effort to make Polish authorities impose force. US officials did not rule out a Soviet invasion, according to the press accounts, but most believed Moscow much preferred that the Poles institute their own crackdown.[15]

---

[13] The explicit identification of the views as being those of "the Intelligence Community" is unusual for a *NID* article, and is usually reserved for interagency products produced under the aegis of the National Intelligence Council. The term "Intelligence Community" is not used to identify the source of the judgments in any of the declassified *NID* reports on Poland in the months preceding or following this article.

[14] "Moscow Orders Poles to Control Anti-Sovietism," *The New York Times*, 18 September 1981, p. A1; "Warsaw Declares Union Jeopardizes Nation's Existence," *The New York Times*, 19 September 1981, p. 1; "Warning From Moscow," *The New York Times*, 19 September 1981, p. 1; and "Text of Letter," *The New York Times*, 19 September 1981, p. 4. Information now available from Soviet and Polish archives indicates the letter was drafted under instructions by the Soviet Politburo on 10 September (see Document 17, in Kramer, "Soviet Deliberations on the Polish Crisis") and delivered by 14 September (see document "CPSU CC Communication to the PZPR," circulated 14 September 1981 to Polish Party officials, *Poland 1980-82: Compendium*).

[15] "US Says Soviet Message is Intervention in Poland's Internal Affairs," *The New York Times*, 19 September 1981, p. 4.

The next day, the US Embassy dispatched its response to the State Department request for an assessment of the situation. It concluded that the Polish regime might employ some form of martial law, "if it considers its own existence at stake, or if the situation has deteriorated to the point where Soviet intervention is inevitable." The Embassy said Solidarity's recent actions already had gone a substantial way toward meeting the first criteria. As a consequence, the existing situation contained "the two generally agreed conditions that could trigger a Soviet intervention—a threat to the leading role of the party, or the integrity of Poland's system of alliances, the Warsaw Pact."

The Embassy nonetheless rated the prospects that the regime would attempt to impose martial law "in the existing situation" as "less than fifty-fifty." It was clear that by "less than fifty-fifty" the Embassy meant better than one chance in three.[16]

The Embassy saw *far less* chance that an attempt to impose martial law might succeed. This was because:

- The regime could not be certain of the loyalty of the military and internal security forces. "In fact, it knows their reliability is suspect."

- Declaring martial law in the existing circumstances would at a minimum lead to passive resistance in the form of general strikes and sit-ins, which would be difficult for the army to counter "even if all units remained loyal." The result could be national paralysis. There was also a good chance, in the Embassy's view, that the resistance would erupt into civil conflict and a total breakdown of law and order.

- "Either result could lead to the very [Soviet] intervention that introduction of martial law would seek to avoid."

The Embassy also believed that imposition of martial law would move Poland "toward an economic catastrophe." Taken together, these considerations constituted a substantial deterrent to an attempt at martial law, according to the Embassy assessment.

The Embassy concluded that if martial law were to have a chance of success, it would have to be preceded by "a successful regime effort to portray Solidarity as recalcitrant and unyielding after the government had presented itself as forthcoming and willing to compromise." The threat of Soviet intervention also would have to be "less ambiguous than it is now." The regime

---

[16] Declassified State Department Cable, Warsaw 9079, 191626Z, "Martial Law–An Unpromising Option," in *Poland 1980-82: Compendium*.

would need to "preserve the loyalty of the army, split Solidarity and the other opposition groups, and gain at least the tacit approval of the church. This would be a most difficult prescription." The Embassy therefore concluded that: "Martial law may be an option. It could be used with confidence in few cases that the Embassy can see."[17]

At about the same time this Embassy assessment was dispatched to Washington, Polish Government officials were releasing information that an "emergency meeting" of the Council of Ministers on 17 September had "examined concrete measures" that "may turn out to be essential in defending the state." Shortly thereafter, the government put out word that another emergency meeting was held on Sunday, 20 September, at which government leaders "discussed urgent matters...assessed the state of readiness of the organs of state administration...[and made] several necessary decisions." Intelligence analysts as well as Western journalists described these as "ambiguous" or "vaguely" worded expressions that seemed to refer to martial law. On 21 September, in an apparent manifestation of regime reaction to Moscow's tirade, two Solidarity activists were arrested on the charge of anti-Soviet activities.[18] A few days later, the Polish press said Jaruzelski had notified parliament that the police had been instructed to put an end to lawlessness and anti-Soviet behavior, and that army units would be deployed to assist the police and internal security forces.[19]

New Warnings From Kuklinski

By this time, CIA had learned from Kuklinski that the chief of the Polish General Staff, General Florian Siwicki, had told a small group of Polish military officers that Poland was approaching the imposition of martial law. According to Kuklinski, this occurred during a meeting of military officers on

---

[17] The cable also addressed several specific issues of conflict that conceivably could spark martial law. These included Solidarity's outreach for free trade unions in other Pact countries, pressures for free elections to the parliament, a spontaneous law and order breakdown, threats to Soviet logistic connections, media access conflicts, protests over food prices and distribution, and the pressures for enterprise self management. The prospects for one of these to prompt martial law were rated from as high as one in three to as low as less than one in ten. The validity of treating any one of these as separate from the existing situation, rather than as an exacerbation of the existing conditions, can be legitimately questioned.

[18] "USSR-Poland: Moscow's Warning," decl. *NID*, 9 September 1981; "Poland-USSR: Cautious Reaction by Solidarity," decl. *NID*, 21 September 1981; "USSR-Poland: Possible Economic Pressures," decl. *NID*, 23 September 1981; and "USSR-Poland: Soviet Pressures," decl. *NID*, 25 September 1981. Also "Polish Regime Says An Urgent Action is Being Prepared," *The New York Times*, 21 September 1981, p. A1.

[19] "USSR-Poland: Soviet Pressures," decl. *NID*, 25 September 1981; and "Premier In Poland Calls On Police To Put An End To Anti-Soviet Activity," *The New York Times*, 25 September, p. A1.

9 September, the day after Solidarity's message to workers in the USSR and other East European countries was published in the union's weekly bulletin. General Siwicki reportedly had assured the Polish officers, in response to their questions, that they would receive help from the Soviets if their attempt to impose martial law by themselves proved unsuccessful. He also told them that proclamations to be issued when martial law was declared were being printed in the USSR—presumably to prevent someone involved in the printing process from warning Solidarity.[20]

Another report from Kuklinski described a pivotal meeting held on Sunday, 13 September, by the National Defense Committee, the select body of senior military and political officials responsible for strategic military policy decisions.[21] As noted above (p. 90), this was the oversight authority for martial law planning, for which Jaruzelski—with his dual hats as Prime Minister and Defense Minister—served as both chairman and deputy chairman.[22]

Kuklinski had not attended the National Defense Committee meeting, but was briefed on it afterwards when he was assigned to tasks that had been directed as a result of the meeting, and he dispatched his report two days later, on 15 September. He was told that "almost all of the participants [at the meeting] supported it [martial law]." He said this was the first meeting of this committee that Kania attended, who reportedly had been somewhat surprised that there was near unanimity for implementing martial law. Kania did not challenge the inevitability of martial law, according to Kuklinksi's information, but said he wanted to continue to pursue political avenues and "if that should fail, repression may be adopted."

Kuklinski said that during the next two days, he had been assigned to a small group that included representatives of the Army, Ministry of Internal Affairs, and the party Central Committee tasked with drawing up a "unified plan of command for the surprise introduction of martial law." He said the plan was still being put together, and he could therefore give only a brief summary:

> In brief, martial law will be introduced at night, either between Friday and a work-free Saturday or between Saturday and Sunday, when industrial plants will be closed. Arrests will begin

---

[20] Gates, *From the Shadows*, p. 234.

[21] This cable from Kuklinski is one of three of his original reporting messages that were released for his use in the early 1990's to prepare for a judicial review of his case in Poland. One of the other documents is his message sent on 4 December 1980. See p. 36 above. The full texts of all three messages are in Kramer, "Colonel Kuklinski and the Polish Crisis, 1980-81," *CWIHP Bulletin 11*, Winter 1998, p. 48ff.

[22] As also noted above, pages 20 and 90, Jaruzelski had similar dual roles in the Party-State Crisis Staff, which authorized the initial martial law planning.

about midnight, six hours before an announcement of martial law will be broadcast over the radio and television. Roughly 600 people will be arrested in Warsaw, which will require the use of around 1,000 police in unmarked cars. That same night, the army will seal off the most important areas of Warsaw and other major cities. Initially, only the MSW's [Ministry of Internal Affairs] forces will take part. A separate decision will be made about 'improving the deployment of armies,' that is, re-deploying entire divisions to major cities. This will be done only if reports come in about larger pockets of unrest.

The Embassy assessment that was sent to Washington on 19 September almost certainly would not have had the benefit of this recent reporting from Kuklinski. The senior CIA officer and no more than a very few other CIA officers probably would have been aware of Kuklinski's recent reports. For security reasons—which had become all the more imperative with Kuklinski's latest message—they clearly would not have introduced it into the Embassy team's deliberations. The Ambassador was aware of the mission Kuklinski was performing, but has said he did not see any of the original reporting, only "summaries from time to time."[23] All of the information specifically cited in the Embassy's assessment was available from public media. Nonetheless, the political dynamics by themselves led the Embassy team to rate the chances of martial law somewhere between one in two and one in three.

Whether Kuklinski's reporting was a factor in the heightened concern for martial law expressed by the Special Analysis in the 18 September *NID* has not been disclosed. That assessment would have been drafted no later than 17 September, and perhaps earlier. Kuklinski's report of the National Defense Committee meeting probably did not arrive in Washington until 16 September, so it would have been a quick turnaround, but possible. The assessment's declaration that the Polish regime "has" drawn up a detailed martial law plan seems to have been informed by Kuklinski's reporting, but he had made this clear in his reporting months earlier. If the conclusions were *not informed* by knowledge of Kuklinski's latest report, then one has to ask how strongly the judgments might have been expressed had the authors been aware of it.

At the same time, CIA learned that reporting from this special source was quite likely coming to an end. In his 15 September message, Kuklinski said he had been told that during a National Defense Committee meeting held two days earlier that Solidarity knew the details of the martial law plans, including the codename for the operation. Kuklinski pointed out to his CIA contacts that

---

[23] See Ambassador Francis Meehan's article, "Reflections on the Polish Crisis," *CWIHP Bulletin 11, op. cit.*, p. 46.

only a small circle of people engaged in preparing the plans were privy to this codename, and that "it will be easy to compile a group of suspects." He said a counterintelligence officer had already visited him the day after the meeting. He concluded his message with an admonition:

> Because the investigation is proceeding, I will have to forego my daily reports about current developments. Please treat with caution the information I am conveying to you, since it appears that my mission is coming to an end. The nature of the information makes it quite easy to detect the source. I do not object to, and indeed welcome, having the information I have conveyed serve those who fight for the freedom of Poland with their heads raised high. I am prepared to make the ultimate sacrifice, but the best way to achieve something is with our actions and not with our sacrifices.
>
> Long live Poland!
>
> Long live Solidarity, which brings freedom to all oppressed nations!

For obvious operational reasons, this part of Kuklinski's message would have been confined to the intelligence operations officers who would ultimately be charged with his safety. The substantive information relating to martial law would have been disseminated separately to the already small "compartment" of analysts and policy officials who had access to the intelligence from this source. The fact that the source was involved in a momentous, life-threatening situation also meant that this compartment would become even more closely guarded.

Nonetheless, intelligence analysts responsible for assessing the evolving situation in Poland continued to have access to Kukinski's information on martial law preparations right up to and after his escape from Poland. There may have been constraints on how explicitly Kuklinski's information could be cited in disseminated products, but the analysts certainly were able to use it to help interpret the overall body of evidence, and to form their assessments of the level of danger.[24] The tenor of the *NID*'s description of the unfolding evidence in the next two and a half months, however, raises significant questions as to how much attention the analysts gave to this unique information.

---

[24] This is based on the author's understanding at the time, and on subsequent confirmation from discussion with CIA officers who were at the time involved on both the collection and analysis sides of the issue.

Signals Missed?

On 24 September, the *NID* reported newly acquired information that the Polish Politburo had discussed a martial law plan at a meeting held on 15 September. This report said the plan had been submitted by the Polish military authorities, but rejected by a majority in the Politburo. The intelligence assessment commented that "the *apparent* backing by the military for emergency measures *suggests a possible* hardening of attitudes among *some* senior officers"[25] (emphasis added).

This assessment did not address whether or how the military authorities could have submitted a plan of such magnitude to the Politburo without approval by the top military officer—the Minister of Defense—and why this did not "suggest" that he was among the "some" military authorities whose attitudes were "possibly" hardening. And this top military officer was also prime minister and head of the government, a member of the Politburo, chairman of the National Defense Committee overseeing martial law planning, and arguably the most powerful official in the Polish regime. Nor did the intelligence report explain how submitting the martial law plan indicated only "apparent" backing, or why such backing and the "possible hardening of attitudes" would have been confined to military officials.

The failure to address these issues and the low-key treatment of the potential significance of this Politburo debate are striking by themselves. They are even more baffling in view of the fact that by the time this *NID* was disseminated, CIA had been informed that a meeting on martial law had preceded the Politburo meeting by two days. Jaruzelski chaired this meeting of the National Defense Committee (NDC), at which most of the participants reportedly wanted to go ahead with martial law. CIA also had been told that Kania provided the main resistance to martial law at that session, and even he did not rule it out, arguing only that political measures should be continued until it was demonstrated that they would not resolve the situation. It is hard to see how analysts could avoid concluding that the 15 September Politburo discussion was a follow-up to the National Defense Committee meeting. A special working group set up by the NDC was in the process of refining details of the martial law plans.

The intelligence report on the 15 September Politburo meeting also failed to mention that a day after it was held, the party released a statement that the US press described as its "hardest yet." Nor did the *NID* address the possibility that the two meetings of the Council of Ministers that followed—both chaired

---

[25] "Poland: Differences Over Martial Law," decl. *NID*, September 1981. This appears to be the meeting described by Gates, *From the Shadows*, p. 234, as having taken place "in mid-September."

by Jaruzelski and both followed by statements that the press and intelligence analysts alike described as seeming to refer to martial law—might have been linked to the Politburo debate on martial law.

This apparent absence of analytic linkage of these events and the potential implications of the trend continued to be evident in the intelligence reporting in the following weeks. The public media, by contrast, even though it did not have the advantage of Kuklinski's information, began painting a more threatening picture. A *New York Times* article at about this same time, for example, posed in its title the fundamental question "For How Long Can Poland Practice Its Brinksmanship?" It characterized the reported Politburo discussions as indicating the leadership was "seriously considering declaring a state of emergency...a drastic step tantamount to declaring martial law," and quoted a "party official speaking privately" saying such a step would be accompanied by arrests.[26]

Escalating Threats to Regime Pre-Eminence

Signs that the regime was gearing up for more drastic moves surfaced at the same time that Solidarity was heading into the second round of its congress. The US Embassy in Warsaw, while rating the chances for martial law "under existing conditions" as less than fifty-fifty, had nonetheless judged Solidarity's actions in the first round of its Congress as having "gone a substantial way" toward creating the kind of threat to the regime that could cause it to resort to such measures. An Intelligence Community Special Analysis disseminated about the same time as the Embassy assessment had said that the Polish regime was determined "to prevent a further erosion of its authority and to employ force if the union refuses to back off," and that chances for the use of force had risen considerably unless Solidarity managed "to tone down those union actions most objectionable to the government."[27] Solidarity actions in the next few weeks showed no such signs.

On 25 September, the day before the congress's second session began, the Polish regime suffered a significant defeat in a head-to-head contest with Solidarity. On that day the Sejm passed new laws for "Workers' Self-Management" and "State Enterprises." On the most contested point—the authority to

---

[26] "For How Long Can Poland Practice Its Brinksmanship?," *The New York Times,* 27 September 1981, p. 4E. The date of the article and the fact that it described the Politburo meeting it referred to as having taken place "last week" could lead to a conclusion that it was referring to another, subsequent Politburo meeting on martial law, and this cannot be ruled out. Nonetheless, the article was drafted by *The New York Times* reporter covering events from Warsaw, John Darnton, a few days before its publication in the editorial section of the Sunday *New York Times*, which would put the date of the meeting it referred to in the week of 13-19 September.

[27] *Op. cit.*, footnotes 12 and 47.

appoint and dismiss directors and managers of enterprises—the parliament approved language that differed in only minor phrasing from compromise wording that government and Solidarity negotiators had agreed to a few days before the vote.

The Polish party leadership subsequently rejected the compromise, however, and informed the parliament of this two days before the vote. The parliamentary commission in charge of drafting the laws nonetheless continued to support the compromise language, and—over the government's objections—submitted it to a vote of the full parliament, where it passed. The party thus found it had issued what it considered to be instructions to the parliament, only to see the parliament disregard those instructions, adding insult to injury by supporting the compromise the union had accepted and the party had rejected.

Parliament's action granted elected workers' councils the right to appoint and dismiss directors at plants and factories except for those defined by the new law as "state enterprises." The Council of Ministers would identify "state enterprises" on the basis of the facilities' role in defense and security, law enforcement, or national functions such as communications, finance, and transportation. Even at these enterprises, the law granted workers' councils the right to appeal managerial selections, while the government would have reciprocal appeal rights at enterprises where appointments and dismissals were under the initiative of the workers' councils.

Most outside observers and the Polish regime itself saw this as a major victory for Solidarity, and a strategic erosion of the party's authority. Many of the Solidarity delegates, however, thought the new laws still conceded too much to the government. They also were particularly incensed at how the compromise was reached, accusing Walesa of again assuming too much authority. Apparently only four members of the union's "presidium" were present when he presented the compromise language for approval, and even then he had a tough sell.[28]

These issues became subject to acrimonious debate when the second round of the union congress opened on 26 September. The delegates ultimately voted to accept the parliamentary action for the time being, but extracted agreement that proposed amendments to certain portions of the new laws be submitted to union-wide referenda. Walesa and the other members of the union presidium who authorized the compromise received a censure vote by the congress for

---

[28] "New Polish Laws Give Workers Role In Running Plants," *The New York Times,* 26 September 1981, p. 1. For further background see Garton Ash, *The Polish Revolution,* pp. 213-214; and Raina, *Poland 1981,* pp. 390-395. The texts of the laws approved by the Sejm were published in *Trybuna Ludu* on 28 and 29 September 1981. An English translation is in Raina, pp. 396-419. On the issue of authority regarding managers, see article 24:2 of the Law on Self-Management, and Article 4:1 through Article 6 of the Law on State Enterprises.

exceeding their authority. The Solidarity delegates also sent Walesa a message in the vote for union chairman. While he beat the closest of his three opponents by better than two to one, he still received only a little over 55 percent of the vote—an indication of the growing divide between what were by then being described as "moderates around Walesa" and "militants" supporting more confrontational tactics.[29]

Western media described the parliamentary action on workers' self-management laws as a "considerable erosion in the power of the communist party," and said it was "moving Poland away from the orthodox Soviet model." A press article on 27 September said Western diplomats believed that the Soviets could not accept the transformation of Poland into the liberalized, social-democratic system that seemed to be evolving. The consensus among these diplomats, according to the press report, was that "prospects for the Poles were as dark as they have been at any time since Solidarity's rise a year ago." Accounts in the *NID*, on the other hand, focused on the contention aroused within Solidarity over the compromise language and the indications of growing factionalism in the union.[30]

A Rival Constitution

On the last day of the congress—7 October—Solidarity upped the level of challenge to the regime yet again with the formal passage of its program, the drafting of which had been under way since early in the year. A sampling of its provisions for transforming economic and political life included:

- Public control over government decisions for dealing with the economic crisis, elimination of the practice of appointing party apparatchiks to management positions, and creation of a "new socioeconomic system based on self-government, and the market;"

- "Pluralism of views" as the "foundation of democracy in the self governing republic;"

- New electoral laws insuring free elections for local and provincial self-governing councils and also for the national parliament, and an

---

[29] "Poland: Solidarity Militants Attack Compromise," decl. *NID*, 28 September 1981; "Poland: Central Committee Meeting Called," decl. *NID*, 30 September 1981; and "Poland: Walesa's Victory," decl. *NID*, 3 October 1981, Also "Union Militants in Poland Attack Leaders Over Government Accord," *The New York Times,* 28 September 1981, p. A1; "Polish Convention Chastises Walesa," *The New York Times*, 30 September 1981, p. A9; and "Walesa Wins Union Vote With Ease," *The New York Times*, 3 October 1981, p. 3.

[30] "New Polish Laws Give Workers Role in Running Plants," *The New York Times,* 26 September 1981, p. 1; and "Soviet Fears For Empire In Crisis," *The New York Times*, 27 September 1981, p. 4E. For *NID* reporting see declassified articles cited in footnote 29 above.

examination of the possibility of creating a second parliamentary chamber;

- Creation of a tribunal for identifying and punishing individuals responsible for past violence against workers and citizens, going as far back as the 1956 suppression in Poznan and including the 1970 and 1976 violence against strikers and the recent Bydgoszcz incident. If the government did not institute this process by the end of 1981, Solidarity's National Commission would "appoint a social tribunal [that would hold] a national trial [and] pass a verdict on and brand the guilty;"

- Protection of the rights of citizens groups, including Solidarity, to own and control the content of their own publishing agencies, and establishment of true "public control over radio and television."[31]

The New York Times described the program as "like a new constitution...." It said the demand for a tribunal, especially, presented a new level of challenge for the regime. The article postulated that the extent of Solidarity's moves to date suggested the union "might push for changes in other fields to establish a democratic system of government not based on the communist model."[32]

NID reporting, by contrast, characterized the program as a "mixture of moderation and militancy." The specific "moderate" aspect cited in the *NID* was preliminary information that a section on foreign affairs that had appeared in earlier drafts of Solidarity's program had been toned down.[33] In fact, the program as finally published had no section on foreign affairs. Foreign affairs aside, however, it is hard to see how any reading of this program could interpret it as compatible with the Soviet communist model, or consider its advocacy as anything other than an effort to break with that model. On the contrary, with the exception of the "appeal" to workers in other Soviet Bloc countries, actions in the first round of the congress that an earlier intelligence assessment had listed as "most objectionable to the government" had been significantly expanded and codified in a formal, printed program that was a direct challenge to the regime.

---

[31] The full text of the program was distributed in a special edition (No. 29) of Solidarity's weekly *Tygodnik Solidarnosc* on 16 October 1981. An English version is in Raina, *Poland 1981*, pp. 326-365. The samples presented here are from Theses 1, 2, 21, 22, 26, and 29.
[32] "Polish Union Adopts Economic Plan," *The New York Times,* 8 October 1981, p. A3.
[33] "Poland: Solidarity Congress Ends," decl. *NID*, 8 October 1981.

Chapter 12

Bringing Down the Curtain

A week after the union congress ended, a new warning of martial law appeared in one of Solidarity's own publications. The Solidarity news bulletin for the period 26 September–12 October reported that Politburo member Alban Siwak had told representatives from the party-fronted trade unions that special units of army and police had been established to put down popular resistance. He reportedly said the forces would be employed in about two months, by which time it was expected that popular support for Solidarity would have weakened. Siwak's revelations included a description of a six-person "Committee of National Salvation" that had been formed, headed by Jaruzelski and Interior Minister Kiszczak.[1] Solidarity's publications were a source of information on events in Poland, and Siwak's comments presumably were known by US intelligence analysts, but there is no reflection of them in the declassified reports from the *NID* or any of the other declassified intelligence assessments.

On 16 October, the Polish Government announced that the active duty service of army conscripts scheduled to be discharged at the end of October (about 40,000 troops) had been extended for two months. The induction of new conscripts was to proceed as originally scheduled. The government justified this move on the grounds of a need for the military to increase its contribution to the national economy.[2]

The *NID* said the extension of conscript service probably was a step by the regime to "show its resolve to act," and also indicated the regime's desire to be prepared in the event martial law became necessary.[3] Not addressed in the intelligence reporting was the belief of some CIA analysts that an extension of conscript service would be a virtual necessity if the Polish regime were forced to consider imposing martial law within a few months of the normal conscript

---

[1] Both Andrews, *Poland 1980-81*, p. 204, and Garton Ash, *The Polish Revolution*, p. 234, who were in Poland at the time, quote *Agencja Solidarnosc*, Bulletin 44 (26 September–12 October 1981), p. 205.
[2] "Poland Says Union Seeks Dictatorship," *The New York Times*, 17 October 1981, p. 3.
[3] "Poland: Party Policy Toughening," decl. *NID*, 17 October 1981.

rotation date. Attempting a crackdown after a recent replacement of about 40,000 troops with brand new conscripts was seen as an unnecessary risk, if it could be avoided. The simple way of avoiding it was to extend the service of the active troops. Going ahead with the callup of new conscripts at the same time offered a means of removing potential resisters from the civilian ranks, while at the same time keeping them out of martial law implementation by confining them to barracks.

The same day the military service extension was announced, the party Central Committee held a plenum that proved critical to the approaching climax of the drama begun in Gdansk the previous year. This meeting had been preceded by stories that party hard-liners were stepping up pressures to impose a "state of emergency" that would include the banning of Solidarity. There were also rampant rumors of new efforts under way to remove Kania.[4]

At the opening session of the plenum, Kania came out with his toughest line yet. He accused Solidarity of seeking "dictatorship," and called for a ban on strikes for the remainder of the fall and winter. His tough opening, however, did not spare him from heavy criticism the next day. The Central Committee also tabled a resolution calling on the government to declare a state of emergency. The press quoted one Central Committee participant as having said privately that a state of emergency—painful as it might be—would at least "generate the basic means of living and the rule of law and order."[5]

On the plenum's third day, 18 October, the party announced Kania's resignation and his replacement by Jaruzelski. The plenum also passed a resolution demanding that parliament impose a temporary suspension of the right to strike, and calling on the government to invoke if necessary "its constitutional prerogatives to guarantee peace in the country," which the press interpreted as a reference to martial law. This party resolution also demanded that all existing agreements between the government and Solidarity be renegotiated, and said the party intended to tighten control over the media, rejecting union demands for greater access.[6]

An official US State Department press release said the US Government viewed the resolution as a move to acquire authority for using force against Solidarity, and declared that "We see no reason for martial law in Poland." In

---

[4] "Poland: Criticism of Leadership," decl. *NID*, 15 October 1981; "Polish Union Seeks Freeze in Rise of Prices," *The New York Times,* 16 October 1981, p. A1.
[5] "Poland: Pressure on Solidarity," decl. *NID*, 17 October 1981; "Poland Says Union Seeks Dictatorship," *The New York Times,* 17 October 1981, p. 3; and "Polish Party Meeting is Critical of Leadership," *The New York Times,* 18 October 1981, p. 10.
[6] "Poland: Party Policy Toughening," decl. *NID*, 19 October 1981. "Kania is Replaced: Polish Party Gives His Post to Premier," *The New York Times,* 19 October 1981, p. A1; and "Soldier In Power, 19 October 1981, p. A1."

response to a question during the press briefing, the State spokesman said it was "too soon to tell" if Jaruzelski's accession to party first secretary and other events at the Central Committee meeting meant hardliners were in control.[7]

The next day's *NID* said the leadership change foreshadowed "a tougher policy by the Polish party toward Solidarity that, while continuing the union-government dialogue, also increases the chances of confrontation." This assessment said the selection of Jaruzelski "seems intended to exploit popular respect for the military...and possibly to place the party in a position to manage any 'state of emergency' more easily." It said the Central Committee resolution "obligated" Jaruzelski to measures "that could bring the government directly into conflict with the union." The assessment also pointed out that the Central Committee had nonetheless left the door open to negotiations. The intelligence analysis concluded that Jaruzelski seemed likely "to move cautiously in using more forceful measures," and that he probably realized the importance of creating the right atmosphere for any declaration of martial law.[8]

The *NID* report on Kania's "resignation" said its "acceptance... reflected heightened frustration within the party over its inability to contain Solidarity. Some moderates may have felt that Kania had to be sacrificed because he had become a symbol of inaction and thus an impediment to his own pragmatic policies."[9] The NID did not address the possibility that the "inaction" which led to Kania's demise was his continuing resistance to carrying out the martial law plans that had been prepared.

This would have been simply speculative proposition. There had already evidence a month earlier that support for martial law was growing, that the plans being debated at the highest political level, and that a working group had been tasked with refining implementation plans. CIA had evidence from Kuklinski that, contrary to the description in the *NID*, the growing support was not limited merely to "some military" officers, and that Jaruzelski was among those at least leaning toward carrying it out. CIA had been informed that in a National Defense Committee meeting in mid-September, Kania reportedly had been virtually the only participant who resisted going ahead with the implementation of martial law. And since that meeting, the challenge to party supremacy—had continued to escalate, with the parliamentary rebuff on the workers self management law and Solidarity's publication of its "program."

---

[7] "Polish Statement Disturbs the US," *The New York Times,* 19 October 1981, p. A14.
[8] "Party Policy Toughening," *NID,* 19 October 1981; and "Kania is Replaced...," *The New York Times,* 19 October 1981, p. A1.
[9] "Poland: Political Maneuvering," decl. *NID* article, 19 October 1981. The Defense Intelligence Agency would offer a more ominous interpretation two weeks later.

The subsequent opening of the Central Committee Plenum at which Jaruzelski was named to replace Kania was accompanied by the extension of active duty for military conscripts—an important element of the regime's preparedness for carrying out martial law. The same Central Committee meeting passed a resolution that even the western press interpreted as a call for martial law "if necessary."

Gates has said that by this time CIA was aware that Jaruzelski had been having a number of unpleasant phone conversations with Brezhnev, from which Kania had been cut out. And CIA had also learned, according to Gates, that Jaruzelski had been persuaded by his own Ministries of Defense and Internal Affairs, as well as by the Soviets, to favor imposition of martial law. It may be that some of this information was conveyed to US policy officials in special, restricted reports, but it does not appear to have had an impact on the interpretations of events given in the *NID*.[10]

The Regime Launches Its Counteroffensive

On 20 October, two days after Kania's removal, police used force and tear gas to disperse a crowd of protesters in Katowice, an industrial center in southern Poland, in what the US press described as "the worst outbreak of street violence in 14 months." The crowd was protesting the arrest of three Solidarity activists who had been distributing anti-Soviet leaflets. The next day, at least three more Solidarity activists in Wroclaw, a provincial capital in southwest Poland, were detained on the same charge—"anti-Soviet propaganda." This time the government accompanied the arrests with a ban on public gatherings in the entire province. The regional chapter of Solidarity threatened a general strike if the activists were not released, and local transit workers initiated preliminary steps to carry out a strike independent of the Solidarity decision.

After one day, the police released the detained activists and lifted the ban on public gatherings, causing the local transit workers to call off their strike. The *NID* suggested that the government actions may initially have been intended to prompt Solidarity leaders to make some effort to control anti-Soviet agitators. This intelligence reporting also said that the regime "may be reluctant to push too hard for a confrontation," pointing out that the conciliatory action taken by the government and the Polish official media's portrayal of Solidarity's positive role had helped contain reactions in Wroclaw.

Solidarity's leadership, however, had a darker view, claiming the arrests were a calculated move to spark local confrontations and divide the union. The violent attack on the protesters took place on the eve of the meeting at

---

[10] Gates, *From the Shadows*, pp. 234-235.

which Solidarity's National Commission was scheduled to decide whether to go ahead with a national strike to protest the government's latest price hikes. While the release of the arrested activists headed off the local transit workers' strike, the government's actions eliminated whatever wiggle room Walesa and other Solidarity moderates had to avoid carrying out the threat of a national strike.[11]

The government had announced the price increases during the final days of the union congress. At that time, union leaders had already indicated that they understood some price increases on consumer goods were unavoidable. They had their own concerns that the disastrous state of the economy was eroding control of their local organizations, and that failure to stem the economic deterioration would lead to disintegration of grass-roots support for the union's larger program of social renewal. Solidarity's leaders were in the midst of trying to get their congress to agree to a program that set up a framework for union and government consultation on such actions, when the government made its announcement.

Union leaders considered the government's action preemptive and dictatorial, and protested vehemently. Walesa dispatched a letter to Jaruzelski, who sent a representative to meet with Solidarity leaders. The union demanded that the government rescind the increases until after the congress, and then engage in consultations. The government refused, and Solidarity responded at the end of its congress by threatening a national one-hour "warning" strike within two weeks if there were no progress on the issue.

The *NID* described Solidarity's threatened action as a "token" strike and one of the "moderate" outcomes of the union's congress. Intelligence analysts nonetheless said that the government decision to go through with the price hikes would intensify militant pressures within the union, and this proved to be correct. While Solidarity's leadership urged local union organizations not to yield to the temptation to engage in wildcat strikes pending the outcome of the talks with the government, the situation's volatility offered little chance that such urging would have much effect. Less than a week after the Solidarity congress, strikes began to erupt around Poland to protest food shortages and price increases, and pressures mounted on Walesa to call a nationally coordinated strike, if only to bring back some cohesion to the increasingly rebellious local unions.[12]

---

[11] "Poland: Incident in Katowice," decl. *NID* article, 21 October 1981; "Poland: Government Resolve," decl. *NID* article, 22 October 1981; and "Divisions Within Solidarity," decl. *NID* article, 23 October 1981. "Polish Police Battling 5,000 Protesting Arrests," *The New York Times*, 21 October 1981, p. A15; and "Poles In Katowice Angry Over Brawl," *The New York Times*, 22 October 1981, p. A3.

The calls at the mid-October party Central Committee meeting for parliamentary action to ban strikes further inflamed the confrontational atmosphere. Intelligence assessments said that Solidarity's leaders would not risk the anger of an already rebellious union rank and file by surrendering—even for a short time—what they considered the union's chief weapon. The *NID* said that if the regime persisted with its demands for a strike ban—which parliament had to approve—Solidarity probably would feel compelled to carry out its threatened general strike. Pressures against any union leadership concessions were already mounting anyway, as wildcat strikes and strike alerts had spread to at least eight provinces. Militants were insisting that a counterattack was necessary to retain credibility with rank and file and to contain widespread uncoordinated strike activity.[13]

Under these circumstances, the government's provocation on the eve of Solidarity's strike meeting left the union leaders with no practical reply to the militants' arguments. They announced that the strike would be carried out on 28 October and added that if the union's demands were not met, Solidarity would conduct more strikes and also take over the food distribution system.[14]

An hour after Solidarity's announcement, the government said that the Polish military was being assigned a major role to help ensure "law and order." Groups of soldiers were to be deployed nationwide with authority to suppress "street provocations across the country," "counteract problems on the spot," and "solve disputes." They also would help distribute food and fix transportation breakdowns. Additional details provided by the government over the next few days disclosed that some 800 groups of three to four soldiers each would

---

[12] "Poland: Moderates Gain Time," decl. *NID* article, 5 October 1981; "Poland: Government Stands Firm," decl. *NID* article, 6 October 1981; "Poland: Solidarity Congress Ends," decl. *NID* article, 8 October 1981; "Poland: Walesa Wins," decl. *NID* article, 9 October 1981; and "Poland: Central Committee Meeting Postponed," decl. *NID* article, 14 October 1981. Also "Poland Announces Price Rises and Union Protests," *The New York Times,* 5 October 1981, p. A4; "Poland Enforces Price Increases," *The New York Times,* 6 October 1981, p. A4; "Polish Union Adopts Economic Plan," *The New York Times,* 8 October 1981, p. A3; and "Wildcat Strikes Erupt in Poland," *The New York Times,* 14 October 1981, p A6.
[13] "Poland: Criticism of Leadership," decl. *NID* article, 15 October 1981; and "Poland: Pressure on Solidarity," decl. *NID* article, 17 October 1981; "Poland Says Union Seeks Dictatorship," *The New York Times,* 17 October 1981, p. 3.
[14] *Op. cit.,* decl. *NID* articles of 22 and 23 October 1981; and *The New York Times,* 22 October 1981.

be assigned to cover some 2,000 villages in the Polish countryside. The deployments would begin on 26 October and take about two to three days to complete.[15]

The *NID*'s assessment said the regime apparently hoped to use the widespread respect for the military to curb local unrest. It said the incidents in Katowice and Wroclaw may have convinced the Polish leadership of police ineffectiveness in enforcing the new, tougher policies. Another objective suggested by intelligence analysts was to intimidate Solidarity in its call for a national strike. Intelligence analysts said the plan to initially dispatch groups of soldiers to rural areas, where Solidarity's presence was low and respect for the military high, reflected the regime's desire to enlarge the role of the military in a manner designed to avoid negative reactions.

This intelligence assessment said the move "does not appear to include any restrictions on civil liberties...even though the measures are a plausible step toward some kind of martial law." The analysis nonetheless pointed out that "the government has moved closer to its final option because it now may be testing the reliability of its military to perform a domestic police function and the willingness of the Polish populace to respect the military in that role." One more step occurred on 28 October with the announcement that General Siwicki (chief of the Polish General Staff and overseer of the detailed martial law planning) had been elevated to candidate member of the party Politburo.[16]

The US Administration reflected a mix of concern and uncertainty in its public reactions. On the day the deployment of soldier groups was announced, the State Department press conference declared frankly that the US "did not know" what the effect would be, and that "time will tell." The US Embassy in Warsaw was reported to have said the situation was calm at the moment. A day later, Secretary of State Haig repeated the "time will tell" caution, and said the United States was closely watching the developments. Secretary of Defense Weinberger, on the other hand, was quoted a day later as saying the Poles were in danger of being "forced by the USSR to take action." He also

---

[15] "Poland: New Role for the Military," decl. *NID*, 24 October 1981; and "Poland: Deployment of Troops," *NID*, 26 October 1981; "Poland Deploying Troops for Action in Local Disputes," *The New York Times*, 24 October 1981, p. 1; and "Warsaw Demands Solidarity Cancel General Walkout," *The New York Times*, 26 October 1981, p. A1.

[16] Decl. *NID* articles, 24 and 26 October 1981, *op. cit.*; "Poland: Tough Government Stance," decl. *NID* article, 27 October 1981; "Poland: Solidarity's Strike," decl. *NID* article, 28 October 1981; and "Poland: Continuing the Dialogue," decl. *NID* article, 29 October 1981. Also *The New York Times*, 24 and 26 October 1981, *op. cit.*; and "Warsaw Deploys Small Army Units Across the Nation," *The New York Times*, 27 October 1981, p. A1.

said that an "armed intervention by the USSR is an even greater danger," and that the United States hoped "the Polish government and people will be able to work out their own destiny."[17]

Meanwhile, wildcat strikes continued to erupt throughout Poland. The largest involved a regional Solidarity chapter in western Poland at Zielona Gora, where as many as 150,000 workers were carrying out an open-ended work stoppage. On the eve of Solidarity's scheduled national strike, local strikes were underway in 36 of Poland's 49 provinces, with some 280,000 workers reported to be participating. More strikes were threatened, as workers at a major factory in Warsaw declared their intent to strike in support of an ongoing sit-in by 12,000 textile workers.[18]

The regime mounted a strong propaganda campaign, asserting that Solidarity's intent to impose a national strike on top of the pre-existing ones, was "an impending national disaster [that]…would destroy the economy and any possibility of agreement." The *NID* described the propaganda campaign as an effort to erode support for Solidarity and depict the union as "irresponsible for having gone ahead with its action in the face of Poland's severe economic problems." This intelligence assessment said the regime was attempting to "contrast Solidarity's move with its own dramatic efforts demonstrated by sending military groups throughout country."[19]

On 28 October, Solidarity's one-hour national general strike took place without incident. The Polish regime asserted the strike failed to achieve its participation goals, an assertion that both the intelligence analysts and Western media interpreted as an effort to portray ebbing support and cohesion in Solidarity. US intelligence assessments agreed with Solidarity's claim that the strike had been a successful demonstration of the union's effectiveness in marshaling the workers' movement. High-level union officials were quoted in the Western press admitting that a driving motivation for the strike had been the need to reverse the fragmentation caused by the wildcat strikes.[20]

Two days later, Jaruzelski formally addressed the Polish parliament. Referring to discussions already taking place behind the scenes, he said he "knew" that a group from the parliament intended to submit a resolution to end the

---

[17] "US Unsure of Impact," *The New York Times,* 24 October 1981, p. 5; "Haig Says US Watches," *The New York Times,* 25 October 1981, p. 21; and "Weinberger Warns of Repression," *The New York Times,* 26 October 1981, p. A10.

[18] Declassified *NID* articles of 23 and 26 October 1981, *op. cit.* "Strikes Spreading, Solidarity Meets," *The New York Times,* 23 October 1981, p. A1; and "Poland Strikes Ignore Army Plan and Union Appeal," *The New York Times,* 25 October 1981, p. 1.

[19] "Warsaw Demands Solidarity Cancel General Walkout," *The New York Times,* 26 October 1981; "Poland: Tough Government Stance," decl. *NID* article, 27 October 1981.

[20] "Poland: Solidarity's Strike," decl. *NID* article, 28 October 1981; and "Poland: Continuing the Dialogue," decl. *NID* article, 29 October 1981; "Millions of Poles Strike For An Hour in Food Protest," *The New York Times,* 29 October 1981, p. A1.

strike action. He declared that if the resolution failed to pass or failed to end the strikes, he would seek approval of a law banning strikes. He also announced that, because of the "existing dangerous situation," he had presented to the parliamentary presidium a draft law granting the government "extraordinary means of action in the interests of protection of the citizens of the state."[21]

The parliament passed the resolution demanding an end to strikes. It did not pass the government's proposed law authorizing "extraordinary means," but did include in its strike ban resolution a declaration that, if the strikes continued, the parliament would "examine proposals to provide the government with such legal means as are required by the situation." At least one Western journalist on the scene interpreted this as a commitment to consider a law banning strikes if Solidarity did not comply with the appeal.[22]

The description of this action in the *NID* said that Jaruzelski "chose a moderate course by not confronting Solidarity with a legal ban on strikes." This intelligence assessment also said that even though he had "temporized" on the issue, his public commitment to follow up with a request for legislation would reduce his future room to maneuver. According to at least one press report, however, there was some evidence that Jaruzelski made his "choice" not to push harder for a formal law against strikes only after learning there was still strong resistance in the parliament, and that it was unlikely to pass. Thus an alternative interpretation could have been that the confrontation Jaruzelski chose to avoid was not with Solidarity, but with the parliament. Under this interpretation, by showing himself willing first to try the more moderate parliamentary action, he may have hoped to enhance his leverage in the predictable event that Solidarity did not comply with the resolution.[23]

Jaruzelski's parliamentary moves were in fact interpreted by the US Defense Intelligence Agency (DIA) as part of a larger pattern with more ominous implications than were described in *NID* reporting. In an "Intelligence

---

[21] "Polish Chief Asks Aid of Parliament to Stop Walkouts," *The New York Times,* 31 October 1981, p. 1. According to Andrews, *Poland 1980-81,* ch. 14, note 22, Jaruzelski's speech to the Parliament is printed in FBIS (EE) of 2 November 1981, pp. G1-G11. A summary is in Raina, *Poland 1981,* p. 433-434.

[22] "Parliament Bids Polish Workers Stop All Strikes," *The New York Times,* 1 November 1981, p. 1.

[23] "Poland: Political Maneuvering," decl. *NID,* 31 October 1981. The evidence that a majority of parliament members would oppose a formal law banning strikes was reported by John Darnton in the 31 October *New York Times* article, *op. cit.* Timothy Garton Ash, who, like Darnton, was covering the events on the scene, gives details on this in *The Polish Revolution,* p. 242.

Appraisal" disseminated in early November reviewing the actions of the Polish regime since the mid-October party plenum, DIA analysts concluded that:

> The way has been cleared for Warsaw to declare a state of emergency or to impose martial law. Although factors indicate that full martial law may not be enforced immediately, events suggest martial law may be imposed in Poland this winter.[24]

The DIA appraisal described the factors that led to this conclusion:

- Kania's replacement as head of the party: in contrast to the *NID*, the DIA appraisal specifically listed Kania's opposition to martial law as one of the main factors leading to his resignation under increasing pressure from a growing hard line in the party leadership;

- Indications of a tougher position taken by Jaruzelski, who now held all the formal instruments of state power with the top posts in the party, government, and military: the appraisal pointed out that with his dual hats as Prime Minister and Defense Minister, Jaruzelski was both chairman and deputy chairman of the National Defense Committee. The DIA analysis described Jaruzelski's attitude as hardening in response to the increasing threat to regime authority manifested by Solidarity's national congress and subsequent actions, the mounting threats of both national and wildcat strikes, and pressures from the USSR and his own military hierarchy;

- Increasingly tougher tactics by the regime: these included extending military service for two months, employing military forces to augment police, increasing security patrols, and expelling certain party members who were also members of Solidarity;

- And most recently, Jaruzelski's effort to enlist parliamentary action—resulting in the parliament's resolution demanding a cessation of strikes—and his public vow to seek legislation granting him extraordinary powers if the resolution was ignored. [25]

The DIA appraisal pointed out that the growing disunity of Solidarity, despite the achievement of some economic agreements with the regime, was eroding the union leaders' ability to control regional chapters in the face of mounting food and fuel shortages. The appraisal said this would probably result in heightened civil unrest, which would increase the pressures for a crackdown.

---

[24] "Poland: Martial Law," decl. DIA Intelligence Appraisal, 4 November 1981, p.1, in *Poland 1980-82: Compendium.*

[25] *Ibid.*, pp. 2-3.

Melded with Kuklinski's recent reporting, this appraisal should have generated questions about whether martial law prospects had risen significantly higher than the "less than fifty-fifty" described in the Embassy assessment a month earlier. Apparently, it failed to get much attention at the time.

Setting the Stage

The absence of more widespread concern by other US intelligence analysts and other Western observers may have been the result of Jaruzelski's two-pronged tactics. At the same time he was seeking tougher legislation from the parliament, he also was promoting his "Front of National Accord." He had proposed this concept at the time of the mid-October party Central Committee meeting, characterizing it as an effort "to seek solutions to the economic and social turmoil in Poland." In it he called for a consultative council of government officials which would also include Solidarity leader Walesa and the Catholic Primate Archbishop Glemp.[26] The proposal was notably vague on the question of what authority the non-government participants would have beyond "consultation," which was a source of suspicion on Walesa's part.

The "Front" proposal was discussed at a 4 November meeting of Jaruzelski, Walesa and the Polish Archbishop. In the intelligence reporting as well as in press coverage, the fact that this meeting took place was given as much prominence as its subject. The *NID* said the agreement to hold the meeting "appeared to be a signal from moderates on both sides that some form of cooperation is necessary if the country is to come to grips with its dismal economic condition." The day after the meeting, the Intelligence Community reported that the three leaders "took the first step forward for consultation and cooperation" and that they "discussed setting up a Front of National Accord and agreed to hold further business-like consultations." Walesa reportedly considered Jarzelski's proposed Front a step in the right direction, although Solidarity remained committed to establishing its own "Economic and Social Council" as called for in its program.[27]

For the next three weeks, the budding high-level talks between the regime, Solidarity, and the church were the most prominent issue in the *NID* reporting on Poland. The "big three" meeting of Walesa, Jaruzelski and the Archbishop was assessed as having generated "cautious optimism" and opened the way for what promised to be the "most comprehensive talks" since well before the party and Solidarity had held their respective Congresses. On 11 November,

---

[26] "Poland: Pressure on Solidarity," decl. *NID*, 17 October 1981.
[27] "Poland: High-Level Talks on Cooperation," decl. *NID* article, 4 November 1981; and "Poland: Three-Way Consultations," decl. *NID* article, 5 November 1981. Also "Heads of Party, Union, and Church Confer in Poland," *The New York Times,* 5 November 1981, p. A3.

the party Politburo formally endorsed Jaruzelski's "Front of National Accord," an action that intelligence analysts said indicated support for Jaruzelski's efforts to find a political solution to the country's problems. "Solidarity and regime leaders have emphasized the need for some form of institutionalized cooperation," according to an intelligence report. This report said Jaruzelski had told the Politburo that "Poland can only be governed with the support of the people and that, if this can be accomplished by a coalition of power centers, then it must be accepted."[28]

Solidarity's national leadership already had undertaken a major effort to end wildcat strikes. Walesa's game plan sought to combine a mechanism for disciplining defiant local chapters with a commitment by the national leadership to more actively represent local grievances. He personally visited many of the striking locals to urge them to return to work, in order to give the talks a chance to produce positive results. Not unexpectedly, he had mixed success. Intelligence analysts nonetheless judged that the ongoing strikes were contained at a level that seemed unlikely to endanger the talks between Solidarity and the government.[29]

The first meeting of party and union negotiators following the "big three" summit was held 17 November. Describing the outlook, the *NID* said "the willingness to begin talks indicates that the moderate points of view still predominate, [although] they will be sorely tested in the coming months." The talks could last for months, according to the *NID*. If they succeeded:

> Poland will have made a significant step toward greater stability. If [the talks] fail, there will be additional radicalization of Solidarity's rank and file and leadership that will substantially increase the prospects for serious clashes with the government. At stake is the creation of the legal and institutional base for a pluralistic political structure.[30]

The *NID* pointed out that both sides would have to give some ground if talks were to succeed. It said the party would have to relinquish some powers and Solidarity would have to agree to political structures that enabled the party to retain the appearance of its leading role, but "moderates on both sides are approaching the talks in a positive and optimistic way."

---

[28] "Poland: Talks Slated," decl. *NID* article, 9 November 1981; and "Poland: Jaruzelski Proposal Endorsed." decl. *NID* article, 12 November 1981.

[29] "Poland: Trying to Control Strikes," decl. *NID* article, 3 November 1981; and decl. *NID* article, 12 November 1981, *op. cit.* Also "Industrial Unrest in Poland Persists," *The New York Times,* 11 November 1981, p. A3; and "200,000 Poles End 22-Day Wildcat Strike But Other Protests Go On," *The New York Times,* 13 November 1981, p. A1.

[30] "Poland: Back to the Bargaining Table," decl. *NID,* 17 November 1981.

Intelligence analysts described this as part of a difficult process with an uncertain outcome. They pointed out that although Jaruzelski had some latitude to seek accommodation, if the compromises he was willing to accept did not satisfy Solidarity's requirements, he "seem[ed] willing to take forceful measures." The daily intelligence reporting in this time frame clearly did not, however, convey any sense of a martial law threat other than as a longer-term potential if current efforts at cooperation broke down and confrontations escalated anew. There was no reflection of the information CIA had obtained in the preceding two months that the leadership was moving closer to martial law. On the contrary, reporting in the *NID* in this time period portrayed a greater prospect of some lasting accommodation—mainly because of Jaruzelski's combination of political strength and apparent commitment—than had been seen at any time in the last year.

It did not take long for the talks to become stalemated. The regime insisted that before any serious substantive talks could begin, Solidarity had to sign up for the ill-defined Front of National Accord. Solidarity, on the other hand, said it would join the Front only after the talks demonstrated that the process would produce some concrete results.

Meanwhile, shortly after the talks began, the Polish Government declared that the small groups of soldiers deployed around the countryside four weeks earlier were being recalled. But on 23 November, the government announced that similar but larger groups—of 10 to 15 soldiers each—were to be deployed in all 49 provincial capitals and other large cities. The total number of troops to be deployed in each place would vary from a few dozen to more than 500, depending on each city's size. The groups would include specialists in medical support, supply, communications, and other technical areas to help people prepare for the hardships of winter. The troops were tasked with insuring the efficient utilization of local resources, including the provision of fuels, electric power, transportation, and health services.

The *NID* initially speculated that Jaruzelski may have decided to withdraw the troops from the countryside because they had not succeeded in removing bottlenecks from the economy, and the regime already had gained as much as could be expected from the show of determination. Upon learning of the new groups to be deployed, intelligence analysts said the move indicated that the regime saw a need to demonstrate its willingness to do the same thing for the urban areas that it had done earlier for country villages. No mention of any potential connection with martial law appears in the declassified *NID* report of this deployment, although the final paragraph is redacted.[31] (The report on the deployment of soldier groups to the countryside a month earlier had included

---

[31] "Poland: New Troop Deployment," decl. *NID* article, 25 November 1981.

an observation that it was a "plausible step toward some kind of martial law," although the same report said there was no indication that this was its purpose.)

At the same time, CIA learned that meetings were taking place between Polish military authorities and high-level military delegations from Moscow. On 18-19 November, a group of nine Soviet and other Warsaw Pact General Staff officers met in Warsaw with the Polish General Staff. This delegation was led by the deputy chief of the Main Operations Directorate of the Soviet General Staff. The principal subject of the meeting, according to Gates, was "documentation" pertaining to the implementation of martial law. Less than a week after that, the Polish press announced that an even higher-ranking Soviet military delegation—led by Marshal Kulikov and his deputy, General Gribkov—was back in Poland for two days of meetings with a Polish delegation headed by Jaruzelski. This press article obviously did not say this visit was related to martial law, but the US Intelligence Community (and most of the Western press corps) knew that Kulikov was the Soviet point man for coordinating martial law, whether it was to be conducted with or without outside intervention.[32]

The Soviet and Polish military officers participating in these meetings knew the US had the details of the martial law plans, including the implementation preparations of the last two months. And *they knew that the US knew they knew.* At the same time they were meeting in Poland, Kuklinski was meeting with CIA officers in the United States. It is plausible, albeit speculative, that this was what had prompted the meetings with Soviet General Staff officers on 17-18 November.

---

[32] Gates describes the first of these delegations in *From the Shadows*, p. 235. He did not address the Kulikov delegation that arrived a few days later. No mention of either of these visits appears in the declassified *NID* articles, but the author can testify that both visits were known and reported. The Kulikov visit was in fact reported by the Polish media in a 25 November 1981 Tribjuna Luda article, "W. Jaruzelski przyjal A. Kulikowa i A. Gribkowa." See Kramer in "Soviet Deliberations During the Polish Crisis," Document 20, Translator's Note No. 261. The visits may have been addressed in the redacted final paragraphs of the *NID* articles for 18 and 25 November. Given the open-source knowledge of the Kulikov visit, redacting the paragraph describing his visit would doubtless have been due to its linkage to other activities going on at the time that were known through more sensitive sources.

Kuklinski Escapes

In an operation that the Ambassador at the time has since described as a "real cloak and dagger affair," Kuklinski and his wife and two sons escaped Poland on 7 November and made it into West Germany the next day. On 11 November, he was flown by military aircraft to the United States.[33]

As soon after his arrival in the United States as the stress of his escape permitted, Kuklinski began exhaustive "debriefing" sessions with his CIA interlocutors. Unfortunately, nothing from the information he provided after his escape from Poland has been declassified. (Indeed, nothing has been made available on the substance of his reporting after his 15 September message described above. And even what was done with the information in that message remains a matter of some debate, as described below.) Kuklinski has, however, related in subsequent public interviews some of the events and discussions he was involved in just prior to his departure from Poland. It would be reasonable to presume that, at a minimum, he gave to CIA at the time of his arrival in the United States the same information that he has since given to the public.

Kuklinski has said that toward the end of September (i.e., sometime following the meeting he mentioned in his message to CIA on 15 September), preparations for martial law accelerated. He said the Operations Directorate of the Polish General Staff, of which he was a deputy chief, was designated as the main center for directing the martial law conditions. For this purpose officers from the internal security services and from key civilian ministries had augmented the Operations Directorate. At the end of September, as Solidarity was engaged in its national congress and media reports were circulating that the party leadership was examining martial law options, work stations were set up with special communications equipment for directing operations under martial law.

After what Kuklinski called a month of hectic activity, a highly placed Polish military officer informed him on 31 October that "The decision [to impose martial law] has been made. At this moment Jaruzelski is coordinating the deadline and plan for the operations with the Allies." Two days later, Kuklinski and a small group of his colleagues were summoned to the office of

---

[33] Kuklinski gave a partial description of his escape in his 1987 interview. See "The Suppression of Solidarity," in Kostrewa, *Between East and West*, pp. 90-95. Ambassador Meehan describes his perspective on Kuklinski's escape in "Reflections on the Polish Crisis, *CWIHP Bulletin 11*, p. 46. The "cloak and dagger" quote is from a personal conversation with Mark Kramer. See "Colonel Kuklinski and the Polish Crisis…," *CWIHP Bulletin 11*, p. 49. According to Kramer (footnote 8 of the same article), Kuklinski gave more details on his departure "itinerary" in an interview in October 1997, parts of which were broadcast on Polish radio a month later.

a deputy chief of the General Staff and told that a "reliable source" had reported that the United States knew about the latest version of the martial law plan. After narrowly eluding a direct "confess or deny" confrontation at this meeting, Kuklinski saw what he believed to be signs that he was under surveillance, and he began preparing for his escape. Years later in, in his first public interview, he said that one of the factors that persuaded him to leave was the clear indication that martial law was going to happen and there was nothing he could do to stop it.[34]

Based on the detailed information Kuklinski had already provided, CIA informed top US national security officials that the Polish regime, at the same time it was pushing its "Front of National Accord," had essentially completed preparations for implementing military suppression. In providing this sensitive information, CIA military analysts pointed out that with Polish forces in this posture, martial law could occur suddenly with little warning (especially since Kuklinski was no longer in Poland). CIA did not address in this report the question of whether this meant a decision had been made, despite what "a highly placed military officer" told Kuklinski. As described below, this information apparently was not sent to policy officials until sometime in the first week of December, and then only to a select few at the most senior level.

The Final Act

On 27 November, shortly after the meetings with Soviet military officials headed by Kulikov ended, the Polish party put out word that during the past three weeks (i.e., the three weeks following the initiation of talks on the "Front of National Accord"), the government had begun surveillance of "opposition groups and started investigations of some 400 crimes against the state." The Western press already had reported signs a few days earlier of a tougher policy on dissident groups when police raided the flat of prominent dissident Jacek Kuron. The official charge against the group was "setting up an organization of a political character." That same weekend, the State Prosecutor warned a group "For Defense of Political Prisoners" meeting in Radom that they were in violation of the law and subject to arrest.[35]

Also on 27 November, Jaruzelski announced at a party Central Committee meeting that he had instructed the government to present a draft anti-strike law to the parliament. The *NID* described the action as Jaruzelski's fulfillment of

---

[34] "Suppression of Solidarity," Kostrewa, *op. cite.*, pp. 90-95.
[35] "Polish Police Break Up Meeting in Dissident's Home," *The New York Times,* 23 November 1981, p. A12; and "Poland: Consideration of Anti-Strike Law," decl. *NID* article, 28 November 1981. The raid on Kuron's flat and the threat levied at the Group for Defense of Political Prisoners is not addressed in any of the declassified reporting.

his pledge at the end of October to seek binding legislation if the parliamentary resolution for a voluntary end to strikes was ignored. The details of the draft strike ban law were not known at the time, but the intelligence report said:

> ...it is likely to be confined to laying the groundwork for prohibiting some strikes and perhaps to giving the parliament the right to limit the duration of all strikes. Such provisions were included in a draft trade union law—agreed to by Solidarity earlier this year—which was never enacted....
>
> A total ban on strikes would be strongly resisted by Solidarity's leadership, would scuttle current union-government talks, and would provoke considerable opposition in parliament.[36]

Other Western observers, according to press reports, were less sanguine about the likely terms of the draft law, pointing out that a major ban on strikes would go to the heart of the Gdansk agreement. In fact, as the terms of the law were revealed in the press a day later, they called for total bans in industries considered "critical" and for "constraints" on strikes in other industries. Who would define which industries were "critical" was not specified. The party publicly demanded that its deputies in parliament put the draft strike-ban law up for an immediate vote, saying the government must have extraordinary powers to curb labor unrest. On 29 November, Jaruzelski proclaimed that "the destructive process has to be stopped or it will lead to a confrontation, to a state of war." These follow-up actions are not addressed in the declassified intelligence materials available.[37]

A few days later the regime employed its most extreme use of force since the Bydgoszcz incident. The cadets at the firefighters' training academy in Warsaw had been on strike since 26 November protesting a government move to place the academy under the sole jurisdiction of the Ministry of the Interior. When the Ministry countered by shutting down the academy, some 300 cadets occupied the building. On 1 December the building was surrounded by police squads equipped with water cannons, and a large crowd gathered to watch the events. A report in the 2 December *NID* said the regime had denied intending to use force. Using force, said the intelligence report, risked setting off a reaction by the crowd of observers, and provoking other strikes and demonstrations.[38]

---

[36] Decl. *NID* article, 28 November 1981, *op. cit.*
[37] "Politburo Tells Poland to Pass Anti-Strike Law;" *The New York Times,* 28 November 1981, p. 1; "Polish Party Urges Special Attention," *The New York Times,* 29 November 1981, p. 1; and "Jaruzelski Warns Poland on Labor Unrest," *The New York Times,* 30 November 1981, p. A13. There are no declassified intelligence reports on Poland for 29 November through 1 December.
[38] "Poland: Tense Confrontation," decl. *NID,* 2 December 1981.

But the regime did indeed use force, with some 1,000 police crashing through the barriers and landing helicopters on the roof. The cadets put up no resistance and were removed without serious injury. The *NID* posited the next day that the regime's motive in resorting to force was to demonstrate to the population as well as to the Warsaw Pact defense and foreign ministers—who were then holding their annual meetings—its resolve to oppose future strikes. The intelligence report also said that conservatives in the regime may have pushed for the use of force in the hope that Solidarity would react with a strike, which could be used as further justification for pushing the parliament to enact the anti-strike legislation. Union leaders were indeed likely to press for some response, according to the intelligence assessment, but Walesa was expected to try to calm the situation.[39]

The following afternoon and evening a long and heated meeting of Solidarity's presidium took place in Radom. At its conclusion, Solidarity issued a statement that listed the violence at the firefighters academy as only one of many unacceptable recent actions by the regime. The statement also attacked the regime's unwillingness to change the system of industrial management and its efforts to push through a law granting the government extraordinary powers. Solidarity threatened a general strike if the parliament adopted the emergency powers law. Other, far more radical steps were raised in Solidarity's meeting, some going so far as to include setting up worker militias and a provisional government.

Walesa temporarily deflected the more radical proposals by insisting that only the full National Commission meeting scheduled to begin on 11 December could commit the union to action. The union leaders then publicized a list of demands to be considered at this meeting—demands which, if implemented, would in effect give Solidarity power-sharing with the government on economic and social matters. In reporting this, the Intelligence Community noted that there was no information to indicate that Polish military units had been placed on alert.[40]

Some of the wilder proposals reaching the floor during Solidarity's meeting in Radom were shortly hung out for public scrutiny. Excerpts from tape recordings that had been made of the meeting began to appear in the government-run media three days later. The Polish media asserted that the tapes disclosed that local union chapters were preparing for physical confrontations with the government and that union leaders were "madmen" with "sick

---

[39] "Poland: Response by Solidarity," decl. *NID*, 3 December 1981.
[40] "Poland: Statement by Solidarity," decl. *NID*, 4 December 1981. The full text of the Solidarity statement was published in the Solidarity New Agency Bulletin, *Agencja Solidarnosc*, No. 58, and a copy is in Raina, *Poland 1981*, p. 455.

ambitions." Among the taped segments that drew the most attention was an exclamation by Walesa that "confrontation was inevitable," and polemics by others regarding a "provisional government." Solidarity did not attempt to deny the comments, but claimed they were taken out of context.[41]

The *NID* described this as "the most coordinated and vitriolic media campaign ever against Solidarity." The analysts said the regime was "probably trying to demonstrate that it was not impotent in the face of union pressure...hopes to encourage greater opposition to the union in local disputes...and probably hopes the campaign will further discredit the union." Additional objectives, according to the intelligence assessment, may have been to split the moderates and militants in the union, and to provide additional justification for the extraordinary powers law being sought from the parliament. The intelligence assessment said the regime's actions would "raise tensions and prevent serious substantive negotiations until after the new year."[42] Such serious substantive negotiations, however, were not to occur.

Solidarity's National Commission opened its meeting in Gdansk on 11 December with a full agenda. It had to design the union's future policy in the face of the government's increasingly tougher line. On the first day, the commission approved a resolution for a 24-hour general strike if the parliament passed the bill granting the government extraordinary powers. The commission also rejected the provision in the draft trade union law then before parliament that would allow 90-day suspensions of the right to strike. The union threatened to shut down national radio and television if the government persisted in its efforts to weed out employees who belonged to Solidarity.

On the evening of 12 December, word arrived in Washington that telephone and telex communications between Poland, Western Europe and the United States had been cut, that the Polish border had been closed, and that many Polish citizens were being arrested. At CIA Headquarters, an alert was sent out to the analysts who had been following the situation, and they convened in the CIA Operations Center. The DCI and his Executive Assistant also came in later, as did the director and deputy director of the office in charge of the operations center.

A debate ensued over how to interpret the events and whether and how to report them to the White House and senior national security officials. Was this another of the localized crackdowns that had been seen in recent days, or the beginning of martial law? Those arguing that it was far more than a local

---

[41] "Warsaw Releases Secret Union Tapes," *The Washington Post*, 8 December 1981, p. A1.
[42] "Poland: Regime's Media Campaign," decl. *NID*, 9 December 1981.

action included analysts who had studied the contents of Kuklinski's reporting of the martial law plans and who were convinced the actions taking place fit those plans. Others were more uncertain, suggesting that what was taking place was indeed a localized action. They did not want to be accused of issuing a false alarm.

Shortly after midnight Eastern Standard Time, one of the military analysts—who knew the martial law plan called for its formal announcement at 6:00 a.m. Warsaw time, the morning after the arrests and the deployment of army and internal security units had begun—left the discussion to check for what he expected to be incoming information. He returned not long afterward with the message that Jaruzelski had just announced over Polish radio that martial law had been declared.

CHAPTER 13
Caught Off Guard

For more than six weeks before Poland's imposition of martial law, the US Government had been notably silent on the subject. This silence was in stark contrast to the klaxons sounded and reprisals threatened on earlier occasions, when the concern was a Soviet invasion or Soviet military intervention in collaboration with Polish leaders.

Jaruzelski has repeatedly said that he interpreted Washington's silence, with no protests to the Polish Government or warnings to Solidarity of imminent martial law, to mean that the US administration endorsed his "internal solution" to head off an "inevitable" Soviet invasion. He has said that when Kuklinski disappeared from Warsaw, he knew the United States had the details of the martial law plans, and of the preparations that had recently been initiated for carrying them out.[1] Since he knew that the *Americans knew* that *he knew*, it would have been logical for him to assume US officials would be aware that the Poles probably were watching for signals of Washington's reaction.

Jaruzelski met with the US Ambassador to Poland, Francis Meehan, about two weeks after Kuklinski's escape (and three weeks before martial law was imposed). The meeting was at the Ambassador's request, just prior to his scheduled return to Washington for consultations. Ambassador Meehan has since suggested that because Jaruzelski already knew by then that the United States had the martial law plans, he could have avoided the meeting had he been concerned about what message or questions the Ambassador would be offering under instruction from Washington. Meehan has speculated that Jaruzelski went through with the meeting as a deliberately misleading effort to present a "business as usual facade."[2]

---

[1] Jaruzelski interview cited in "Polish Officer Was US Window on Soviet War Plans," *The Washington Post*, 27 September 1992, p. A1; also his memoir, *Stan Wojenny Dlaczego*, pp. 356-358 (see Dobbs, *Down With Big Brother*, p. 73), most recently "Jaruzelski: Le Mur est d'abord tombé en Pologne," *Le Figaro*, 7 November 1999, p. 4.

[2] Francis J. Meehan, "Reflections on the Polish Crisis," *CWIHP Bulletin 11*, Winter 1998, p. 46.

An equally plausible motive, however, could have been Jaruzelski's desire to find out what the United States was going to do with this information. He might have assumed that the US Ambassador to Poland had been given the latest—and most authoritative—US intelligence on martial law. Under these circumstances, it would have been naive for Jaruzelski to expect to "sell" a business-as-usual image simply by having the meeting and not raising the subject. He would have had every reason to suspect that a meeting requested by the US Ambassador, about two weeks after Kuklinski presumably had informed Washington that the Polish leadership was close to imposing martial law, was for the purpose of conveying the initial US reaction. Under these circumstances it would have made sense to see if the US Ambassador would raise the subject. The Ambassador has noted that the hour of the meeting was unusual—from 8:30 to 10:00 p.m. After the meeting, Jaruzelski would have had reason to believe the United States intended to do nothing.

Some Western scholars at least partly share the interpretation that the lack of US action reflected Washington's view that martial law was the "lesser evil." Earlier US public statements, condemning Moscow for threatening military force while emphasizing the Poles' right "to solve their problems on their own," had already been described by the press as ambiguous toward a purely internal military crackdown. In the initial stages of martial law, some US officials said Jaruzelski's move might offer a solution to Poland's problems short of a violent crackdown, and a *Washington Post* editorial suggested that Jaruzelski was "Poland's Last Chance." Several US officials have since been quoted saying there was a sense of relief in some US Government quarters after the declaration of martial law. Former Secretary of State Haig has written that at the beginning of Jaruzelski's move, "we recognized...that...for the time being at least, martial law, rather than something worse, had been imposed in Poland."[3]

Haig also has said that he did not want to warn Solidarity and risk stirring up a violent resistance when the United States had no intention of attempting to deliver assistance. Then-Assistant Secretary of State for European Affairs Lawrence Eagleberger has offered much the same reasoning for not threatening Jaruzelski, claiming "We would have figured that martial law would have happened anyway," and then what would the United States have done?

---

[3] One of the stronger presentations of this view, citing several on-the-record statements by individuals who were in the US Government at the time, is in Tina Rosenberg, *The Haunted Land*, pp. 208-210. See also Dobbs, *Down With Big Brother*, p. 73. For an initial US Government interpretation of Jaruzelski's move, see declassified State Department memorandum of 16 December 1981: From A/S EUR Eagleberger to the Secretary, "General Wojciech Jaruzelski," in *Poland 1980-82: Compendium*. The portrayal of Jaruzelski as "Poland's Last Chance" is in *The Washington Post*, 14 December 1981, p. A16. The Haig quote is in *Caveat*, p. 247.

Ambassador Meehan has expressed a similar view.[4] (These concerns had not, however, prevented the United States in earlier situations from warning of potential Soviet invasions and threatening the USSR with reprisals.)

While this outlook almost certainly played a role in shaping US behavior, it is noteworthy that these statements were made after the fact. On 13 November, a month *before* martial law was imposed, Secretary of State Haig sent the President a memorandum calling attention to the fragile situation there, and emphasizing "the importance of Poland's peaceful revolution as a demonstration that Moscow's power could be challenged and confounded." He said that if Polish gains could be consolidated, it would be an historic event for the people of Eastern Europe and for Western values, but he was concerned that the democratic forces in Poland could not prevail without additional US assistance.[5]

On 1 December, the Secretary sent the President another memorandum, saying that in the short interval since his earlier memo:

> ...it had become even clearer that Poland is on the verge of a potentially catastrophic economic crisis...that could demoralize and discredit the democratic forces and *lead to the re-imposition of an inflexible Soviet-style communist dictatorship. ... [O]ur entire tradition and security interests dictate prompt action to avert such an outcome....* We are backing a struggle for national self-determination and political liberalization against a failing communist regime.[6]

(emphasis added)

The Secretary's memorandum said he believed that American assistance could be "implemented in a way that not only minimizes the risk of Soviet intervention or counteraction, but strengthens the already formidable power of Solidarity."

All of which suggests that *if* US policy officials had been persuaded somewhat earlier that there was a good chance of martial law, they might have sought a wider range of options. They might have attempted to prevent martial law from happening. That certainly was the objective conveyed in Haig's

---

[4] The Haig and Eagleburger quotes are in Rosenburg, *The Haunted Land*, p. 210. Ambassador Meehan's observations are in "Reflections on the Polish Crisis," *op. cit.*

[5] Haig, *Caveat*, p. 246. A reference to the concerns he expressed in this memorandum and the need for US assistance appears in a later memorandum, described below, a copy of which is available at the National Security Archive.

[6] Memorandum to the President from Alexander Haig, 1 December 1981, "US Assistance Program for Poland," in *Poland 1980-82: Compendium.*

1 December memo. And deterrence of a Soviet-engineered military suppression certainly had been the aim of US public and diplomatic offensives in late 1980 and in the spring of 1981.

The administration let it be known, however, that it had been surprised and was unprepared for the sudden imposition of martial law. In the first few days after martial law was declared, Secretary of State Haig said publicly several times that it had been a surprise to him, and that Western governments were "caught off guard." He said that while he thought the administration had received "a fair, acceptable level of intelligence in terms of what the Polish armed forces *might* do," the West was nonetheless surprised by the willingness of the Polish armed forces to carry it out, and by its timing. (He later gave a similar description in his memoirs.) He commented that just two days before the crackdown, the National Security Council had authorized $100 million in grain credits to Poland (as proposed in his 1 December memo), but an imminent threat of martial law had never been raised at this meeting. Assistant Secretary of Defense Richard Perle, at that time the Pentagon's lead official on Soviet and Warsaw Pact political-military affairs, also told the press that the US Government "was taken by surprise." The press quoted several other officials—unnamed and speaking on background—to the same effect.[7]

(I can add personal testimony from my presence at intelligence briefings of three principal members of the National Security Council shortly after martial law was declared. Each briefing was held separately as an informal, private session attended only by the principal official and no more than one or two personal staff officers. In each case, the official said he had not had any warning that martial law might be imminent.)

Perle said in his press interview that the failure to anticipate that the crackdown on Solidarity would be carried out by the Polish army rather than the Soviet army resulted from a "collective failure in intelligence gathering and assessment." One "senior State Department official speaking on background" publicly took issue with this statement, claiming in a press interview that the administration had concluded that "drastic Soviet intervention was less likely than a crackdown by the Polish military." (This official did not, however, attempt to argue that the Polish crackdown had been foreseen.) According to

---

[7] Haig's comments are in "US Informs Poland, USSR of 'Serious Concern,'" *The Washington Post*, 14 December 1981, p. A1; and "US Lacks Info, Acts Warily," *The Washington Post*, 15 December 1981, p. A1. Perle's remarks are in "Pentagon Aid Says US Failed to Anticipate Polish Moves," *The Washington Post*, 18 December 1981, p. A41. The views of other officials are described in "Polish Situation Sets Up Complex Choices for US," *The Washington Post*, 15 December 1981, p. A16; "Caught Off Guard," *The Washington Post*, 15 December 1981, p. A23; and "High Officials Make No Secret They Were Caught Off Guard," *The New York Times*, 18 December 1981, p. A17.

press accounts, most US officials willing to comment on the issue said the Reagan administration had been poised to confront a Soviet invasion, but had not developed plans to deal with martial law. The State Department representative on an interagency Poland working group at the time has said that "the prospect of martial law was discussed, but in a way that was completely wrong. The idea underlying all of our scenarios was that martial law would be a gradual escalation."[8]

From what is now known of the information available to CIA at the time, it is clear that there was not a failure in intelligence "gathering." There was a failure in the use—or non-use—of the information that had been gathered. This can be illustrated in the following chronology that *could* have been provided to US policy officials six weeks prior to the imposition of martial law.

This chronology is not a hindsight interpretation of the evidence, but simply a presentation of the information now publicly known to have been available to intelligence officers at the time. Because most of what Kuklinski reported and evidence from other sensitive sources has not been declassified to date, this information must be viewed as the *minimum* that could have been presented.

This chronology—by itself, with no further analytic interpretation—makes its own case for the threat of impending martial law. It would not have "proved" that martial law was certain, but it certainly met the criteria that had prompted earlier US policy efforts at deterrence. If, for example, this summary had been delivered to senior policy officials in early November, it is hard to believe that it would not have generated demands for an immediate, rigorous analytic review of prospects for martial law. As Secretary Haig's memoranda to the President on 13 November and 1 December demonstrate, the State Department already was preparing US policy recommendations for "backing a struggle for national self-determination and political liberalization against a failing communist regime." Indeed, it seems implausible that the preparation of such an evidential chronology would not have motivated the Intelligence Community itself to conduct such a review.

For example, the Polish Politburo discussion of martial law on 15 September had been initially described by CIA analysts as reflecting "apparent" backing by the Polish military that "suggested" a "possible" hardening of attitudes by "some" military officers."[9] The change in PZPR leadership that followed less than a month later was described as the result of "frustration within the

---

[8] *Ibid.* For the "senior State Department official," see "US Calls for Release of Walesa," *The Washington Post*, 19 December 1981, p. A1. Haig's later description is in *Caveat*, p. 242. The quotation from the State Department officer is in Rosenberg, *The Haunted Land*, p. 206.

[9] As was described on p. 153, this was the interpretation given in the *NID*, 24 September 1981.

Chronology September-October 1981: Key Evidence Relating to Martial Law

1. On 8 September Solidarity, during the first session of its National Congress, took what even some sympathetic Western observers have described as a step too far, publicizing a message inviting workers of the other Soviet Bloc countries—including the USSR—to follow Solidarity's example in forming an independent union.

2. On 9 September, the chief of the Polish General Staff met with a small group of military officers charged with preparing martial law plans and informed them that the regime was approaching the implementation of the plans. He reportedly said that proclamations to be delivered when the move was made were being printed in the Soviet Union. He assured the officers the Soviets would provide military backup assistance if needed.

3. Four days later, on Sunday, 13 September, the Polish National Defense Committee, the body of military and political authorities responsible for major decisions on strategic military affairs, held a special meeting to address the implementation of martial law. Jaruzelski serves as both chairman and vice chairman of this committee, in his dual capacity of head of the government (Prime Minister) and head of the military (Minister of Defense). The committee also includes the Minister of Internal Affairs (a military officer appointed by Jaruzelski) and other high level military and civilian officials. Kania attended the meeting, the first time he has done so.

   a. Nearly all participants in the meeting favored going forward with implementation of the martial law plans. Kania reportedly was surprised by the tenor of the meeting. He did not question that such a move was inevitable, according to the reporting, but did argue for first continuing to pursue political means of suppressing Solidarity and then, if these failed, forceful repression could be adopted.

   b. After the meeting, working groups were formed and tasked with refining the martial law implementation measures. The basic plan is for martial law to begin at midnight on a night before a day when industrial plants will be closed (either Saturday or a Friday before a work-free Saturday). Roughly 600 union officials and prominent dissidents are to be arrested in Warsaw alone; the arrests are to be carried out by the Internal Security Forces while army units are deployed to seal off major cities.

4. On 15 September, the party Politburo met to discuss a martial law plan submitted by the military authorities. (According to press reports, the meeting went on well into the night and the Politburo "seriously considered the plan.")

    a. A majority of the Politburo reportedly rejected the plan, but the day after this meeting the Politburo issued its strongest public condemnation yet of Solidarity and the "threat" posed by the union.

    b. On 17 September and again on Sunday, 20 September, the government Council of Ministers, also chaired by Jaruzelski, held what were described in official Polish Government statements as "emergency meetings" to address "urgent matters" and assess "the readiness of organs of state administration."

5. On 7 October, at the end of its National Congress, Solidarity published its program for changing economic and political procedures in Poland. It called for free elections at all government levels from towns and provinces up to and including parliament; establishment of a tribunal to punish those responsible for violent acts against strikers and protesters as far back as the 1956 workers suppression; guarantees of public control over radio and television, and the right of private citizens' groups to own and control the content of publishing agencies.

6. On 16 October, the PZPR Central Committee held a special plenum, which coincided with the announcement that the term of service for military conscripts due to be discharged at the end of the month (about 40,000 troops) had been extended until at least mid-December. The call up of new conscripts, however, would proceed on schedule.

7. On 18 October, this party Central Committee meeting announced that Kania had resigned as head of the party and had been replaced by Jaruzelski, who now held all the major power positions. There were reports that he had been persuaded by his own Defense and Internal Security officers, as well as the Soviets, that martial law should be imposed.

8. That same day, the Central Committee issued a resolution demanding that parliament pass an anti-strike law, and that the government "invoke its constitutional prerogatives to guarantee peace in the country," an expression all observers agreed referred to authority to employ force.

9. On 20 October, in what on-scene observers have described as the worst outbreak of violence in Solidarity's 14-month existence, police used force and tear gas to disperse a crowd protesting arrests of three Solidarity activists who were distributing anti-Soviet leaflets. The next day (21 October) three more Solidarity members were arrested, also on the charge of "anti-Soviet propaganda," and the government issued a ban on public gatherings in that province.

10. These actions took place on the eve of a Solidarity meeting that already had been scheduled—and publicly announced—to decide on whether to go ahead with a threatened strike to protest the government's latest price increases. Solidarity went ahead with its meeting the next day, and on 23 October announced that a one-hour national protest strike would take place on 28 October.

11. One hour after Solidarity's announcement, the government announced that some 25,000 soldiers would be deployed in small groups in villages around the country to help in "establishing law and order," suppressing street demonstrations, assisting in food distribution, and ensuring transportation lines were kept open. The soldier groups were empowered "to counteract problems on the spot."

12. On 28 October, Solidarity carried out its strike; two days later, Jaruzelski asked the parliament to pass a resolution calling for an end to strikes and submitted a draft law granting the government authority to take "extraordinary means of action." The parliament passed the resolution calling for strikes to cease, and declared that if this appeal was ignored parliament would then address the proposed law granting the government extraordinary powers.

party over its ability to contain Solidarity." The "acceptance" of Kania's "resignation," according to the analysts, indicated that "party moderates" had become persuaded that he had to be "sacrificed because he had become a symbol of inaction and thus an impediment to his own pragmatic policies." Jaruzelski's selection as the new party head "seems intended to exploit popular support for the military...and possibly to place the party in position to manage any 'state of emergency' more easily," according to the description given at the time by CIA analysts. The *NID* did say that the leadership change foreshadowed "a tougher policy toward Solidarity that...increases the chances of confrontation," but given the number of "confrontations" that had already taken place over the past year, this hardly could be read as a forecast of martial law.

Viewing these events as part of an integrated package of evidence, however, makes it difficult to avoid a more ominous prima facie interpretation. The Politburo discussion on 15 September was only one of four meetings on martial law held by top Polish leaders over an eight-day span immediately following Solidarity's first national congress session. Two of the meetings were held on consecutive Sundays, and three were chaired by Jaruzelski. Kuklinski's account of the National Defense Committee discussion of martial law plans two days before they were taken up by the Politburo certainly conveys more than just "apparent" backing by "some" military officers. He also disclosed that detailed preparations for carrying out the plans were going on at the same time the Politburo meeting was taking place.

An uncomplicated interpretation of this information would have been that, although Polish leaders still were divided on the question of martial law, there was at minimum a strong contingent pushing for implementing it, and preparations were moving ahead. And the circumstantial evidence as well as Kuklinski's description of the National Defense Council meeting indicated that Kania was one of those resisting, while Jaruzelski appeared to be at least leaning towards it. Proceeding from this premise, it would have been difficult to avoid the obvious implication that Kania's removal one month later was due to his resistance to using force, and that Jaruzelski was named successor specifically because of his willingness to do so. The only declassified intelligence document to examine this reasoning seems to have been the DIA appraisal of 4 November 1981, which reached the same conclusion.[10]

Even if this had been only one alternative interpretation of the developments, it also would be one premise for examining the meaning of the events that accompanied the leadership change. For example, on the opening day of the party plenum at which the leadership change would take place, the Ministry of Defense announced that conscripts due to be discharged at the end of the month would be retained on active duty until at least Christmas. CIA analysts posited that this was probably a step by the regime to "show its resolve to act," and said it also indicated the regime's desire to be prepared "in the event martial law became necessary." Extending conscripts' service was on the list of warning signs for martial law, and now it had taken place two days before a leadership change that also could be read as a move toward martial law. How many warning lights are enough?

The *NID* said the violent police actions taken just two days after the party leadership changeover may have been to pressure Solidarity to control anti-Soviet agitators, and noted that after a few days the regime eased off. What was not pointed out was that the party leadership change had been accompanied by a resolution that called for a suspension of the right to strike and which made a thinly veiled call for the government to use force "if necessary." No examination was given in the *NID* of the fact that the police action was launched on the eve of Solidarity's meeting to decide on a strike, or of the validity of Solidarity's charge that the violent assault was a deliberate provocation to ensure the strike took place just as the regime was pressing parliament to ban strikes. And two days after Solidarity carried out the strike, Jaruzelski, as the head of government, was standing before parliament pro-

---

[10] See above, p. 160.

moting the ban on strikes called for in the resolution issued by the party of which Jaruzelski was chief. The parliament did, in fact, pass a resolution calling for an end to strikes.

A broader consideration of the evidence also might have made analysts less sanguine about Jaruzelski's promotion of "dialogue" during November. Viewing this action against the bigger picture would have brought out the contradictions in the two modes of behavior seen since mid-October. An attempt to reconcile these might have produced speculation that Jaruzelski's support for dialogue was really an effort to show that he was more reasonable than a militant Solidarity. The US Embassy in Warsaw had said such a move would be necessary for martial law to succeed, and CIA analysts also had said that Jaruzelski probably realized the importance of creating the right political atmosphere for imposing martial law.[11]

Perhaps if intelligence analysts had been forced to work through a comprehensive layout of the evidence and its potential meanings early enough, they might have been more inclined to sound louder warnings as events began to blossom in December. And perhaps, if policy officials had received such a presentation earlier, the later warnings would have been better heeded.

The above is not intended to support arguments about who was right and who was wrong, or who was smart and who was not. Rather, it is meant to demonstrate that the fundamental fault was in the professional practice—the failure to produce a comprehensive presentation of the evidence and demonstrate the origin of analytic conclusions derived from this evidence. This is not just a matter of providing intelligence products to policy officials. The first beneficiaries of this process of "externalizing"[12] evidence in this way—setting it down on paper—are the analysts themselves. One of the purposes of such practices is to highlight the tough questions that too often get passed over in day-to-day reporting, and to develop alternative explanations that have not been given prominence. The first task in putting together a puzzle is laying out all the pieces on the table. In the case of intelligence, pieces will always be missing, but that makes it even more important to pore over what is available. Looking at one piece alongside others helps to bring questions to the fore that might otherwise slip by.

---

[11] See pp. 148 and 161.
[12] Regarding the origins and use of the term "externalizing" as an analytic tool, see Heuer, *Psychology of Intelligence Analysis*, p. 27, and Chapter 7.

No such integrated analysis was produced on the Polish situation in the months before martial law. There was no established procedure at the time requiring such overview summaries to be prepared. Creation of such products depended on someone taking the initiative, and in this case no one did. Why this was not done is likely to remain a matter of some disagreement.

A commonly held perception is that overprotecting Kuklinski's information caused it to be so restricted that it was "rendered useless."[13] It certainly is true that there were rigorous controls on access to this reporting and how it could be characterized, including tight restrictions on who could receive these sensitive products. Even tighter controls were placed on distributing his reports after he sent word in September that he was in jeopardy, which was certainly justifiable.

This did not, however, prevent analysts covering Poland from producing the kind of integrated assessment described above. At minimum, an assessment integrating what was known from Kuklinski with all the other evidence could have been produced for the DCI and the few senior officials who already were cleared for Kuklinski's reporting. Key reporting from Kuklinski had periodically been written up and provided to a select group of senior officials. The analysts who wrote these reports were mainly the same ones who wrote the *NID* reports on Poland. The details of the martial law preparations provided by Kuklinski were regularly examined and distributed—within restricted dissemination channels—by CIA's military analysts, and these reports could have been integrated with the evidence on political developments. Instead, they were disseminated separately, even to the select group of readers, and tended to be treated as a separate matter of military contingency measures.[14]

Moreover, nothing prevented analysts from drawing on the Kuklinski reporting to shape the interpretations they presented in other products, including the *NID*, for mid-level policy officials not specifically cleared for Kuklinski's information. As noted earlier, a Special Analysis in the 18 September *NID* assessing the situation in the aftermath of Solidarity's first national congress session, said that "The Polish regime has drawn up a detailed plan of military measures, including curfews, arrests, shows of force, total military control of the country, and arrest of Solidarity leaders. The Pol-

---

[13] Rosenberg, *The Haunted Land*, pp. 205-207; Dobbs, *Down With Big Brother*, p. 73. Prominent scholars described the same views to this author at a seminar held by the Davis Center for Russian Studies at Harvard University in winter 1997.
[14] Kuklinski's reporting is not explicitly identified in any of the declassified intelligence reports written prior to the imposition of martial law, but examples of the general tendency to portray actions that clearly raised readiness for martial law as purely contingency steps can be seen in the declassified *NID* reports described above, p. 153 (footnote 25), p. 161 (footnote 9), and p. 165 (footnote 16).

ish leadership appears to be readying itself for the possible employment of at least some of these measures in the near future." This cleared statement, with no references to sources and methods, could have been explicitly included in the *NID* report a week later on the Politburo discussion of martial law. Had it been included, some readers might have questioned why the interpretation of the Politburo meeting was so sanguine.

By mid-October, Kuklinski had provided information that Jaruzelski favored going ahead with martial law, as soon as the political conditions could be set. Again, while this was passed to senior policy officials, it appears to have had no effect on descriptions of the potential implications of Jaruzelski's becoming head of the party, nor on the *NID* interpretations of the potential motives of his "Front of National Salvation."

Critics of CIA's performance have made much of the fact that Kuklinski was in the United States nearly a month before martial law was implemented. The natural question is, since at this point his physical jeopardy had been relieved, and the Poles and Soviets knew the United States had the details of martial law preparations, why was no effort made to publicly expose the Polish scheme?[15] This is a legitimate question.

At a minimum, the operational handlers of Kuklinski's escape are vulnerable to criticism for failing to spotlight the potential implications of the escape itself within the larger political context. Kuklinski's flight from Poland did not take place in a vacuum. Kuklinski had already warned CIA two months earlier that the Polish intelligence service knew the United States had knowledge of the martial law plans, including the code name. There can have been no question that by the time Kuklinski arrived in the United States the Polish regime would have known he was gone, and concluded that he was the source of US knowledge about martial law.

The Poles would have been uncertain about the extent of the information on martial law that Kuklinski had provided the United States, but they would have presumed that after arriving in the United States, he would have provided whatever additional details he had not reported already. No one seems to have called attention to the obvious fact that this could affect how US actions were interpreted in the coming weeks, and thus added urgency to getting the martial law information to policy officials as quickly as possible.

This does not, however, explain the failure to produce an integrated assessment of the kind outlined in the chronology above. All of that information was available to intelligence analysts before Kuklinski left Poland. Once he was in the United States, the absence of any alarm or note of urgency—from intelli-

---

[15] *Op. cit.*, footnote 120.

gence analysts, operations officers, or policymakers—caused his debriefing to be rank-ordered according to standing collection requirements, which meant strategic military information came first. Within the standing military priorities, martial law ranked lower than nuclear plans and posture. The same lack of warning that allowed policy officials to be caught off guard also impeded CIA's use of its own asset.

A summary of the information Kuklinski could provide on martial law did go in special, restricted channels to senior policy officials. They were told that preparations for a military crackdown were for all practical purposes complete, and that given this level of preparation, the Intelligence Community probably would not be able to provide much tactical warning if the regime ordered the plans to be carried out. But all this still was treated as a description of "military contingency moves," and even this special report was not disseminated until three weeks after Kuklinski arrived in the United States—about a week before martial law was launched—at about the same time the Polish regime was publicizing the tapes of Solidarity's meeting at Radom.[16]

Some analysts have argued that US senior policymakers were indeed warned about martial law. They say that senior policymakers were provided with sensitive information from Kuklinski indicating that by mid-October, Jaruzelski, the military hierarchy, and an unknown number of civilian authorities had concluded that martial law should proceed. Senior US officials also had been told the plans and preparations were essentially in place and the crackdown could thus occur with little tactical warning. This defensive argument contradicts the charge that the reason CIA analysts did not provide a more forceful warning was that they were prevented from using Kuklinski's information.

This outlook does, however, point to what appears to have been a central factor in the failure to produce an integrated, comprehensive assessment. It might be called the "current intelligence trap." Analysts report each piece of incoming intelligence, sometimes with time gaps. For the analyst working full time on a particular issue, the day-to-day intelligence reported, even though sometimes with notable time gaps, is placed in a single mental "file," at the top of the priority list. The policy official, on the other hand, and most especially the most senior officials, receive a steady, daily stream of reports involving a wide range of complex issues, many requiring immediate action. This flood of information and maze of issues make it difficult to piece together a path of incident reports spread over time.

---

[16] This is based on the author's knowledge.

What analysts think is obvious in current intelligence reporting often is not so to the recipients. The analysts are at risk of thinking they have conveyed the whole message, while to readers, the reporting seems incremental. Several analysts who covered the Polish crisis have observed that, looking back, the ongoing frequent reporting on every aspect of Polish politics for a year and a half, whether threatening or encouraging, tended to have this effect.

The purpose of intelligence analysis is not just reporting, nor is it crystal ball-gazing and pontificating about the future. It is to assemble the evidence, examine its potential meanings, and convey it to policy makers. Every study of CIA's formation emphasizes this as its *raison d'être*. This mission was set down in a presidential directive while debates still were going on about how to organize collection and well before the covert action mission was inaugurated.[17] As described above, how this function is carried out is critical not only to communicating the intelligence but to the quality of the analysis itself. In this case, for example, for analysts to insist that Kuklinski's basic message— that the martial law plan was set and the leadership was prepared to carry it out—was sufficiently communicated makes the absence of a comprehensive integrated assessment all the more glaring. The first customer for such a product is the DCI himself, for whom there are no constraints on reporting details about sensitive sources and methods.

In the end, the judgment in the Intelligence Community and the administration that Polish leaders would not impose martial law on their own people prevented the writing of an intelligence product that might have made a difference in US policy deliberations. Not surprisingly, recollections from almost 20 years ago may be fuzzy, but one can read the *NID* reporting and draw one's own conclusion. The debate underway in the CIA Operations Center on the night martial law began, illustrates the extent to which this underlying judgment was still a factor late in the game. There can always be found a sentence here or a paragraph there that suggests preparations for use of force, but even these are offered in "also may/possible/suggests" formulations. Without the benefit of hindsight, there is nothing in the daily intelligence reporting to convey that a sudden crackdown might occur.

It also should be pointed out that this was not a matter of being smart or of expertise. The analysts were smart, and they were experts. Their perspective on the likelihood of the Poles' use of force was the same as that of experts in the policy community (as the Embassy cable vividly illustrated). Ambassador Meehan said that on the same day he met with Jaruzelski, Polish Archbishop

---

[17] Anyone questioning this statement should review the hundreds of archival documents offered in *Foreign Relations of the United States: Emergence of the Intelligence Establishment 1945-1950*, (Washington, DC: Department of State, US Government Printing Office, 1996).

Glemp told him that there was "a good chance of martial law." Meehan said he reported this to Washington, but "without giving it particular weight."[18] Records from Polish and Soviet archives show that their perspectives were shared in varying degrees by participants in Warsaw and Moscow. The analytic pitfalls discussed here have been routinely encountered in other fields of analysis.

Had a requirement been in place to lay out all available evidence in the type of chronology outlined earlier, an analytical breakthrough probably would have emerged that cast events in a different light. If the CIA had required such an analytical review, based on the seriousness of the circumstances, there is little question that a warning would have been sounded. Absent such rules of professional practice, the human failings of mindset, bureaucratic turf-guarding, inadequate communication, and simple distraction were free to wreak their damage. No one emerges blameless.

---

[18] Meehan, "Reflections on the Polish Crisis...," *CWIHP Bulletin 11*, p. 45.

Chapter 14
Would It Have Made a Difference?

Jaruzelski's claim that he imposed martial law as a lesser evil to preempt an inevitable Soviet military intervention has enjoyed fairly widespread acceptance, as illustrated by the comments of US policy officials at the time, and by much of the literature since.[1] This interpretation is a logical outgrowth of the strongly held conviction of both US intelligence analysts and policy officials, before martial law was imposed, that the Poles would not impose martial law (unless forced by the Soviets.) Indeed, the many statements and writings from Western officials and analysts were given public resonance well before Jaruzelski's assertion. Up until the time of the Soviet breakup in late 1991, Jaruzelski staunchly denied that the USSR intended to invade Poland. His public offerings of the "lesser evil" argument have been since then. This may have reflected his continuing deference to the Soviets,[2] but it is also worth noting that his change in position occurred at a time when it was clearly in his interest to do so.

While the evidence leaves no doubt that the Soviets had worked out detailed plans for deploying military forces into Poland in a crackdown on Solidarity, all the information available so far shows that the planned military intervention—with Polish knowledge—was to be a collaborative operation with the Polish regime. It called for forces from the USSR and other Warsaw Pact states to enter Poland under a joint exercise cover that was to have been supported by the Polish regime. Once in Poland, these forces were to provide back up for martial law that would be imposed mainly by Polish military and security forces. Soviet and other "fraternal" Warsaw Pact forces were to intimidate resistance, and if necessary to substitute for Polish army forces whose willingness to impose force on their own populace was suspect.

---

[1] In addition to the comments of US officials cited above, pp. 180-181, Garton Ash, *The Polish Revolution*, pp. 287ff, discusses the extent to which this had gained "surprisingly wide acceptance in Western foreign policy establishments." Rosenberg, *The Haunted Land*, p. 208, also refers to it as the common view.
[2] See, for example, Kramer, "New Evidence on the Polish Crisis 1980-81," *CWIHP Bulletin 11*, Note No. 3.

This was the plan prescribed in the December 1980 "maneuvers" scenario that was subsequently postponed. It was also the plan being organized under the cover of the *Soyuz '81* exercise in spring 1981, and has been described in documents and statements by former Soviet and Warsaw Pact military officers in recent years. It is consistent with the size of the forces set out in the Suslov Commission directive at the beginning of the crisis in August 1980.

The evidence also strongly suggests that through mid-1981 the Soviets were prepared to carry out this plan, and probably were expecting to do so in spring 1981 under the cover of the *Soyuz '81* joint Warsaw Pact exercise taking place on Polish territory. They were prevented from doing so then by the adamant opposition of Kania and Jaruzelski—opposition that left Moscow with the alternative of going ahead with a unilateral invasion or accepting at least a temporary postponement while continuing to push the Poles toward martial law. On that occasion, the Soviets opted for the latter course.

US intelligence on Soviet military force postures shows that—invasion warnings notwithstanding—Moscow never mobilized and prepared forces commensurate with an invasion to be carried out against potential armed resistance. Experts can challenge CIA's estimate that 30 or more divisions would have been prepared for such an operation, but there should have been more than just three to four Soviet divisions mobilized in the western USSR. Yet even during the critical periods of December 1980 and April 1981 when US intelligence warned of a possible invasion, no larger numbers of Soviet forces were observed mobilizing. Contrary to some allegations made since then, no preparations for Soviet military intervention—even the relatively small size called for in the collaborative scenario—took place in the weeks prior to martial law. Indeed, the absence of preparations for a back up Soviet intervention force in the weeks before martial law was one of the reasons the United States remained complacent.

Moscow sought to utilize the specter of an invasion for political leverage. Even so, most of the evidence shows this was aimed more at the Polish opposition and at Western perceptions than at the Polish leaders who were being pressed to carry out the martial crackdown. One document from the Soviet archives, for example, points out that the reason Solidarity had not yet exploited the weakness of the Polish regime to "take de facto power into its own hands" was "primarily because of its fear that Soviet troops would be introduced." This document was produced by the Suslov commission on 16 April 1981, just after Moscow failed to get Jaruzelski and Kania to exploit the *Soyuz '81* exercises and impose a military crackdown. In recommending future measures, the Suslov commission recommended "as a deterrent to counterrevolution, maximally exploit the fears of *internal reactionaries and international imperialism* that the Soviet Union might send in its troops."[3] (emphasis added)

There is ample evidence that Polish leaders were aware of Soviet reluctance to carry out a full-fledged military invasion, and that they were counting on being able to coerce the Poles into imposing a martial crackdown. Jaruzelski participated in planning as far back as December 1980, and the Polish General Staff was fully involved in the spring 1981 exercise scenario, which called for "fraternal forces" to be inserted into Poland under the cover of a joint exercise. The browbeating sessions with Soviet leaders usually involved threats of retaliation against irresolute Polish leaders—and implied efforts at their replacement—rather than threats of invasion. According to East German records, Soviet Marshal Kulikov explicitly emphasized to Jaruzelski in April 1981 that Moscow did not want to intervene unilaterally, and insisted that the Poles had to make the first effort; then Soviets could portray their actions as assistance. As described above, Jaruzelski's face-down of Soviet pressure to implement martial law in April 1981 indicated that he understood the leverage he derived from confronting the Soviets with the alternative of having to conduct an invasion on their own.

There also is increasing evidence that, although Polish leaders clearly dreaded the potential violence and repercussions of Soviet military intervention, they still were counting on being able to call on Soviet backup forces as a last resort if their own efforts went awry. An archival document on martial law plans dated 25 November 1981, released in 1997 by the Polish Interior Ministry, posits the worst case as widespread violence, and concludes with the statement "The assistance of Warsaw Pact forces is not ruled out."[4] Jaruzelski has sought to dismiss the relevance of this document on the grounds that it was a "draft" from a file containing "preliminary materials" and was not signed[5] (which is probably why it survived in the records).

---

[3] "Extract from CPSU CC Protocol No. 7, 23 April 1981," with attached Politburo [Suslov] Commission report "On the Development of the Situation in Poland and Certain Steps on Our Part," *Poland 1980-82: Compendium*.... A subsequent KGB document said the threat of military intervention by Warsaw Pact members must be "a constant factor in the minds of *all Polish political forces*." It is not clear whether this was the KGB's description of the same Suslov Commission recommendation described above or a later version by the Commission. See Christopher Andrew and Vasili Mitrokhin, *The Sword and the Shield: The Mitrokhin Archive and the Secret History of the KGB* (New York: Basic Books/Perseus Group, 1999), p. 524.

[4] Pawel Machewicz, "The Assistance of Warsaw Pact Forces is Not Ruled Out," *CWIHP Bulletin 11*, pp. 40-42.

[5] Wojciech Jaruzelski, "Commentary," *CWIHP Bulletin 11*, pp. 32-39.

But CIA had received reports in September 1981, as the momentum for martial law increased, that Polish General Staff officers had pressed General Swicki on whether Poland could get help from the Soviets if necessary. Swicki reportedly assured them it would be there. Other reports received by CIA described the martial law plans presented by the General Staff to the Polish political leaders as not excluding the need to request assistance from the USSR and other Warsaw Pact members. These reports said for this reason the chief of the Polish General Staff specifically called for martial law plans to be coordinated with the Soviets and other potential Warsaw Pact participants.[6]

A sizable body of evidence indicates that on the eve of martial law, Polish leaders were actually seeking explicit assurances that they could count on military assistance from Moscow if necessary. This information comes mainly from former Soviet officials and documents, who assert that these Polish requests for assistance were rebuffed, and the Poles were told not to expect such aid. The sources include a September 1992 article by Soviet General Anatoli Gribkov, who at the time of the Polish crisis was deputy to Warsaw Pact commander in chief Marshal Kulikov. Subsequent statements by Mikhail Gorbachev, at the time a member of the Soviet Politburo, independently corroborate much of Gribkov's account, and similar descriptions have come from the former chief KGB officer in Warsaw. Records of Soviet Politburo meetings also refer to the Poles' expectations of Soviet military assistance. The notebook of Marshal Kulikov's personal adjutant shows that Soviet military backup for the martial law measures was a major issue in several exchanges between Polish and Soviet leaders and military officers shortly before martial law was launched.[7]

Jaruzelski has of course vehemently denied this charge, and has sought to rebut each piece of evidence cited in support of it.[8] He faces a tough sell, because there are many sources and their information is consistent. Adding to his burden is new evidence made public in late 1999, after Jaruzelski had published his latest rebuttal. Copies of KGB documents smuggled out of Russia by a former KGB archivist, Vasili Mitrokhin, include a report from the KGB station in Warsaw describing Jaruzelski's meeting with Marshal Kulikov on 8 December. According to this report, Jaruzelski exhibited concern over the prospects that the martial law plan would succeed, and said it might be necessary to appeal for assistance from the USSR and other Warsaw Pact forces, although he asked that East German forces not be included. Kulikov

---

[6] Gates, *From the Shadows*, p. 234. Gates does not specify whether this was from Kuklinski.

[7] Mark Kramer, "Jaruzelski, the Soviet Union, and the Imposition of Martial Law in Poland: New Light on the Mystery of December 1981," *CWIHP Bulletin 11*, pp. 5-31.

[8] Jaruzelski, "Commentary," *op. cit.*

responded that "I can assure you that you have no need for concern on that score. The question of assisting you in the event that your own resources become exhausted is being addressed at the General Staff level."[9]

This KGB report fits with, and adds some insight to, the record of a Soviet Politburo meeting held on 10 December. The record of this meeting has been available for several years, and has been a controversial part of the evidence used to support allegations that Jaruzelski in fact sought guarantees of Soviet military backing if his own forces failed. According to this record, the CPSU Secretary for Inter-Party Relations in the Warsaw Pact (K. V. Rusakov), referring to meetings that took place in Poland "the day before yesterday," claimed Jaruzelski had said that "if the Polish forces are unable to cope with the resistance put up by Solidarity, the Polish comrades hope to receive assistance from the other countries, up to and including the introduction of armed forces on the territory of Poland." Rusakov said that in expressing this hope, Jaruzelski has been "citing remarks by Comrade Kulikov, who supposedly said that the USSR and other socialist countries would indeed give assistance to Poland with their armed forces." [10]

Others joined Rusakov at this meeting—Andropov and Ustinov in particular—in what some have interpreted as statements tailored for the record asserting that Kulikov did not say this, and that the USSR had no intention of inserting forces into Poland.[11] At one point, however, Andropov commented that "If Comrade Kulikov actually did speak about the introduction of troops, then I believe he did this incorrectly." This has been interpreted as suggesting that Kulikov indeed had made some statement about willingness to commit military assistance, and that Andropov was aware of it and thus felt compelled to record that the Politburo had not authorized any such statement.[12] The KGB description of the Jaruzelski-Kulikov discussion on 8 December supports this interpretation. As KGB head, Andropov would have received this report, and its description of Kulikov's statement may well have been more explicit than what was communicated through other channels.

---

[9] Andrew and Mitrokhin, *The Sword and the Shield*, pp. 529-530.
[10] Kramer, Soviet Deliberations on the Polish Crisis...," Document 21. An earlier translation by Kramer appearing in *CWIHP Bulletin 5*, Spring 1995, used the term "speech by" rather than "remarks by" Kulikov.
[11] See, for example, Ambassador Meehan's comments in "Reflections on the Polish Crisis," *CWIHP Bulletin 11*, p. 44.
[12] See, for example, Kramer, *Soviet Deliberations on the Polish Crisis*, Translator's Note No. 282.

This Politburo meeting also was not the first time this issue was recorded. The record of a meeting on 29 October also includes a statement by Andropov that "the Polish leaders are talking about military assistance from the fraternal countries. However, we need to adhere firmly to our line—that our troops will not be sent to Poland."[13]

Although the new evidence reinforces the case that Jaruzelski was indeed looking for a Soviet guarantee of a military back up, it also underscores the phoniness of Soviet protestations that the Poles had no reason to expect such support. All their declarations for the record at official meetings in December 1981 cannot erase their record throughout most of the previous 12 to 15 months.

None of this rules out the possibility that, ultimately, faced with a liberalization in Poland and—at a minimum—uncertainty regarding Poland's place in the Warsaw Pact military alliance, the Soviets might have resorted to an invasion. But it does indicate that at the time the Poles instituted martial law, the prospect of a Soviet invasion was speculative, rather than based on evidence. Jaruzelski himself, in his latest public rendition of his defense, said that "The Russians truly did not want to undertake an intervention, but the circumstances would have made its imposition inevitable."[14]

It is plausible and even likely that Soviet military planners did at least examine the requirements and options for a unilateral military intervention, if for no other reason than to be able to answer questions from the political leadership. As has also been pointed out, the Soviets had the military might to overcome Polish resistance. Moscow in the end could have won such a war.[15]

But whether Moscow, in late 1981 and early 1982, was willing to pay the price of such a war is uncertain at best. Poland was a bigger military challenge than Hungary in 1956 or Czechoslovakia in 1968. The USSR already was suffering significant economic strains, and Moscow's capacity in the 1980s to bear the political and economic costs of the Western—not just US—reaction to an invasion was far less than in the earlier Cold War years. Some Western economic penalties already had been imposed in reaction to the invasion of Afghanistan, and the conflict there was escalating, as was its cost. The Soviets could ill afford to take on the new expenses that would come with a military occupation of Poland, the probable imposition of stringent Western economic

---

[13] Kramer, "Soviet Deliberations on the Polish Crisis...," Document 20.
[14] "L'état de siège était un moindre mal. ...Les Russes ne souhaitaient pas vraiment si livrement une intervention, mais les circonstances pouvaient la rendre inevitable," *Le Figaro*, 7 November 1999, p. 4, "Jaruzelski: Le Mur est d'abord tombé en Pologne."
[15] See, for example, Garton Ash, *The Polish Revolution*, p. 296.

penalties, and the political isolation that occurred after Afghanistan, as well as the burden of replacing at least some Western economic support to Poland itself.

The Soviets also had every reason to believe, based on their experience in December 1980 and April 1981, that if an invasion force were to be readied near Poland, the US would ensure the whole world heard about it well before the assault could be launched. This would add uncertainties to the military calculus for Soviet planners, adding the prospect of even higher costs. This of course was precisely the purpose of the public and diplomatic offensive the Carter administration launched, albeit relatively late in the game, in December 1980. Nothing in that effort had hinted at some kind of military aid or assistance. No one would have assumed that such a public and diplomatic offensive would, by itself, be a decisive deterrent. But for Moscow, the prospect of carrying out its planned invasion of a forewarned state under a public spotlight and widespread censure, would be a far different matter than the fait accompli in Czechoslovakia in 1968. In a close call, this added dimension faced by the Soviets could tip the balance—if it came early enough, before too many irreversible decisions had been made.

Much the same can be said about the Polish martial law action. The evidence is fairly conclusive that Jaruzelski and other players in Poland were greatly concerned that events could spiral out of control. Jaruzelski's effort to rationalize his action may appear duplicitous, but his concern for the consequences of widespread violence, and his repugnance at the thought of having to draw on Soviet military participation, seem genuine.

The main reason a crackdown was not attempted earlier clearly was that Kania and Jaruzelski believed then that an attempt to do so would result in widespread resistance, quite likely accompanied by rebellion in parts of the military and security forces, and a complete breakdown of control. Apparently, both Kania and Jaruzelski viewed the worst of all outcomes as one in which this occurred *and* resulted in the defeat of the military crackdown. Thus they thought martial law was so risky that they feared having to call for assistance. They were concerned that the attempt to institute a forceful suppression could bring about the very thing they were seeking to avoid.

Kania's perspective is contained in a report the Hungarian Ambassador in Poland dispatched to his leaders describing a meeting he had with the Polish First Secretary on 18 September 1981. In this discussion, Kania informed the Hungarian Ambassador of the earlier National Defense Committee deliberations on martial law (which the United States already had learned about from

Kuklinski) and by the party Politburo and various other party and government organs. Comparing the situation in Poland to that of Hungary in 1956, Kania said that if martial law plan were imposed "today" it would provoke:

> ...a wide-spread national strike and it would certainly bring the masses out on the streets too. In that case force would have to be used not against hostile elements but against the masses.... Polish communists have assessed their forces. For such action their resources would be insufficient and thus the support of allied forces would be necessary. The consequences of this would, however, set back the development of socialism by decades.[16]

In his discussion with the Hungarian Ambassador, Kania presented this as an argument for delaying martial law until the regime had more time to "win over the masses." The KGB reporting from Warsaw, however, concluded that Kania had no intention of ever being forced to call on outside military intervention, and that he was therefore unwilling and unable to carry out "the necessary means." This also was the KGB view of Jaruzelski through the summer of 1981. At one time, the KGB recommended that Moscow engineer the replacement of both, initially aiming at the party congress in July as the opportunity. The Soviet political leadership agreed that Kania had to be ousted, but concluded that Jaruzelski was the only Polish leader who possessed the authority to carry out martial law.[17] The initial effort to replace Kania with one of the party hardliners at the July party congress failed, mainly because of Jaruzelski.

In August and September 1981, KGB assessments concluded—as did at least some US intelligence assessments—that Jaruzelski's attitude was hardening. By September, the KGB station in Warsaw reported that it was convinced Jaruzelski was ready to institute "decisive measures." The KGB reporting shows a significant Soviet role in Kania's replacement by Jaruzelski at the mid-October party plenum. Whether the replacement was due to Soviet pressure or was mostly an independent action by the Poles can be debated, but both sides apparently agreed on what to do.

The divergence in views between Jaruzelski and Kania at this point was not over whether martial law imposition carried a great risk of exploding. But Jaruzelski had become convinced that an attempt was necessary, and made it known he was prepared to do it. His reasoning was complex, and even the Soviets continued to have some reservations about his reasoning and his com-

---

[16] "Report to the Politburo" from Hungarian Ambassador Jozsef Garamvolgyi, 18 September 1981, *Poland 1980-82: Compendium.*

[17] The KGB assessments of the situation in Poland in the final months before martial law are described in Andrews and Mitrokhin, *The Sword and the Shield*, pp. 520-528.

mitment. At the 10 December Soviet Politburo meeting, for example, Rusakov complained that in declaring martial law Jaruzelski did not intend to speak about the party, but instead planned to "appeal to Polish nationalist sentiments" and "proclaim a military dictatorship of the sort that existed under Pilsudski." The Pilsudski analogy is probably an apt description of how Jaruzelski perceived his decision.

All this is background for the judgment that the United States and its European Allies were in a position to influence events in Poland in late 1981. What policy choices and courses of action the US Government might have chosen, and what impact they might have had, however, can never be more than speculation. In theory, the United States might have chosen to do just what it did—nothing. For the record, this author believes that no US administration could have chosen such a course. Rightly or wrongly, everything the United States claims to stand for, would have compelled some effort to deter a plan to impose a military suppression of a popularly based movement seeking greater democracy and economic openness.

No such policy choices were made, because no one believed they were necessary. Although there is enough blame to go around, the principal failure was in the use of intelligence.

Sources

Andrew, Christopher and Mitrokhin, Vasili, *The Sword and the Shield: The Mitrokhin Archive and the Secret History of the KGB* (New York: Basic Books/Perseus Books Group, 1999).

Andrews, Nicholas G., *Poland 1980-81: Solidarity vs. the Party* (Washington, DC: National Defense University Press, 1985).

Ascherson, Neal, *The Polish August* (New York: Penguin, 1982).

Brzezinski, Zbigniew, *Power and Principal: Memoirs of the National Security Advisor* (New York: Farrar, Straus, Giroux, 1983).

_____, "A White House Diary," in *Orbis: A Journal of International Affairs,* Winter 1988.

Cynkin, Thomas H., *Soviet and American Signaling in the Polish Crisis* (New York: St. Martins Press, 1988).

Davies, Norman, *God's Playground: A History of Poland: Vol. II – 1795 to the Present* (New York: Columbia University Press, 1982).

Dobbs, Michael, *Down With Big Brother: The Fall of the Soviet Empire* (New York: Alfred A. Knopf, 1997).

Garton Ash, Timothy, *The Polish Revolution: Solidarity* (New York: Vintage Books, 1985).

Gates, Robert M., *From the Shadows: The Ultimate Insider's Story of Five Presidents and How They Won the Cold War* (New York: Simon and Schuster, 1996).

Haig, Alexander M., Jr., *Caveat: Realism, Reagan, and Foreign Policy* (New York, MacMillan, 1984).

Kuklinski, Ryszard, "The Crushing of Solidarity," in Kostrzewa, Robert, ed., *Between East and West* (New York: Hill and Lang, 1990). (Translation of main portions of interview originally granted to the Paris-based émigré magazine *Kultura* in 1987.)

Raina, Peter, *Poland 1981: Toward Social Renewal* (London: George Allen and Unwin, 1985).

Rosenberg, Tina, *The Haunted Land: Facing Europe's Ghosts After Communism* (New York: Random House, 1995).

Walesa, Lech, *A Way of Hope* (New York: Henry Holt and Company, 1987).

Weschler, Lawrence, *The Passion of Poland* (New York: Pantheon, 1984).

U.S. Archival Sources

Cold War International History Project, Bulletin No. 5, "Cold War Crises," Woodrow Wilson International Center for Scholars, Washington, D.C., Spring 1995.

- "Declassified Soviet Documents on the Polish Crisis," translated and annotated by Mark Kramer, pp. 116-117, and 129-139.
- "Warsaw Pact and the Polish Crisis of 1980-81," Mark Kramer [includes translation of Honecker letter to Brezhnev of 26 November 1980].

Cold War International History Project Bulletin No. 11, Winter 1998.

- "Colonel Kuklinski and the Polish Crisis, 1980-81," Mark Kramer, pp. 48–59.
- "In Case Military Assistance is Provided to Poland," Mark Kramer, pp. 102–109.
- "Jaruzelski, the Soviet Union, and the Imposition of Martial Law in Poland: New Light on the Mystery of December 1981," pp. 5-31.

Andrzej Paczkowskki and Andrzej Werblan, *On the Decision to Introduce Martial Law in Poland in 1981: Two Historians Report to the Commission of Constitutional Oversight of the SEJM of the Republic of Poland,* Cold War International History Project Working Paper No. 21 (Washington, DC: Woodrow Wilson Center, 1998).

Mark Kramer, *Top Secret Documents of Soviet Deliberations during the Polish Crisis, 1980-81.* Special Working Paper No. 1, Washington, DC: Woodrow Wilson Center, 1999. [22 documents/records of meetings from archives of former USSR.]

Malcolm Byrne, Pavel Machcewicz, Christian Ostermann (eds.), *Poland 1980-82: Internal Crisis, International Dimensions, A Compendium of Declassified Documents and Chronology of Events,* Washington, DC, National Security Archive, 1997.

Declassified intelligence documents, on deposit at National Security Archive, 2130 H Street, NW, Suite 701, Washington, DC, 20037.

- *National Intelligence Daily* reporting from July 1980 through December 1981. (A total of 364 documents from the Intelligence Community's daily reporting, which includes "Situation Reports," reporting and analytic commentary on unfolding events, and periodic "Special Analyses." Alert Memoranda warning of potential crisis events usually also appeared in the NID one day after they were disseminated to the President and a few top policy officials.)

- CIA Intelligence Memorandum, *Approaching the Brink: Moscow and the Polish Crisis*, November–December 1980 (late December 1980, specific date for document not given).

- National Intelligence Estimate 12.6-81, "Poland's Prospects Over the Next Six Months," (date of information listed as 27 January 1981).

- CIA Intelligence Memorandum, "Photographic Summary," 30 March 1981.

- Intelligence Article, "Poland: Concessions Ease Tensions," 31 March 1981.

- Intelligence Memorandum, "Implications of a Soviet Invasion of Poland" (date blocked out, approximately late May to mid-June 1981).

- Intelligence Memorandum, "Polish Reaction to a Soviet Invasion," 30 June 1981.

East European/Warsaw Pact Archival Sources and Compendia

Woldek, Zbigniew, ed., *Tajne Dokumenty Biura Politycznego: PZPR a "Solidarnosc,"* [Secret Documents of the Politburo: The PUWP vs. "Solidarity"], London: Aneks, 1992, provides a compilation of minutes of Polish Politburo meetings during 1980-81. These documents are in the original Polish.

Kubina, Michael, and Wilke, Manfred, *Hart und kompromisslos durchgreifen: die SED contra Poland,* 1980-81 (Berlin: Academie Verlag, 1994), [contains a compilation of East German documents in German language].

Gutche, Reinhard, Kubina, Michael, and Wilke, Manfred, *Die SED-Feuhrung und die Unterdrueckung der Polischen Oppositionbewegung* (Cologne: Bundesinstitute fuer Ostwisenschaftliche und Internationale Studien, 1994), [a collection of essays drawing on documents from the archives of the former East Germany, in German].

Virtually all *New York Times* articles in 1980-81 dealing with Poland, and most articles on Poland appearing in *The Washington Post* for the months of December 1980 and December 1981.

Index

A
Andropov, 199, 200
   Brest meeting, 115, 116, 117

B
Brezhnev, Leonid,
   and Moscow meeting with Kania, 53, 54, 55, 56
   on Jaruzelski and Kania, 122
   Soviet Party leader, 34
Brown, (Secretary of Defense) Harold, 34
Brzezinski, Zbigniew, 40
   talks with AFL-CIO leader, 17
   tells SCC meeting that strong reaction might deter Soviets, 23 September 1980, 15
   urges press briefing on consequences of Soviet intervention, 26
   view of Gdansk agreement, 11
   warns that Soviet intervention probable, December 1980, 33
Bydgoszcz incident, 96, 99, 100, 101

C
Carter, (President) Jimmy,
   December 1980 letter to allied leaders, 61
   warning letter to Brezhzev, 34
Christopher, (Deputy Secretary of State) Warren, 38, 40
Committee for Defense of Workers (KOR), formed by dissident intellectuals, 2

D
d'Estaing, (French President) Giscard, 10, 31

E
Eagleberger, (Assistant Secretary of State for European Affairs) Lawrence, 180

G
Gates, Robert, 13, 14
   on value of Kuklinski's reporting, 123
Gdansk Agreement, 7
Gierek, Edward,
   becomes head of Polish United Workers Party, 1
Glemp, (Polish Archbishop), 192
   meets with Jaruzelski, Walesa, 169
Gomulka, Wladyslas,
   replaced as head of Polish United Workers Party, 1
Gorbachev, Mikhail, 198
Gribkov, (Soviet General) Anatoli, 198
Gromyko, (Soviet Foreign Minister), 137

H
Haig, (Former Secretary of State) Alexander, 104, 108, 180
   reaffirms Carter's warning to Moscow, 75
Honecker, Eric, 54, 57
Husak, Gustav, 54

J
Jagielski, (Deputy Prime Minister),
   on party-state staff to plan use of force, 20
Jaruzelski, (General) Wojciech, 56, 90, 91, 107, 119, 125, 166, 167, 175, 184, 185, 198

and "Front of National Accord," 169, 170
and Bydgoszcz incident, 96
and Soviet Party criticism, 130, 131
announces martial law 178
at Soviet Party Congress, 91
becomes prime minister, 83, 84, 86
Brest meeting, 115, 117, 121
justification for martial law, 195, 197, 198, 199, 200, 201, 202
meeting with Kulikov, 13 April 1981, 118, 119, 120
November 1981 meetings with Kulikov, 172
on party-state staff to plan use of force, 20
opposition to Warsaw Pact "exercise," 51
replaces Kania as head of Polish Party, 161, 162, 187

K

Kadar, Janos, 54
Kania, (First Secretary) Stanislaw, 57, 85, 91, 107, 125, 127, 138, 184
and Soviet Party criticism, 130, 135
at Soviet Party Congress, 91
becomes head of Polish United Workers Party, 8
Brest meeting, 115, 116
meeting with Kulikov, 13 April, 1981, 118, 119, 120
position taken in October 1980 Moscow meeting, 53, 54
replaced by Jaruzelski, 160, 161, 162, 187
unexpected Moscow trip in October 1980, 18
views on martial law, 201, 202
Kruchkov, (KGB Deputy Director) Vladimir, 104, 114
Kuklinski, (Colonel) Ryszard, 48, 51, 57, 90, 104, 105, 123
begins drafting martial law plans, 20
escapes, 173, 174
reports martial law coming, 149, 150, 151, 152
reports planned Warsaw Pact intervention, 36
restrictions on his reporting, 189, 190
Kulikov, (Soviet Marshal), 17, 78, 114, 198

meeting with Jaruzelski, Kania, 13 April 1981, 119, 120, 197
November 1981 meetings with Jaruzelski, 172, 174

M

Meehan, (US Ambassador to Poland) Francis, 179, 181, 192
Milewski, (Internal Affairs Minister) Miroslaw, 138
on party-state staff to plan use of force, 20
Mitrokhin, Vasili, 198
Muskie, (Secretary of State) Edmund, 34, 40

N

Narozniak, Jan,
and "Narozniak Affair," 25, 27

P

Perle, (Assistant Secretary of Defense) Richard, 182
Pinkowski, (Prime Minister) Josef, 79
replaced by Jaruzelski, 83
unexpected Moscow trip in October 1980, 18

R

Reagan, (President) Ronald,
holds first policy meeting on Poland, 75
Rural Solidarity, 88, 105
and Bydgoszcz incident, 96
established, 70
Rusakov, K. V., 199

S

Schmidt, (West German Chancellor) Helmut, 10, 31
Siwicki, (General) Florian, 149, 150
Chief of Polish General Staff,
heads drafting of martial law plans, 20
Solidarity, 106, 125, 185, 186
benchmark strike of 3 October 1980, 17
compromise agreement with government, 79, 80
massive work boycotts in January 1981, 73
national congress, 141, 142, 143, 144, 145
passes program, 156, 157

reacts to Wroclaw arrests, 162
strike committees adopt the name, 6
view of Jaruzelski, 88
Soyuz '81, 196
exercise begins, 95
exercises extended, 102, 103, 104, 119
Suslov Commission 196
Suslov, Mikhail, 128
and "Suslov Commission" plan, 48

T

Thatcher, (British Prime Minister) Margaret, 10, 31
Tikhonov, (Soviet Prime Minister), 90
Turner, (DCI) Stansfield, 12
briefs Special Coordinating Committee, 23 September 1980, 13, 14
warns of Soviet intervention, 2 December 1980, 32, 38

U

Ustinov, (Soviet Defense Minister), 52, 113
Brest meeting, 115, 117, 122

W

Walesa, Lech, 88, 95, 176
and Bydgoszcz incident, 96
meets with Jaruzelski and Archbishop, 169
reaches compromise agreement with government, 79
takes leading role in Gdansk shipyard strike of 1980, 4
Weinberger, (Secretary of Defense) Caspar, warns of Soviet military intervention, 104, 110

Z

Zhivkov, Todor, 54

www.ingramcontent.com/pod-product-compliance
Lightning Source LLC
Chambersburg PA
CBHW061258110426
42742CB00012BA/1967